T0354534

Books in the series 'The Colonial Economy of NSW 1788-1835'

A Brief Economic History of NSW

The Colonial Economy of NSW 1788-1835–A retrospective

The Government Store is Open for business–
the commissariat operations in NSW 1788-1835

The Enterprising Colonial Economy of NSW 1800-1830–
Government Business Enterprises in operation

Guiding the Colonial Economy - Public Funding in NSW 1800-1835

Financing the Colonial Economy of NSW 1800-1835

Essays on the colonial Economy of NSW 1788-1835

Industries that Formed a Colonial Economy

A Collection of Essays on the Colonial Economy of N.S.W.

Gordon Beckett

For book orders, email orders@traffordpublishing.com.sg

Most Trafford Singapore titles are also available at major online book retailers.

Printed in Singapore.

ISBN: 978-1-4669-2777-3 (sc)
ISBN: 978-1-4669-2778-0 (hc)
ISBN: 978-1-4669-2779-7 (e)

Trafford rev. 08/07/2012

www.traffordpublishing.com.sg

Singapore
toll-free: 800 101 2656 (Singapore)
Fax: 800 101 2656 (Singapore)

CONTENTS

CHAPTER 1

INTRODUCTION AND PREFACE

The economy of the colony (between 1788 and 1856) is by far the most interesting chapter of early Australian history after settlement, and within that chapter the Macquarie economy and its growth and major accomplishments is the most interesting segment. Why those particular dates? Settlement commenced with the arrival of the First Fleet, and their goal of being a self-sufficient penal colony, and full self-government arrived with the Constitution Act of 1855.

Of the Macquarie economy, we can see the economy in transition (from penal, towards a free, settlement); we see the exploration over the mountains, a barrier that was both physically and psychologically a severe limiting factor to the growth of the economy; we see the dramatic changes in agricultural production with the opening up of the Western Plains (both the Bathurst and the Liverpool Plains) and the advent of foreign (British) investment. The growth of manufacturing accompanied a change of policy with the Commissariat, and the financial institutions grew in accompaniment to the British absentee landowners, and the rise in livestock numbers. The desire and need to earn an adequate return on the investment in these pastoral enterprises, created a surge in exporting, as well as the diversification of enterprises and the decentralisation movement (the expansion of settlement boundaries).

The most significant change during the Macquarie Administration was the great movement of convicts into the colony and the Macquarie policy of putting these people to creative work; the by-product of these policies was the investment in public infrastructure of roads, bridges, public buildings and private housing.

The economy flourished and operated at full steam. The Hunter and Bligh years had witnessed very little capital investment in buildings and roads, so Macquarie had a lot of catching up as well as fulfilling his own expansionary plans.

The central theme of the era was not the official congratulations to Macquarie but the unceasing urging by successive Secretaries of State to curb expenditures even those annual local revenues tripled during the decade of 1810 to 1820 and over 50% of those revenues found their way into the public building program.

Consternation that the local revenue and taxing powers had been invalid since 1802 (Gov. King's first revenue raising to re-build the local jail) led to a validating Act in 1819 by the Westminster Parliament, who unctuously appointed a select committee into transportation to review government activities in the colony but then directed Bathurst to send a Commissioner (Bigge) to the colony for a more first-hand and in-depth investigation.

This story is firstly about the growth of the Colonial economy between 1788 and 1856, then about the key aspects of the Macquarie economy between 1810 and 1821 and finally to review the civil and criminal codes under which the colony operated and the variety of statutes imposed on the colonial governance.

There are some notable contributions to studies on many aspects of the colonial economy–that is the period between 1788 and about 1830. This period covers the setting up and establishment of the penal colony to the transition period when most of the economic development and structuring of the economy took place.

- The major contributors to our knowledge of the colonial economy and its growth and structure are Professor Noel G. Butlin (late of Australian National University) and his brother Professor S.J. Butlin (late of Sydney University). Collectively they have contributed numerous books and monographs to the literature His contributions come in his books (two are published posthumously)

My studies have been into more particular issues of and within the colonial economy. I commenced with an assembly and analysis of the financial statements of the two 'funds' from 1802 to 1822, followed by a biography of the first colonial acting treasurer and auditor-general–William Lithgow. Two important structural aspects of the economy as detected by N.G. Butlin are dealt with–the Commissariat and the Government Business Enterprises that commenced in 1802 and were not abandoned as Government policy until about 1830. This led to an analysis of the growth of manufacturing and the role of the early entrepreneurs. One of the most interesting aspects of the early economy (as directed by the British Treasury) is the establishment of 'land grant companies for development of land and pastoral enterprises. The first two are the AA Pastoral Company established in NSW in 1823 and the Van Diemen's Land Company, established in Tasmania in 1824. Both companies operated in the pastoral industry and in pursuit of wool interests held by their major stockholders. Whereas one was successful whilst the one studied in this volume–the VDL Company was close to ruin for much of its existence even though it survives to this day.

I have assembled as a companion volume, 20 of the best essays and writings on the colonial economy. This volume includes writings by N.G. Butlin and other exponents of the development band growth of the economy between 1788 and 1830 and includes my own study of the Aboriginal economy as of 1788.

CHAPTER 2

DEFINING ECONOMIC HISTORY

A good definition of Economic History (relating to Australia) is taken from Colin White **'Mastering Risk, Politics in Australian Economic History'**

'(Man's economic activities which define those parts of the environment relevant to him, and which he can select as being those parts of the environment which can be described as resources'. P. 3)

White spends a large amount of print on questioning the key elements of colonial economic development and concludes (p.78)

"Most accounts of 19th century Australian economic development assume homogeneity with characteristics of uniform government attitudes to development finding expression in common economic policies, and an economic system in which exports of staples are important and that the all-pervasive capitalist system with its associated class struggle"

White is correct that these attitudes are prevalent amongst social; and political historians and for good reason. The colonial society was surging ahead on solid bedrock of private enterprise guided by the government wanting to encourage private and foreign investment and minimize government social expenditures.

However, White could offer an alternative guide to the colonial economy. The size of the economy dictated government involvement at the embryonic stage of private enterprise. It was not only Macquarie's encouragement of private enterprise that fuelled growth but his intervention in cleverly putting government assigned convicts to productive work in the GBEs and then transferring those activities into private hands that created a strongly growing secondary sector and further fuelled foreign investment and loans into the economy.

The encouragement of education, job training and productive labour were the driving force behind development. The conduits of the commissariat and the GBEs gave expression to a successful secondary sector and profitable outcomes.

CHAPTER 3

50 ASPECTS OF (AUSTRALIAN) COLONIAL ECONOMIC HISTORY 1788-1835

			ECONOMIC		COLONIAL		BRITISH
Aspect	**Period**	**development**	**planning**	**natural resources**	**Social**	**Political**	**policy**
Commissariat Operations	1	1					
convict assignment	1				1		
Crime & law enforcement	1				1		
Developing a welfare program	1				1		
Development of export industries	1			1			
Development of Infrastructure	1			1			

Development of Staples	1			1			
discovery and settlement of Australia	1						1
Fishing & Whaling	1			1			
Government farms	1			1			
Growth of Population	1				1		
Growth of religion	1				1		
Growth of the colonies	1					1	
military traders	1	1					
Operating the Female Factory	1	1					
Rum Corp operations	1	1					
Terra Nullius–fact or fiction	1					1	
The Aboriginal Economy in 1788	1		1				
The growth of the timber industry	1			1			
The operations of the Abattoirs	1	1					
The operations of the Naval Yard	1	1					
The operations of the Penal Colony	1					1	
The operations of the Stone Quarries	1	1					
The operations of the Windmills	1	1					
The Transportation Program	1					1	
Advent of Newspapers	2						
Creation of postal services	2				1		
Developing a public service	2					1	
Development of natural resources	2			1			
Drought & Floods	2		1				

Economic Cycles	2		1					
Education Corporation	2				1			
Exploration	2					1		
Government Farms	2		1					
Growth of Agriculture	2		1					
growth of financial institutions	2					1		
Growth of the Pastoral Industry	2		1					
Land Grant companies	2					1		
Spread of Settlement	2					1		
strikes and unions	2					1		
The colonial colony in transition	2						1	
The first Treasury	2						1	
The first audit Program	2						1	
The first bank	2					1		
The government business enterprises	2	1						
The Land Corp.	2					1		
The rise of Manufacturing	2	1						
The spread of Education	2				1			
The Wool Industry	2	1						
Macquarie's farsightedness	2	1						
	25 x 1	12	7	7	8	12	4	50
	25 x 2							

CHAPTER 4

THE ABORIGINAL ECONOMY IN 1788[1]

Recording a model of the Aboriginal economy in 1788 would not be an approach recognised by Aborigines, for they do not appear to distinguish between economic activity and any other necessary activity. We, on the other hand, draw the distinction in order to highlight the difference the Aborigines make between necessary material support, as an economic system, and their philosophy of land care and resource management for survival.

1. The basic difference between European culture and Aboriginal culture is simple. For centuries Europeans relied upon agriculture (and therein 'farming') to feed themselves. For many thousands of years and therefore hundreds of centuries, Aboriginals did not plant crops or tend or domesticate animals or live in towns, nor possess houses worthy of the name, as we would define them. The Aboriginals were survivors by being hunters and gatherers (hunting wild animals and gathering necessary and useful natural resources). But we know now that hunters and gatherers, generally, were knowledgeable and sophisticated managers of the limited natural resources, which allowed them to live off the land with a minimum of effort. Although they appear to have possessed ample time in their busy lifestyle to enjoy a full spiritual, ceremonial

1 Tony Dingle '*A Pattern of Experience: The Aboriginal Economy*' p4

and social life, their need for careful time management ensured that their food needs were always satisfied and occupied a central position in their daily life.

2. The pattern of their lives is something that we of the industrial age require an imaginative understanding to bridge the gap between the Aboriginal lifestyle and the European pretences at fulfilment.
3. Much of what grows is inedible, and many animals and plants that can be eaten flourish only in habitats that suit them. Some birds, animals and fish move over quite an extended area. Consequently the food supply of a locality typically consists of a large variety of species some of which might be available for only limited periods during a year or season.
4. Hunters and gatherers used two approaches to adapt to the ever-changing nature of the food supply.

    i. They lived in small groups thinly spread across the land. Nowhere was its density similar to agricultural or industrial societies. In fact there was never any concentration.
    ii. They moved residence regularly–not necessarily travelling very far, but moving unlike the manner of 'farmers' with a set piece of land for resource extraction.

5. Storage was a limiting factor as well. There was little point in collecting more than is needed for a day or two. They learnt the skills to only collect certain foods but to go out each day to get what they needed. Their move every couple of days was designed to harvest food close to the vicinity of the campsite. Game, which was to be hunted, became less plentiful and more wary, while convenient sources of plant food are depleted. The longer the hunters and gatherers remain in one location the more energy they must expend to feed themselves. This is a neglect of good time management and so the group must move. If people wish to minimise the need for movement it is sensible to keep the tribe size small.
6. Many groups will define their territory and move, during the course of a year, from one campsite to another within the boundaries of its territory. The timing of each move is usually governed by the time it takes to feed itself at that location and the expectation

(availability) of food and water in other locations. Since the food is largely seasonal, and often defined by gluts and shortages of specific foods, the patterns of movement are likely to be repeated year after year.

7. Another characteristic of the hunter-gatherer's economic existence is the adaptation to regularly occurring foods by regular movement and small group living. To suit this lifestyle, material possessions are kept to a minimum; people possess few clothes or furnishings, maintaining only basic (abandonable) housing and small kits of tools, weapons and water containers. In a European society, many material possessions are prized, but if movement is necessary, they become a burden. This western preoccupation with accumulating wealth by way of material goods and possessions makes no sense in the context of hunting and gathering.[2]
8. In western economic thinking, the factors of production are broken down into *land, labour & capital.* If we try to apply this concept to the Aboriginal economy, then most forms of Aboriginal production will require little capital equipment, and are speedily accomplished, and whereas hunting and collecting takes hours instead of months with western farming; simplicity of tools, housing and weapons is also a part of the plan for the Aborigines. Among the primitive people, the labour factor of production is more evenly distributed and specialisation occurs. A significant development is that everyone is trained as an alternative to physical capital, and everyone has access to the group's skills and knowledge and acquisition of this training is recognised as a transfer into adulthood.
9. The 'ownership' of land and capital is concentrated and centralised, whilst the rewards from 'production' are more equally shared in the Aboriginal economy than in the European economy.
10. Ecological management is carefully planned, since the supply of food consists mainly of edible plants and animals in the area of hunting and gathering. The measure of sustainability is not the stock of animals but the productivity of the land resources. In this scenario, people can only eat the equivalent of the annual crop of kangaroos, fruit, or roots. If they go above this level the

---

2 Blainey, G '*Triumph of the Nomads-A Natural History of Australia*'

productive capacity of these renewable resources will be impaired and supplies in future years will be in decline. In this way natural productivity places an upper limit on how many people can be fed and this policy becomes a flexible but natural constraint on population growth. It is flexible because natural phenomena affect the levels of natural productivity. Short–and long-term climate changes such as an increase or decrease of average rainfall, the type of animals and plants will affect the amount of food available. Increased food supply could come not from 'farming' or domestication of wild animals but from increasing and aggressive resource management. Such measures can include: the attempt to develop 'storage' facilities; conversion of inedible plants to edible, by grinding and baking; the careful use of fire can change the environment and allow animals to multiply.[3]

11. Land was vital for physical survival, but was more than an economic resource: People were tied spiritually to a particular locality-this was their 'country' and 'dreaming place', a tangible link with ancestors who lived and died there. Based on an interview with an elder in the Northern Rivers (NSW) 'clan' the following association has been characterised. Each individual belonged to a family, but also to a clan or territorial (estate) group. A number of clans united by shared language, beliefs, customs and kinship ties. Each clan 'claimed' an estate within the boundaries of the larger group territory. The clan would exercise proper rights over its estate and defend it against trespass by unauthorised individual or other clans. Land could not be bought or sold, but was used, cared for and held in trust for future generations. The control was not exclusive but shared, through joint use of its resources, with others. Hunting rights could be temporarily assigned and in return similar permission extended over other estates.[4] Such complex social, spiritual and territorial arrangements ensured that everyone had access to land to sustain themselves physically and spiritually.[5]

---

3 Dingle, T. '*aboriginal Economy: Patterns of Experience*' p 8

4 Bell, Dianne *Daughters of the Dreaming*'

5 Dingle, T. '*aboriginal Economy: Patterns of Experience*' p 11

12. The hunter-gatherer diet was varied depending on the season of the year and the locality that they were temporarily occupying. In some seasons the diets may be exclusively meat or purely game (when catching migratory birds) or simply seafood (when living by the coast). The women appear to be the more reliable food providers, because their food sources were generally more plentiful and stable. Women usually sourced their food from 'gathering' whereas men were not always successful in their hunting'. Foraging was not arduous work–they usually kept within 5 kilometres from the camp and would return within four to six hours, having taken time to rest and talk. Aboriginal women would collect for a day with minimal effort since they were also the child minders. Hunters would be away for a similar time but would travel much further, particularly if there were tracks of promising game. Most hunting was carried out singly or by three or four men. This would become a co-operative effort in tracking, killing and hauling the game. Richard Lee, in surveying surviving hunting and gathering societies in 1960 concluded that "hunting was a high-risk, low-return activity whilst gathering was a low-risk, high–return activity".[6] This combination of hunting and gathering ensured a more diversified and tastier diet. It most probably ensured a more reliable food supply due to the combination of skills.

Before we examine aspects of technology and bartering in the Aboriginal economy, let me find a way of summarising the Aboriginal economy from the viewpoint of hunting and gathering. Harry Lourandos offers his reader a well-developed conclusion about the Aboriginal economy.[7]

> *The hunter-gatherer economy has been viewed traditionally as basic, elementary and subsistence-based, guided by ecological factors. However, the prior distinction between 'food producers' composed of land and resource management strategies, agriculturalists,* ***and*** *food collectors, or 'hunter-gatherers' has been revised. All human societies can be considered as*

6 Lee, Richard 'What hunters do for a living' *Man the Hunter* P30

7 Lourandos, Larry *Continent of Hunter-Gatherers–A new perspective in Australian prehistory* 1997 p.17

'producers' in the sense that food and other commodities are appropriated by a division of labour (Sahlins 1974[8]; Ingold 1980[9]). The hunter-gatherers 'economy' itself can be seen to operate at two main levels: (a) the domestic or local group level and (b) the wider group level.[10]

The Aboriginal Economy In 1788

There was an economy in operation in New Holland at the time of the arrival of the first white settlers in 1788.

Professor N.G. Butlin concludes:-

Early Aborigines were the first discoverers and occupiers of the Australian continent, "the first to establish functioning societies and economies, and the first to make the large-scale adaptations required using almost every type of ecological condition in Australia. The arrival of the First Fleet did not mean merely 'contact' with Aborigines, but the destruction of Aboriginal society and populations and the transfer of their resources *to the benefit of both the new arrivals and those who remained in Britain.*[11] What 'settlement' meant in this case was the cheap acquisition of Aboriginal resources, just as it did in the Americas. In other cases, overt conquest, which led to comparatively small settlement, and provided a mechanism for imperial access to resources without such an overt asset transfer? It improved the terms of trade for the conquerors, opened up opportunities for imperial development and to some extent ameliorated the imperial process by a sharing of the benefits of such development. In the process it recognised property rights, but this option did not apply in the Americas or Australia".[12]

---

8 Sahlins, M. *'Stone Age Economics'*

9 Ingold, T. *Hunter, Pastoralists & Ranchers'*

10 Lourandis, H *'Continent of Hunter-Gatherers'*

11 Butlin, N.G. *Economics of the Dreamtime–A hypothetical history* p.2 (Butlin's italics)

12 Butlin *ibid* p.3

The Cambridge Economic History of Europe explains economic development in the industrial nations of Europe in terms of the growth of inputs of land, labour and capital, plus technology. If we extend this concept to Britain, should we not also recognise that its new acquisitions did not merely imply food but included all natural resources, such as wealth under the surface?[13]

Butlin has specialised in the statistics of the Aboriginal economy in and after 1788.

Here are some observations made by Butlin:[14] Butlin's three works each record some varying aspects, at differing times of the Aboriginal population movement between 1788 and 1850 and the Aboriginal Economy.

He approaches the Aboriginal Economy through a system of time budgeting.[15]

"On that basis, it is possible to order Aboriginal time allocation in terms of a range of categories along the lines of:

Food collection
Environment management and adaptation
Food preparation and distribution
Clothing, bedding and household utensils
Production Planning, including decisions to relocate
Travel and transport
Housing
Equipment production and maintenance
Education
Law and Order
Defence
Religious Observance
Ritual ceremonies

---

13 Cambridge Economic History of Europe

14 Butlin, N.G *Our Original Aggression, Economics of the Dreamtime & Forming a Colonial Economy*

15 Butlin, N.G *Our Original Aggression*

Art & Recreation
Entertainment.

Such a list may, adds Butlin, could be considered common to both the white and Black society, although Aboriginals were more inclined to pooling of resources and to sharing, even though in the penal society the definition of 'convict rations' and 'board and lodging' brings the two societies closer together than first thought". [16]

Butlin models the Aboriginal populations at the time of white arrival, and suggests the NSW/Vic population was 250,000 aborigines, with a total Australian aboriginal population at one million (of which only 10,000 were located in VDL). So obviously the Qld, NT, WA & SA populations were in excess of 740,000

As with the Governors before him, instructions to Governor Darling regarding Aborigines, stressed the need to protect the natives, both "in their persons, and in the free enjoyment of their possessions".[17] The Governor had also been instructed to co-operate with Archdeacon Scott (the former Secretary to Hon. J. T. Bigge) in providing the means by which the Aborigines could be converted to Christianity and 'advanced in civilisation'. In response to Thomas Brisbane declaring martial law in Bathurst, Lord Bathurst informed Darling (Brisbane's successor) that it was his duty "when the aborigines made 'hostile incursions for the purpose of plunder' and only when 'less vigorous measures' had failed, 'to oppose force by force, and to repel such aggression in the same manner, as if they proceeded from subjects of any accredited state".[18]

Attempts by Archdeacon Scott and Bishop Broughton produced reports the need for substantial expenditure on education and general welfare reform. Darling's response was that the expense and the difficulty of finding suitably qualified people posed formidable problems. Darling admitted that his response was more to economy than to any lack of

---

16 Butlin *Economic & the Dreamtime*

17 Governors despatches 1826 HRA 1:12:125

18 Brisbane to Bathurst 1824 HRA 1:11:409; Bathurst to Darling 1825 HRA 1:12:21

interest in aboriginal welfare. He admitted he had little understanding of their culture or way of life. 'Those who he saw in an urban setting depressed him, as the appearance of the natives about Sydney is extremely disgusting, due to the frequent and excessive use of spirits. Tribes living in the interior were not exposed to this evil and appeared to be a much finer race'.[19] Darling was critical of the language problem and the fact that different tribes could not converse with each other.

It would appear that very few of Darling's predecessors or even his successors took the time or interest to understand the Aboriginal economy or society, as a means of making informed judgements and policies about a diminishing but still aggravating problem. Darling was largely pre-occupied with skirmishes (and massacres) between the white settlers and the Aborigines. But neither legislation nor regulation seemed to be the answer to the hostilities and deaths and anger and retaliation.

Perceptions prevailed, as a basis of policy decision-making on behalf of Aborigines. David Day claims 'Officers of the First Fleet of British invaders believed they were stepping ashore on a continent that had not felt the heel of civilised man".[20] Such perceptions of uneducated stone-age peoples unfamiliar with any white man or white man's ways, persisted until the Gipps Administration, and as a result not much got changed to improve their way of life, or their economy. Even Manning Clark perpetuated the myths and false perceptions when he introduces Volume 1 with the thought 'Civilisation did not begin in Australia until the last quarter of the eighteenth century'[21] The implications of that sentence served to justify the continued dispossession of the Aborigines who, Clark argued, had lived for 'millennia in a state of barbarism'[22]

Our conception and perception of civilisation has a European orientation to it, but the Aborigines lived with some form of deliberativeness.

---

19 Fletch, Brian, *Ralph Darling: a Governor maligned*

20 Day, David *Claiming a continent–A New History of Australia* p.3

21 Clark, C.M.H. *A History of Australia* Vol 1

22 Clark, *ibid*

Butlin is concerned with implication not motives of the Aborigine as an 'economic man'. However, the main questions we need to ask relate to:

Was Aboriginal economic behaviour rational or not?

Did the population change with production (mainly climatic) setbacks or did they adapt to known technologies or change their tastes, technology, methods of production and allocation of labour?

Butlin explains "the Aboriginal economy in Australia was established over thousands of years by the successfully arriving migrants from South-East Asia and by their locally born descendents. If we accept prevalent views of very low rates of natural increase amongst hunter-gathers, it would follow that any population build-up to occupy the entire Australian continent even within a time-span of several millennia is explainable primarily by immigration inflow It is not plausible to approach the study of the Aboriginal economy in terms of a static structure and function. The dynamism may be summed up in the proposition that Aboriginals evolved in Australia from hunter-gatherers to resource managers and 'improvers'."[23]

The Aboriginal economy is structured into many segments and activities:

- Food gathering
- Food technology
- Aboriginal culture and society (this is integral to the economic understanding & interpretation
- Inter-group associations
- Property rights in land (individual, centralised or communal)
- Marriage customs
- Property in ritual
- Economic decision-making

This aspect of the pre-history of Australia is still being written.[24]

---

23 Butlin *Forming a Colonial Economy* p.56

24 Lourandos, Harry *Continent of Hunter-Gatherers-New Perspectives in Australian Prehistory*

Becker suggests that hunter-gatherers had a scarce resource, which was time and that the Aboriginal economy could be better considered in this light.[25]

Mulvaney discusses some features of their life-style. He identifies many plants and animals that were common to South-East Asia and Australia in the distant past, as well as the continuous landmass between New Guinea and Tasmania with the mainland.[26] The emergence of two large lakes, one in the Gulf of Carpentaria the other in Bass Strait, provided a large food resource of fish, fowl and habitation for native animals as well as humans. With water being a prime consideration to human and animal (food) habitation, Mulvaney concludes that 60,000 years ago both the Murray and Darling Rivers were much broader than they are today and shows the existence of the active Lake Eyre and Lake Frome in south-central Australia–conditions which deteriorated after 60,000 BP.

David Day puts it in a similar way." It could even be argued that Aborigines were more sophisticated than Europeans have proved to be in Australia. While the Aborigines lived for hundreds of centuries in Australia, changing their lifestyles in reaction to gradual changes in the environment and sometimes even shaping that environment to maximise their returns from it, just two centuries of European occupation have seen almost irreparable harm done to the environment through greed or ignorance. There has been a recent return to Aboriginal methods of land management to take care of national parks and to live successfully in arid areas".[27]

Early attempts at understanding the natives was not left only to Government officials, the churchmen in the colony were assigned the tasks of 'civilising' this race, and the Rev. J.D. Lang records:

> "Their wanderings are circumscribed by certain well-defined limits, beyond which they seldom pass,

---

25 Becker, G.S. *A Theory of the Allocation of Time*', The Economic Journal, September 1965

26 Mulvaney, D.J. & Golson, J (Eds). *Aboriginal Man and Environment in Australia*

27 Day *Claiming a continent* p.7

> except for purposes of war or festivity. In short, every tribe has its own district, the boundaries of which are well known to the natives generally . . ."[28]

Some characteristics of the Aboriginal economy in Australia

- Omnivorous diet
- Limited inter-group trade (usually exchange)
- A marked division of labour by gender
- Education–learning by doing
- Limited storage capacity
- Communal sharing rules
- Communal property rights
- Population control
- Complex kin relationships
- Formal non-literacy
- Limited formal government
- Recognised as 'grass farmers'
- Native animals and sea-food recognised as 'valuable'

Assembling the national income accounts of the aboriginal race 1788

The challenge was issued by N.G. Butlin to compute national income figures for the Aboriginal economy.[29]

In fact on more than one occasion Butlin wrote, "We need to establish the national income of Aborigines. Such statistics have never been collected, nor are they ever likely to be. But we need to recognise, in looking at the use of Australian resources, and in understanding how our well-being improved, that whites gained in part because blacks lost."[30]

---

28 Lang, John Dunmore *An Historical & Statistical Account of NSW* 1833

29 Butlin, N.G. *Forming the Colonial Economy* 1788-1856

30 Butlin, N.G Chapter 8 'Australian National Accounts' *Australian: National Statistics* P126

Aborigines filled the traditional history books as in the following extract

> *"In 1815 the Aborigines were 'killed in great numbers, so much so as to call for proclamations against the cruelty'.*[31]

But rarely, if ever, is any mention made, in those same history books, of the Aboriginal lifestyle or economic activities, and yet the Aborigines survived in great number for thousands and thousands of years, and the land became and remained their life support. How did they manage this?

R.M.Younger reveals (albeit *unsourced)* that Governor Macquarie "up to 1817 had been able to concentrate on the advancement of those in his charge within the framework of a comparatively compact penal establishment. He had settled numerous emancipists, the few incoming free settlers, *and even some Aborigines* on small farms, to grow the food the community needed.[32] This policy was unsuccessful in both the governor's understanding of the natives and their ability to work in this way, and the ability to regiment and anglicise the Aborigine.

McMartin reports that "the fact that only £51,800 was appropriated for native welfare during the whole of the first half-century gives a better idea of the concern that was really manifested during that period.[33]

The sources for such a study as this are scarce but a few writers have developed a theme for understanding the Aboriginal economy. An outstanding work written specifically about the Aboriginal people of the northern rivers area of NSW is 'Wollumbin' by N.C. Keats.

---

31 Mukherjee, S.K. '*Crime & Justice*' Chapter 17 *Australian: National Statistics* P126

32 Younger, R.M. *Australia and the Australians* p.178

33 McMartin, Arthur *Public Servants and Patronage* p.211 *this is the first record that the author has seen reported of the expenditure on Aboriginal Affairs, however, the agreement for the usage of crown lands revenue assigned 15% to Aboriginal matters, and no record exists of any expenditure from this source of funds. McMartin also records that the 'Protector of aborigines and his staff amounted to 34 persons in 1842 (p.210) so there was an appropriation for this expenditure at that time.*

As can be imagined Noel Butlin seemed to enjoy this area of research and wrote a series of articles and books.[34]

Another writer of significance is D.J. Mulvaney.[35]

Altogether, a methodical and a logical approach are necessary for this study. We need to know about the population in 1788, the way of life of the Aboriginal people and their material ways, their food gathering inclinations and their territorial means. Were Aboriginal movements meaningful for food gathering and territorial protection or for another reason?

Let me start with a summary of the population problems arising after 1788.

The Aboriginal Population 1788

Butlin reminds us "it took until 1838 for the combined colonial and aboriginal populations to reach the pre-1788 level Aboriginal level. This downturn of the Aboriginal population was triggered by three factors:

a. The massive early loss of Aborigines due to introduced diseases from the white population
b. An Aboriginal recovery and colonial expansion in the 1820s, and
c. Further Aboriginal loss and rapid colonial increase from the mid to late 1820s

Did the Aboriginal population shrink with production setbacks and expand to absorb increased productivity or were per capita gains achieved, particularly with the aid of population control? This raises the question of motivation. Did Aboriginals behave rationally or not? This could be

---

34 Butlin, N.G. *Our Original Aggression: Aboriginal Populations of S.E. Australia 1788-1850; 'Contours of the Australian Economy 1788-1860'; 'Forming a Colonial Economy 1810-1850'; Economics and the Dreamtime–A Hypothetical history*

35 Mulvaney, D.J. *The prehistory of Australia (1969)*

seen as looking at Aboriginal economic behaviour through the eyes of 'economic man'–which would be a misconception, since it would imply rational behaviour. Aborigines may be seen, for example, to prefer more leisure or more ritualistic activity to more consumption goods. They may be seen as being satisfied with a limited range of ends. Neither perception entails the conclusion that they behaved 'irrationally'.[36]

The Aboriginal economy in Australia was established over thousands of years by successfully arriving immigrants, from island south-east Asia and by their locally born descendents. No modelling has been completed that would associate this migration and local net annual increase with the population at 1788. However a back-projection method of population modelling may be valuable in this situation.[37]

Aboriginal Life-Style

It was suggested in *Economics and the Dreamtime*[38] that one might approach the Aboriginal Economy through a system of time budgeting. On this basis, it is possible to order Aboriginal time allocation in terms of a range of categories along the lines of:

- Food Collection
- Environmental management & adaptation
- Food preparation & distribution
- Clothing, bedding & household utensils
- Production planning, including decisions to relocate
- Travel and transportation
- Housing
- Equipment production and maintenance
- Education
- Law & Order
- Defence

---

36 Butlin, N.G. *Economics and the Dreamtime* p.54

37 Wrigley & Schofield *'The Population History of England 1541-1871-a reconstruction using the back-projection methodology.*

38 Butlin, N.G. *ibid*

- Religious observance
- Ritual ceremonies
- Art, and
- Recreation and entertainment

Aborigines were inclined to the pooling of resources and to sharing though the definition of 'convict rations' and even the concept of 'board & lodging' also conveys the same concepts, and thus brings the two societies closer together.

Many food items were consumed in both societies (white and native)–game meats, wild fowl, eggs, wild fruit and nuts, fish, shellfish and crustaceans. This short list illustrates a cross-cultural food transfer that accounted for a large part of Aboriginal diets (even if colonists and convicts drew the line at snakes and lizards). Both sides prized animal skins and sealskins. Aboriginals took sheep and cattle meat when they could. There was Aboriginal technical superiority in the capture of game and birds and colonial superiority in production of domesticated livestock.[39] The explanation for social adjustment, and the alteration to division of labour and resource exploitation in the Aboriginal lifestyle have important implications for our perceptions of Aboriginal demography and social organisation at the time of European settlement They also have significance for the dynamics of Aboriginal economy over the past 50,000 years and for any appraisal of its structure and function.

The choices for dominant population growth are:

1. Through continuous migration and a learning-by-doing for newcomers
2. Essentially by net natural increase of a small number of ever arriving migrants with primary emphasis on the inter-generational transfer of ecological understanding and a socially managed gradual adaption to change in the environment.

The predominantly migrant source of population increase would imply the likelihood of technological transmission from Southeast Asia to

---

39 Butlin, N.G. *Forming a Colonial Economy* p.214

the Australian continent, but would also suggest an increased conflict at arrival points between earlier and later arrivals. Therefore it is not possible to assess the Aboriginal economy in terms of a static structure and function. Economic behaviour was certainly reformed and contained by water supply conditions in central Australia and the rising seawater levels in the period 40,000 to 17000BP. Other elements of the dynamics of the Aboriginal economy in more recent times is evident from regional differences in consumption patterns, production structure, division of labour and other characteristics[40] This transition from hunter-gathers to resource manager and 'improvers', is understandable from the argument as to why Aborigines 'failed' to become 'farmers'. It is generally agreed that the Aboriginals achieved a large-scale alteration in the natural landscape and environment through burning and this practice evolved from 30,000BP.

Likewise many side issues affect and impact on a study of Aboriginal economic behaviour. Jones in 1977 believes that Aboriginal social structure and function are part of the consideration of economic behaviour as are inter-group associations, property rights in land, marriage customs, property in ritual and so forth.[41]

Jones also stresses the point that "in the absence of any clearly defined market, individual property rights or central direction with communal property, and with little in the way of government or overt laws, Aborigines nevertheless achieved an orderly system of economic decision-making.

Butlin concludes his chapter on the Aboriginal economy by "it was the attempt to achieve modes of satisfying many competing demands (such as food consumption, ritual, reproduction, warfare, leisure and education) that made up the problem of the Aboriginal economy, as it does the modern household. Hunting and gathering was only a small part of the total behaviour in which economic considerations were relevant."[42]

---

40 Keats, N.C *'Wollumbin-The Aboriginals of the Tweed Region'.*

41 Jones R. *The Fifth Continent: Problems concerning the Colonisation of Australia*-Vol 8 Annual Review of Anthropology.

42 Butlin, N.G. *Economics and the Dreamtime* p.56

Diversity of Culture

Did Aborigines prefer foods from the land or the sea?

Did they prefer animal or plant foods?

A variety of limitations influenced local preferences. Interesting as these limitations are (for example scale fish, ritualistically-imposed constraints), they are less significant than the variety of consumption patterns across the continent: the dominance of seafood consumption in some areas, or the exploitation of grains in others, or of cycads or yams elsewhere. Some of this differentiation was linked to ecology or production practicalities. For instances, root crops were scarcer in the arid inland and thus grains were more important; cycads spread across northern Australia and down the east coast; seafood were more abundant in northern Australia; waterfowl were seasonally available in south-eastern and northern Australia; freshwater fish depended on inland water sources; the concentration on wild animals was influenced by supplies of drinking water and grasslands or open woodlands.[43]

A major influence on diet was the movement of the peoples. The people of eastern Cape York appear to have followed a strongly seasonal pattern of movement. Many peoples showed quite strong preferences for certain foods and did not consume all the variety of foods available to them. On the west of the Cape, tribes appear to have been stable on the seashore for periods of six months, before moving inland for the balance of the year, and changing their diet to living off the land.

Tribe sizes influenced dietary patterns. Although the average appears to have been about 40 there were considerable variations from this mean. Smaller numbers were more prevalent in the arid areas whilst higher numbers prevailed in the 'richer' environs, where harvests were readily accessible in one or a small range of particular foods.

Storage or a limited ability to store foodstuffs was another limitation of movement and tribal numbers. Water carriers were developed in a large

---

43 Coghlan *Wealth & Progress 1886-1887*

variety of moulds–from human skulls to wooden implements and the skins of animals.[44]

Although land was fundamental to Aboriginal culture, it was also a basic means of production. Our premise must be that the hunting and gathering way of life forms the basics of sustenance for the Aboriginal people for well over 50,000 years of existence in Australia. Of all the economic systems, which human ingenuity has devised, hunting and gathering is the most ancient and long lived and it survived longer in Australia than anywhere else in the world.[45]

Put into perspective, it is now widely accepted that over 2,000 generations of Aborigines have been living on this continent for those 50,000 years sustained by hunting and gathering. By comparison the two hundred years of white community is a mere infant not yet demonstrated to be durable for an extended period. The Aborigines had a deep-rooted respect for and appreciation of the ecology of the land as a means of production and regulated their existence to fit in with and be sustained by the changing climate patterns. To this we compare the current abuse and constant optimising the use of natural resources without recognising the limitations naturally imposed. It appears the Aborigines did not need 'farming' as we understand it, nor the envy of permanent food sources without challenge, but would work within the confines of the ecological system and prepare for a limited lifestyle, limited only, that is by a sustainable lifestyle rather than rampaging excesses.

---

44 Mulvaney *ibid*

45 Dingle, Tony *Aboriginal economy–patterns of experience* p.2

CHAPTER 5

WILLIAM LITHGOW 1824-1852– A GREAT PUBLIC SERVANT

The working life of William Lithgow paralleled the most interesting period of colonial history between 1824 and 1852, from the end of the Macquarie Administration to the strains of self-government approaching fast. Born in Scotland in 1784, his life tracked closely the growth of the Colony of New South Wales, however, his contribution to the colony did not commence until his transfer from Mauritius in 1823.

As characterized by Governor Darling in 1827, Lithgow was a man with great quantities of devotion and dedication, but mostly he was 'full of zeal'.

This then, is the story of Lithgow's contribution through his work and advice to the five Governors he so ably served during 28 years in the New South Wales colonial public service. Lithgow's contribution has not been verified sufficiently by previous historians, as we will see, and in economic history terms his gift to the people of the colony was unsurpassed in 'value'.

His life was as varied as the times in which he lived. A more interesting and varied Colonial would be hard to find. A lifetime of Public Service was rare for the 1800s, but Lithgow successfully divided his time between his salaried position and numerous Boards and Committees, many of which he sat on by request of the governor of the day, as a community service. He was selected for these tasks and assignments because of his broad experience, insight and loyal government service.

His mantle was broader than that offered through Commissariat accounting, to which he devoted the first 10 years of his working life. He had risen to the position of assistant deputy-commissary of accounts in Mauritius, before turning to the arduous and demanding task of auditing the Colonial Accounts under the umbrella of the Colonial Secretary's office. This experience of dealing effectively with British Commissary and Treasury bureaucracy was invaluable in the new settlement, and his know-how was called upon frequently in the struggling colony. Although he eventually became second in command under the Colonial Secretary, his activities were never fully recognised, at least publicly. He was just another Public Servant trying to set down the financial affairs of the Colony in the format demanded by the British Treasury. By today's auditing standards Lithgow's tasks were mundane, regimented and routine; however, his title of Colonial Auditor-General may well have been too generous for his real and more exacting role was as financial advisor to the colonial governors, and the implementer of practical solutions to keeping the colony on an even economic keel. The procedures of fiscal governance were demanding and bureaucratic–vouchers, vouchers and more vouchers. Each one having to be verified, firstly for authorisation within the appropriation of public funds, and then approved for payment with supporting paper work of 'receipt of goods', matched against Purchase Orders, and finally 'passed for payment' by a supervisor, within each government department. But even that wasn't the end of the process. Lithgow, as Auditor, had to confirm the trail of paperwork, and to finitely confirm that all the paperwork was in order. Each piece had to bear the correct number of signatures, carry the correct supporting vouchers and then be authorised, appropriately, for payment. Bureaucracy was rampant, but even so we find as Lithgow carried out his onerous tasks that even he was capable of making simple arithmetic errors. The Accounts forwarded over Lithgow's signature to the British Treasury in 1825, for example, contain some arithmetic errors, but any notation of weakness in this regard was more than compensated by his insatiable contribution to other aspects of the Colony.

Lithgow was made a Magistrate in 1828, a Board member of the Female Factory in Parramatta and a Board Member of the newly created 'Board of

General Purposes' who's role, as defined and laid down by Governor Ralph Darling, was to oversee the Colonial Planning Operations on behalf of the Governor.

From May 1824 until October 1825, Lithgow held the senior post within the Commissary System of being both Assistant Commissary General and also of being in charge of the Accounting Records and Returns. A second position was created after the British Treasury released in 1826 the revised 'Recording and Reporting Procedures'. These updated guidelines for Colonial Accounting were partly in response to the relatively unprofessional (and essentially 'privatised') accounting system invoked by Macquarie and his predecessors who, from 1802 to 1821 relied on amateur 'treasurers' to collect, record, disburse and report on Colonial funding. Some responsibility for this temporary clerical assistance is due to the fact that the Colony had no Treasury. Nevertheless the two 'treasurers', being Reverend Samuel Marsden and Mr (Surgeon) Darcy Wentworth, handled all the locally raised revenue and expenditures.

After Macquarie left the Colony, Brisbane and then Darling had been instructed to install the 'Blue Book' system of recording and reporting, and so from 1822 the British Treasury received two copies of the hand compiled reports whilst the Governor kept the third copy. These records were only compiled at the end of each year and rather than assist in reducing the work load of the Colonial Secretary's office, this procedure increased it substantially, since the Blue Books were summaries taken from other summaries but then recompiled into the format required by the British Treasury. The 'Blue Book' process was a marked improvement on the Orphan Fund, the Police Fund, the Land Fund and the many other 'funds' that were really an extension of have a separate bank account for each process of government.

Lithgow fulfilled the duties of Commissary of Accounts and Colonial Auditor admirably and impressed Governor Darling to the extent that when the Governor was given approval to form an 'Executive Council', Lithgow was offered the role of 'acting' secretary to the Council. It did not take long for Lithgow to move from mere scribe to active participant and he later filled a vacancy on the Executive Council itself.

Brisbane saw the need to create the position of Auditor of government accounts, having seen first-hand the benefits of having Lithgow fill the extra role of Auditor of Commissary accounts. Brisbane thought nothing of the potential conflict of interest of the one officer acting as both accountant (preparer) and Auditor (reviewer) of Commissary accounts, nor did he see the potential for conflict by having the one officer fill the roles of commissary accountant and government auditor. Today these roles would be arms length and very independent. However Brisbane's problems were of a more practical nature than considering conflicts of interest. Brisbane found a dearth of experienced public servants in the colony and having an officer of Lithgow's experience was like a godsend. Likewise Brisbane desperately wanted and needed some 'financial' advice to assist his economic planning for the economy. Again Lithgow filled that role in terms of experience and background.

Soon, however, the dual roles of Commissary Accountant and Colonial Auditor were growing too much for one man to handle, and it was Brisbane's successor, Ralph Darling who sought the approval of The Secretary of State in London to make Lithgow a full-time Auditor (in 1825) at an increased salary. Governor Darling's salary recommendation was not accepted and Secretary of State Huskisson imposed his own limits on the Lithgow remuneration.

Even after Lithgow settled into his new restricted position (as Colonial Auditor-General) he continued to take an active role in economic analysis and future planning for the Colony, by becoming an active participant in the Governor's exclusive but unofficial 'executive council'.

Four interlinking roles (which will be explored more fully in the main text) included:

a. Lithgow working with Major Ovens, before Oven's premature death, on assessing the organisation of and work practices for the convicts. The idea for and organisation of the work gangs used at the dockyard, the Lumber Yard, the timber yard, the land clearing, road making gangs was that jointly of Ovens and Lithgow, although Ovens placed his name alone on the final report, lest it be thought by Governor Bourke that Lithgow had surplus time on his hands.

b. Working on and with the Board of the Female Work Factory to develop outputs that were worthwhile and meaningful. As a former Commissary principal, Lithgow was in a good position to gauge what could be produced within the colony by the growing 'army' of female prisoners. The numbers for the Female Factory are interesting, as the private placement of 381 of the 573 women meant that the government was denied the working output of these people, although on the other hand the government was saved the direct cost of clothing, defending the morals, housing and feeding of these women.
c. The Land Board prepared a detailed series of reports (they were authored and assembled by Lithgow) for the governor that established the role and needs of land sales, land clearing; surveying and set aside land for townships, schools, churches and the need for town planning including communications and transportation.
d. His association with the Bank of New South Wales was long and successful. Lithgow was a Director, initially representing the Government, but was re-elected in his own right, an association that lasted almost 20 years. He became a trustee of the Australian Society for Deposits and Loans. Lithgow also became an initial shareholder (nominal value 100 pound) in the Bank of Australia.

Lithgow filled his position for 19 years as a member of the Legislative Council admirably and used his participation to assist in interpreting the all-important Appropriation Bills for the benefit of the other members.

The Lithgow committee work would have brought him in touch with most, if not all, of the notable and significant members of the Colonial community. His voluntary associations and community interests including those already mentioned, as well as the Southern Cattle Association and the Railway Association and the Steam Navigation Company. These committees were then extended to the Board of Trustees of the Clergy and School Lands; the New South Wales Legislative Council; The Bank of NSW and the Savings Bank of NSW; Magistrate and J.P; followed by his nomination to the Executive Council in December 1835, and membership of the Coal Board in October 1847.

Lithgow served under five governors, one of which he also served as acting Private Secretary. He liaised with eight British Secretaries of State and five British Prime Ministers. He was threatened with termination by Sir George Gipps, who was being chastised for failing to deliver the 'Blue Books' for 5 years past the due date. Gipps blamed Lithgow; Lithgow blamed the down the line record-keepers, but in the end Lithgow delivered six years of audited annual records (the Blue Books) in less than six months.

We have yet to learn very much about his early life, except that he was born and raised in the Scotland of the late 1700s. It is most likely, that the Lithgow family home was in the Lanark district in the Clyde River region of south-central Scotland. He graduated from the University of Edinburgh as a licentiate of the Church of Scotland, but shortly after graduating chose instead to join the Commissary Operations of the British Military abroad. Another conjecture, by this author, as yet unverified, is that Lithgow was a second son, expected by tradition to enter the 'church', but as the Church of Scotland was, at that time in turmoil and undergoing major change, it is likely that young clerics were paid very little and Lithgow saw a larger benefit in a secure, government position. Scottish Home Office records do not include references to the early Lithgow family, and so we are left wondering if William was a descendent of the famous Scottish explorer from the early 1600s who bore the same name We could attribute, in yet another giant leap of imagination that Lithgow's decision to remain an unmarried loner all his life could have been due to a family tragedy before he joined the army, or possibly he had the predilection of this forebear, William Lithgow (1583-1637) to roam, adventure and travel. The British Military had headquartered their commissary operation for Europe in Edinburgh, and after two years of pounding the streets following his graduation, earning a small pittance as a stipend and feeling he was going nowhere, Lithgow decided to join the military in as non-military field as he could find. He spent the next two years in the original quartermaster's stores in Edinburgh and found he had a flair for numbers, clerical organisation and a good judgment for forward planning. The military decided, following the initial training period that his commission should be made permanent and his knowledge and instruction extended. Thus commenced a lifelong period of public service.

His first appointment was to Heligoland, a small piece of British Territory–an island in the North Sea. When the British were relieved of control over Heligoland and it was handed back to the Germans, he was transferred (July 1812) to Mauritius, still with the Commissary division of the British Military, where he rose through the ranks to become assistant commissary. He was in Mauritius at the same time as Ralph Darling, who, upon his appointment (in April 1823) as Governor of New South Wales, requested the transfer of Lithgow as Assistant Commissary-General for 'Accounts' at the same destination. Lithgow had sailed directly to Sydney, via Hobart, arriving May 1824, whilst Darling took himself and family back to England for twelve months before sailing for Sydney. Whilst in London he received two commissions–one as Governor of the colony of New South Wales and the other as Governor-in-Chief of Van Diemen's Land, with a lieutenant governor, resident in Hobart responsible for day–to-day operations. Thus Lithgow's journey into Colonial Australia began in Sydney in 1824, but he was serving Governor Brisbane until Darling arrived in 1826.

Lithgow had grown up in a Scotland that had unified in 1707 with England to form a creative and beneficial union as Great Britain, and he chose to contribute to the growth of the British Colony in New South Wales. Lithgow's participation in just about every aspect of the future government of the colony made him a potentially formidable force in Colonial public affairs, and he was an influential adviser to each successive governor of the day. Darling anticipated this potential and Lithgow was the first of a number Darling had worked with prior to 1825 who he selected to gather around him in Colonial New South Wales. This 'team' included Major Ovens, his son in law, William Dumaresq, and the other Dumaresq brother–Henry.

The post Macquarie colony was a rapidly changing place–the colony had matured remarkably since Macquarie had generated unparalleled growth in the land, through his building program and his placement of the swelling ranks of male and female convicts into productive, both private and public, work. Macquarie's encouragement of new colonial industry sustained the growing levels of British investment and speculation in the colony. Decentralisation and the need to open up new settlements including Van Dieman's Land, Port Phillip and Morton Bay continued to grow the local revenue and de-emphasise the need for British Treasury funding. However the Commissary operations grew increasingly important, as they were the sole support programs for both the convicts and the military remaining in the colony, whilst also being the defacto Treasurer until 1817.

Lithgow received at least three land grants: a rural grant of two thousand acres in the Hunter district, and a residential site in Sydney town (on the North Shore at St. Leonard's), on which he built a cottage, and a grazing property on the banks of Lake George in the Monaro Plains area of Southern N.S.W. He also held a 'grazing' licence in the then Riverina District, but in an area we know today as Gundagai. His 'run' was on the eastern bank of the Murrumbidgee River, where the township of Gundagai now stands. This property was managed on his behalf and records show that he only visited this area once in the 8 years he operated the 'lease;' but this pastoral activity made him think a great deal about the agricultural planning in the colony and its potential, and he then spent many years in the two agricultural societies that became so influential during the rise of the pastoral and squatting industries.

Lithgow retired in the Colony in 1852 on a pension of £339/3/4 per annum, and relocated from Sydney to his cottage on the rural property in the Hunter region. He retired also from the Legislative Council in 1848 (after 19 years of service), and from his position of Auditor-General in 1852. Lithgow died in 1864 (11June) at the age of 80. Lithgow's was a remarkable career, stretching 50 years in the service of his country and leaving a legacy of contribution to the colony, and such a contribution would be difficult to ever match again. His memorials are few, other than a town that retained his name and became an established settlement in the area known originally as 'Lithgow's Valley' (the name was given by Lithgow's friend and colleague (Surveyor-General John Oxley). We learn from newspaper reports of his land-sales (first at Kissing Point and then Lithgow Valley) and of his sheep 'run' at present day Gundagai in the Monaro Region of southern New South Wales.

CHAPTER 6

THE STORY OF THE NSW COMMISSARIAT

The HRNSW contains numerous references to original records reporting the instructions on how to operate, or anecdotal reports on how the commissariat operated. In 1786, Phillip wrote[46]:

> *'It is planned that a quantity of provisions equal to two years consumption should be provided, which will be issued from time to time, according to the discretion of the Superintendent, guided by the proportion of food which the country and the labour of the new settlers may produce.'*

He added that 'Clothing per convict was estimated to cost £2.19.6 including jackets, hats, shirts, trousers, shoes' but 'the type of clothing was not always suitable for the climate, and should be ready made rather than relying on the convicts to sew their own.' He noted that 'The *Sirius* brought seed wheat and barley and four months supply of flour for the settlement, together with a year's provisions for the ships company,' and:

> *'Supplies of grain or flour from England will be necessary to maintain the colony until there is sufficient local crops in store rather than 'in the ground', because of grub, fire, drought and other accidents'.*

---

46 HRNSW Vol 1 Part 2

On 9 January 1793, he noted that 'I have directed the commissary to make a purchase and have thus augmented the quantity of provisions in the colony to 7 months at the established ration.'

On 6 January 1793, Phillip recorded his opinion that the projected expense for the settlement for 1794 for the 5,500 population was £25,913. With 3,000 convicts included in the population, this translated to of £13.14.0 per head per annum, (approximately 9d. per day) and pointed out 'this sum cannot increase, but must gradually diminish'. Phillip was allowing only 1,900 persons 'on the store' or less than 40% of the population. His numbers were obviously incorrect but the cost he calculated conveniently came within the official allowance of 14d. Per head per day.

On 9 November 1794, the Colonial Office reported that 'the stock of stores of provisions and ready-made clothing should now be sufficient for the settlement for one year. With the quantity of clothing shipped in mid-1794, there would be a sufficient supply for 2,500 men and 700 women, according to the last official report of numbers.' Mr. Henry Dundas (British MP) insisted that the convicts should be made 'to wear the allotted clothing for a full year.' On 15 February 1794, the Colonial Office directed that 'Each ship was to carry supplies for the trip and for maintenance upon arrival, for convicts, soldiers and sailors. 'King, as Phillip's Deputy and Governor of Norfolk Island, recorded on the 20 July 1794, that the island had produced 'a second crop in sufficient quantity for storage for the next year.–being 11500 bushels plus 4000 reserved for seed, stock, and the producing families.' 'Stores were ordered from the Cape of Good Hope for the Sydney settlement and the hospital on 22 June 1788 to be selected by John Hunter, as captain of the *Sirius*

On 10 June 1797, Governor Hunter submitted a plan that

> *'. . . were Government to establish a public store for the retail sale of a variety of articles–such as clothing, or materials for clothing, hardware, tools, sugar, soap, tea, tobacco and every article that labouring people require–supported by a reputable shopkeeper who should produce regular accounts and charge a small premium to cover these other costs, then*

> *the people would get what they wanted with ease, and at far less expense than in any other way.'*

On 10 January 1798, Governor Hunter repeated his request for a public store:

> *'If my suggestion is adopted, a branch of the store should be placed on Norfolk Island. Such a store should lessen the expense of maintaining the convicts and into the store; I would also suggest the retailing of liquor and spirits, for the purpose of putting a stop to the importation of that article.'*

Again on the 25 May 1798, Hunter recommended using:

> *'. . . the public store as a means of controlling the high price of grain. Such a store would operate as an encouragement to industry. Without some form of price control on grain the settlers cannot live let alone provide for a family. The speculators and the monopolists all contrive to keep the settlers in a continual state of beggary and retard the progressive improvements of the colony.'*

The success of Simeon Lord's colonial merchandising in 1801 proves that Hunter was on the right track with his 'public' store.

The Colonial Secretary wrote to Hunter on 3 December 1798 about the meat supply:

> *'. . . when the livestock belonging to the crown, added to that of individuals, is in so flourishing a state as to supply the needs at 6d a pound or less, it is evident the Government will gain by supplying the settlement with fresh meat instead of sending salted provisions from England.'*

This request was later modified to limit the store purchases for meat to those from farmer settlers.

On 2 February 1800, William Broughton, a churchman and Magistrate, was also appointed as the storekeeper at Parramatta to replace a man Hunter had sacked for fraud.

Governor King recorded his success in conserving the stores by writing that

> *'. . . since I took office, I have reduced the number of fully rationed people relying on the public stores by 450. This has saved annually the amount of £10,488, using the rate of £23 per head. I have also reduced the price of wheat to 8d per bushel, pork to 6p per lb, and maize to 4s instead of 5s per bushel.'*

When Hunter was recalled to England, the commissariat was left with many debts owed by settlers and he was concerned that they would be denied and he be held responsible. He wrote to the new Governor, Phillip King, and recorded:

> *'I trust it is clear that there has been no lavish waste and no improvident use of the public stores during my authority. These debts are just, even though many of the individuals may doubt their being indebted to the Government for so much. 'It appears there were doubtful debts of over £5,000 due to the store.'*

In response, King made demands on the settlers and accepted grain at a higher price than usual in settlement of the debts. When news of the demands became known, it produced an unusual response from John Macarthur, who suddenly recalled that much of what he had taken from the stores, and charged against the public account, over the previous 12 months was in fact his personal responsibility and he settled with the stores on this basis.

On 7 November 1800, King re-appointed John Palmer to his former position as Commissary. Other appointments included Broughton to Norfolk Island, Deputy Chapman from Norfolk to Sydney and William

Sutter as Storekeeper at Parramatta. In order to conserve grain, King reduced the ration to 13.5 lb of wheat per week.

At the time of his appointment, Palmer had been handed a set of instructions, including:

> *'All troops and convicts in the territory were to be properly supplied and the commissary was to keep a grain stock of 12 months supply*
>
> *He was to transmit annually a list of expected consumption, and all purchases were to be made under the authority of the Governor and prices paid to be no greater than market prices*
>
> *All bills of exchange must be accompanied with an affidavit of purchase countersigned by the Governor.*
>
> *You will also make receipts for all payments in the presence of at least one witness–preferably a magistrate–and make three sets of all vouchers, one for the treasury, one with the accounts and one for the store use.*
>
> *Keep a separate account of all items transmitted from England.*
>
> *Make a survey of any stores lost or damaged–which goods are to be sold or destroyed at the Governors discretion.*
>
> *Make up annually an account of all receipts and expenditures, accompanied by one set of vouchers.*
>
> *You are responsible for the preservation of all stores and provisions and the employees who work for you, and to the public.'*
>
> (Signed)
> Portland (Duke of Portland)

This set of notes on how the commissariat should operate was prepared by the Duke of Portland and handed to Governor-in-Chief Phillip Gidley King on 28 September 1800. They are attached for historical purposes.

A list of some of the main provisions and supplies that arrived with the First Fleet indicated the role and difficulties facing the storekeeper. In addition to foodstuffs, supposedly sufficient for the first six months, some of the provisions and supplies which were shipped with the First Fleet in 1787, were:

TABLE 1.1: SUPPLIES SENT WITH THE FIRST FLEET

700 steel spades	5448 squares of glass	50 pickaxes	30 box rulers
30 grindstones	700 axe handles	140 angers	50 hayforks
700 iron shovels	200 canvas beds	700 wooden bowls	30 pincers
330 iron pots	747,000 nail of various sizes	700 gimlets	42 splitting wedges
700 garden hoes	63 coal buckets	700 wooden platters	100 plain measures
6 hand-carts	100 pairs of hinges	504 saw files	8000 fishhooks
700 West India hoes	80 carpenter's axes	10 forges	12 brick moulds
4 timber carriages	10 sets cooper's tools	300 chisels	48 dozen fishing lines
700 grubbing hoes	20 shipwright's adzes	700 clasp knives	6 harpoons
14 chains	40 corn-mills	60 butcher's knives	10000 bricks
700 felling axes	175 claw hammers	500 tin-plates	12 lances
14 fishing nets	12 ploughs	100 pairs–scissors	
700 hatchets	175 handsaws	60 padlocks	

The complete list[47] of articles sent with the First Fleet was much longer and represented a storeman's nightmare if records of issues and returns were to be maintained. For instance, the unloading of stores and provisions for immediate use commenced on 7 February but; since the settlement held over 1,000 people, there was obviously not sufficient bedding, blankets, cooking utensils, or eating utensils for everyone[48]. The allowance of clothing

[47] HRNSW Vol 1, Part 2 p.16

[48] The list of 'stores' and 'provisions' is found in both the HRNSW and in John Cobley *'Sydney Cove'* Vol 1

for a male convict for a year was equally inadequate; although raw cloth, needles and cotton had arrived with the Fleet and female convicts could be encouraged to hand sew clothing if necessary. The records show that the total costs of all male and female convict clothing was only £4,144.

In '*Botany Bay Mirages*', Alan Frost has raised the question of whether the inadequate quantity of tools and supplies was deliberate, or merely poor planning. A case can be made for improper planning rather than deliberate mismanagement. Phillip was left in sole charge of the voyage and received very little guidance, support or interest from the Secretary of State's office, the Naval Board or the commissariat division of the British Treasury.[49] It is unlikely that, after a fairly ordinary career as a naval officer, Phillip would suddenly have reverted to poor leadership. Indeed, he had commented to the Naval Board that the vessels allotted to the Fleet were not adequate in size or number. He also questioned the short amount of time allowed for the planning process, but received no worthwhile response. Clearly, this was not regarded as a voyage of high importance compared with British naval activities in other parts of the world. So, the fact that Phillip used a great deal of judgment and commonsense, speaks volumes for his quiet confidence and determination that he was the most suitable choice as the head of this mission.

For the first storekeeper, local circumstances were such that the supplies brought from England needed to be carefully protected against theft and loss. The tools, in particular, were to be issued daily and returned each evening; however according to Marjorie Barnard, within 14 days of arriving in the colony, over one-third of the tools loaned out for chopping trees and clearing land had been lost, stolen or deliberately concealed from the storekeeper.[50] The chief cause was the unwillingness of convicts to work; removing the tools meant they were unable to chop firewood or cut timber framing for the new camp. As a way of keeping the tools in repair, Miller had set up forges on the banks of Sydney Cove and used iron and steel pieces brought out as ballast to forge new tools and replace lost items. Watkin Tench in his '*Narrative of the Expedition to Botany*

---

49 Alan Frost raises this possibility in '*Botany Bay Mirages*' Chapter 8 'No Cheaper Mode…' as does Barnard in '*Phillip of Australia*'.

50 Barnard '*A History of Australia*' *Chapter 3* 'Taking Shape' *p60.*

Bay' provides some useful insights into the conditions faced by Phillip and Miller. In November 1788 he noted: 'Temporary, wooden stores, covered with thatch or shingles into which the cargoes of all the ships have been lodged, are completed, and a hospital erected'.[51] However, the stores were not to remain as such for long as the end of one such building was converted into a temporary church for Sunday services. These frail structures were neither fire-proof nor rat-proof and the summer of 1789 saw the end to these temporary structures when Phillip designed a new, sturdier and more permanent store in a location closer to the settlement's military camp. Later in 1789, Tench recorded that 'the storehouse was finished at Rose Hill (by then renamed Parramatta). It was 100 feet by 24 feet and was built of local brick, deep red in colour, but not as durable as the Sydney product'.[52]

Displaying rare frustration, Phillip wrote to Assistant Secretary of State, Phillip Stephens, in August 1790 'Leather is needed for soles for men's shoes and materials for mending them. Shoes here last but a very short time, and the want of these materials and thread to mend the clothing will render it impossible to make them serve more than half the time for which they were intended'. The following month Phillip wrote to Nepean, the Under-Secretary of State for the Colonies, and made two observations: 'I cannot help repeating that most of the tools sent out were as bad as ever' and, 'the wooden ware sent out were too small; they are called bowls and platters, but are not larger than pint basins. There was not one that would hold a quart'.[53]

Tench also described the development of the new town of Rose Hill and the buildings adjacent to the store: 'the new stone barracks is within 150 yards of the wharf, where all boats from Sydney unload. In addition there is an excellent barn, a granary, an enclosed yard to rear livestock,

---

51 Flannery quotes Tench in '*1788 Watkin Tench*' p81

52 Flannery *ibid* p127

53 Governor Phillip to Under-Secretary Nepean HRNSW Vol 1, Part 2 p481. In terms of the departmental hierarchy, the Colonial Office had a Secretary, an Under-Secretary and then a number of Assistant-Secretaries

a commodious blacksmith's shop and a most wretched hospital, totally destitute of every convenience'.[54]

In 1790 Phillip told Nepean that the colony badly needed 'honest and intelligent settlers, and free men to act as superintendents of convicts'. Phillip also requested a new, more appropriate style of clothing for the convicts, even suggesting a form of mark to protect them from being sold. He badly needed a windmill, and requested axes, saws, combs, iron pots and 'two or three hundred iron frying pans which will be a saving of the spades'.[55] Unlike Macquarie some twenty years later, Phillip was of two minds about free enterprise in the colony. He did approve an open market, but then reverted to government importing 'specialty' items into the colony. According to Barnard, "in April 1792, Phillip established a regular market in Parramatta". It was for fish, grain, livestock, clothing and anything else that might legitimately be bought or sold. It was open to convicts. In October 1790, Phillip reported to Secretary Dundas in London: "The commissary was obliged to purchase various articles brought out by the sailing officers of the *Pitt*, where the private property sold in this settlement amounted to upwards of £4,000, which may serve in some measure to point out what might be bought by a ship loaded wholly on account of government".[56]

During 1792, Phillip was faced with a minor mutiny. The military under the leadership of Major Grose advised Phillip that they (the military) had chartered *The Britannia* to sail to the Cape for supplies. In spite of strong protests from Phillip, the ship sailed on 24 October and thus was born the 'pernicious system of private trading by the military'.[57] Phillip wrote movingly to the Right Hon. Henry Dundas, the Secretary of State in London, of this continuous struggle to get necessities: 'The period at which the colony will supply its inhabitants with animal foods is nearly as distant at present as it was when I first landed'. He added:

54 Flannery *ibid* p 145

55 Governor Phillip to the Rt. Hon Henry Dundas HRNSW Vol 1 Part 2 p595

56 Governor Phillip to the Rt. Hon Henry Dundas HRNSW Vol 1 Part 2 p.613

57 Barnard, *Phillip of Australia*, p. 126

'I beg leave to observe that all those wants which have been pointed out in my different letters still exist: for iron pots, we have been nearly as distressed as for provisions: cross cut saws, axes and the various tools for husbandry are also much wanted; many of the articles are now made here, but the demand is greater than can be supplied because of the shortage of materials; many bales of clothing have been received, but arrive rotten and so injured from the damp that they have scarcely borne washing a second time'.[58]

TABLE 1.2: VALUE OF BILLS DRAWN BY THE NSW COMMISSARY ON THE BRITISH TREASURY[59]

Year	Amount (£)
1806	13,873
1807	31,110
1808	23,163
1809	49,514
1810	72,600

These increases could be directly attributed to the additional population being victualled in the colony, the higher level of rations, purchases by the commissary of foodstuffs and provisions from visiting foreign vessels, and higher prices of produce in England due to the prevailing economic conditions. Secretary Liverpool was also aware of the growing local revenue being raised in the colony from import duties, which he had little control. Macquarie, on the other hand, saw this locally raised revenue as 'cream' and discretionary revenue for his personal use–not to be handed over to the Treasury in London. Liverpool made mention of the growing expenditure on public works and wanted this item to be trimmed; the civil list was growing at the same rate but his goal was to make the 'Police' and 'Orphan' funds pay for these extra persons. He directed that there be 'no increase in the civil staff' unless covered by local funding. He approved the purchase of a brig for the colonial service provided it was paid for from

58 Governor Phillip to the Rt. Hon Henry Dundas HRNSW Vol 1 Part 2 p.643

59 These figures are assembled from Governor Macquarie despatches found in HRA 1: vols 9 & 10

local funds. Macquarie could see his dream dwindling away rapidly unless he could maintain his control over the commissariat, so that he could manipulate expenditures to suit his own needs whilst keeping the majority of local revenues under his control.

Some of Liverpool's premonitions of uncontrolled expenditure may well have been caused by Macquarie, especially as the commissariat pursued a 'support' role. In 1810 Macquarie wrote to Liverpool's predecessor, Viscount Castlereagh, offering his opinion of the condition of the local commissary:

> *'I found the Public Stores almost destitute of dry provisions, which situation had occasioned very serious alarm for some time before my arrival. This very exhausted state of His Majesty's Stores had been very much occasioned by the last dreadful and calamitous inundation of the Hawkesbury River, which had swept away the entire crops in that fertile district–an event not infrequent, and which has repeatedly involved the inhabitants in the deepest misery and distress'.*[60]

In response to this finding, Macquarie acted swiftly, adding 300 acres of grain to the government farms, importing wheat from Bengal and reducing all rations. Castlereagh had expressed doubts about the preference for government over private farms but Macquarie protested that the government herds and farming should be maintained further livestock be imported for breeding purposes. He maintained control over the colonial economy by giving notice of a bank and a local currency and an appropriation of funds for the restocking of the commissariat. He also supported the operations of the Lumber and Dock Yards.

Over the next 10 years, Macquarie commenced what Commissioner Bigge later declared to be 'excessive spending; however, it produced significant results for the economy. He was generally responsive to the needs of the traders, merchants and entrepreneurs who he considered were the drivers of the economy. As shown by his instruction of 8 July 1815, he was intent

---

60 HRA 1:X: 221

on simplifying the process of business in the colony and of making the store receipts, issued by the commissariat, a form of medium of exchange for the local settlers.[61]

Summary of Instructions for Operating the Commissariat in Colonial NSW

Phillip Gidley King arrived as Governor in 1800 and noted that, up to the time of his appointment, there had been no explicit set of instructions issued for the guidance of the Commissary, except for verbal commands from each successive governor or administrator. In October 1800 he appointed Thomas Laycock as acting Commissary to fill the vacancy between the departure of James Williamson and the return in November of John Palmer from England. King saw the need for a set of instructions for the guidance of the 'officer on whom alone the public economy of the colony rests'[62] In the same despatch King advised that on behalf of the colony, he had purchased the wine cellar from retiring Governor Hunter and directed the commissary to pay for it and 'receive it'. The cost was £151.11.6.

King was as good as his word and produced a set of instructions as well as transmitting annual statements of the commissariat's revenues and expenses to the Treasury–the first and last governor to do so. After King, the commissariat handled its own transmittals until 1813, when they were made to Army headquarters (quartermaster's regiment) in England for consolidation and transfer to the Treasury. According to the NSW–SRO, King's commissariat records still exist in the PRO in London, but they do not appear to be part of the AJCP records.

---

61 HRA 1:8:p623

62 HRA 1:2:675 King to Secretaries of the Treasury (Governor's Despatch # 2, September 1800)

The Instructions of Governor King

The HRA[63] offers a complete set of the instructions of Governor King, of which the following is a summary:–

The Commissary was 'to control the receipt and issue of all stores and provisions into and from His Majesty's stores.

No articles were to be received or issued without a written order from the Governor.

Detailed store receipts were required of all 'grain or animal food' purchased or otherwise received into the store.

Accounts of expenditure were to be furnished quarterly and more often if required.

The Commissary was to plan to match ration requirement with food availability. The Governor was to be advised of any shortfall and where it would be covered from and how much it would cost.

The Commissary was 'directed to reform the irregularity that has existed in the mode hitherto followed in making payment for such articles as have been purchased from settlers for public use'. Previously promissory notes had been made out for goods received; but these notes were frequently counterfeited and hence offered little security. King proposed a system of store receipts, which were to show the quantity and nature of goods received as well as their monetary value. At convenient intervals, the Governor would draw a Bill on the British treasury, at which time a call would be made for the return of all store receipts issued to settlers.

King obviously wanted to create regularised recording & reporting for the commissary and required the commissary to present to the governor once a year the following account books for audit.

63 HRA 1:2:632-6 sets out a complete copy of the instructions

'Victualling Book'–containing names of persons who received provisions during the year.

'Clothing and Slop Expense Book'–to record issues of clothing, blankets etc.

'Book to record Receipts of Stores', provisions and clothing, from all sources; also the expense thereof, and an inventory of stores on hand at the end of each year.

'Store Purchasing Book' specifying purchases of food from settlers, noting date, quantity, application and cost, a cross-reference was to be made with store receipts issued.

'Purchasing Book', to set out the quantities and cost of stores purchased from masters of visiting vessels or 'other strangers'–again to be supported by vouchers. Method of payment is to be specified–in kind, in grain, meat or money.

'Book of Particular Expense' showing provisions and clothing issued during the year to non-convicts e.g. civil and military officers. A similar book was to be kept for issues to free settlers.

An open list of all births, deaths and absentees during the year–these details were to be supplied by the clergy in the colony.

Whenever a ship was due to sail to England a 'State of the Settlement Report' was to be prepared for despatch with the vessel. This statement was to include a current population record, the number on stores, inventory in the store and a weekly return of expenditures.

A 'Weekly Victualling and Store-issue Book' was to be kept by each remote storekeeper, and a quarterly summary sent to the Sydney store.

In many ways, the requirements imposed by Governor King were not unlike the range of statistical returns provided in 1822 by the first *Blue Book.* All of the above books and returns were to be delivered to the governor on 31 October each year, prior to their transmission to England, and a 'correct copy was to be kept in the commissariat office' as directed by the British Treasury instructions.

The British Treasury Instructions

The British Treasury must have also seen the need for a formal set of instructions to be issued to the Commissary as, in November 1800, Commissary Palmer returned with a set of instructions for his guidance.[64] These Treasury regulations are more general than those of Governor King but they were not inconsistent. The main difference was a policy change which now authorised the Commissary to draw bills without the approval of the governor, contradicting the earlier written policy that 'all bills drawn for public purposes in the settlement should be drawn by the governor and by no other person'. King's despatch to the Duke of Portland of March 1802 included a State of His Majesty's Settlements in NSW Report[65], which confirmed, essentially down to the last detail, that King's instructions were being adhered to exactly and also showed that the commissariat was becoming of considerable importance in the colony as a market and exchange. King's order of August 1802 authorised the Commissary to sell surplus perishable stores to free settlers at a profit. The commission charged varied at first but was later fixed at 50%. Remuneration to Commissary Palmer was by a small percentage on sales, although from this he had to pay for extra bookkeeping clerks from his own pocket.

---

64 HRA 1:3:5 King's despatch # 3 of 10 March 1801 records Palmer delivered to him a letter from Secretary Long inclosing instructions from Treasury Commissioners for the commissary's guidance. King questioned the third article, which authorised the commissary to directly draw bills, for purchases on the public account, on the Treasury instead of going through the governor.

65 HRA 1:3:418 details the civil establishment in the colony and the lengthy report of the administration of the commissariat department

A period of instability occurred during the military administration, between the time of the Bligh rebellion and the arrival of Lachlan Macquarie. During this time, Williamson, Wiltshire, Fitz and finally Broughton replaced Palmer as successive Commissaries.

Governor Macquarie's Instructions to the Commissary

Macquarie wasted no time in commencing his investigation of the commissariat for on 31 January 1810, less than one month after his arrival in the colony, he issued a general order[66], a summary of which is as follows:

Remote storekeepers were to submit vouchers (Form #1) for requisitions on the general store in Sydney each month.

Form #2 was a return of all foodstuffs received by storekeepers weekly.

Form #3 was a copy of Store receipts for all stores received.

All requisitions for stores had to be counter-signed by the Governor's secretary.

Invoices for all store purchases were to be sent to the Governor's secretary

Statements of receipts and expenditures were be made each June and December and forwarded to the Governor's secretary.

Storekeepers were to furnish to the governor weekly summaries of receipts and issues of stores.

The Commissary was to keep lists of all persons victualled from the public stores.

The 'Statement of the Settlement' was to be sent with each ship sailing for England.

---

66 Found in SRO NC11/5

In February 1811, Macquarie directed that only the commissariat was to import into 'bonded store' all wines and spirits ordered for the colony, with a fee receivable of one-half gallon for every one hundred gallons measured. From 1827 the Bonded Store became part of the Customs Department. He also oversaw the removal of civil servant families from store support–only the civil servant himself could draw rations. By an order dated December 1814, the sale of articles from government stores to any private individual was disallowed, thus introducing freedom of trade–this meant the colonial government would issue permits for imported articles to be distributed amongst the settlers and created a new class of merchants.

Following the Bligh rebellion, Treasury officials in London considered the commissariat to be in need of reorganisation. Up to this time, it had been a separate colonial department under the control of the governor, paid for through the Budget appropriation process. The reform proposal was to transfer responsibility for the colony's commissariat to the Commissary-General in England, who headed sub-branch of the Treasury department. A Deputy Commissary–General was to head the colonial operation and would be subject to instructions issued from the British Commissariat. Another revision was that all deputy commissaries would now be recruited in England and the colonial governor would only have a supervising role[67]. The activities of David Allen have been discussed in Chapter 2 and do not require repeating. However, there was a source

67 HRA 1:8:126 + note 19 (p657) Bathurst to Macquarie February 1814: Note 19 records 'Prior to June 1813, the commissariat department was a distinct colonial entity under the immediate control and direction of the governor. A separate establishment was created for it and salaries were voted annually by Parliament. On 11th June 1813 David Allen arrived holding the appointment of D.C.G. He assumed control of the commissariat and a new *regime* was established. The department became a branch of the commissary-general in England, a sub-department of the treasury and officers held their appointments as part of the general English commissariat staff. The D.C.G. was head of the department generally, qualified by the local supervision of the governor of the colony. He communicated directly with his superiors in England and not through the governor as formerly. It is evident that the functions of the governor were curtailed considerably by this change

of disagreement between the D.C.G and the governor, other than over commissariat personnel and their overt dishonesty. The governor was to be concerned with changes in the methods of payment to free settlers for stores received into the commissariat. The store had been using 'store receipts' as payment and, as Butlin points out in *Foundations*[68]:

> '. . . *because of the lack of money in the colony, the store receipts became in effect the circulating currency. However, this led to difficulties in making up accounts, since it was often quite impossible to obtain the receipts back from the settlers in order to make up quarterly or annual returns. The fact was that many settlers found that the demand in the colony for those store receipts was sufficient to make the return of them unnecessary*'.

Macquarie's attempt to solve the problem came via a government order[69], which stipulated 'all store receipts are to be brought to the D.C.G at the end of every two months. Failure to hand them in would cancel the value of the receipt'.

It was David Allen's excursion into issuing promissory notes to replace the store receipts that eventually brought about his dismissal. Macquarie's reports[70] on the matter show that, at this time, the commissariat had branches in Sydney, Parramatta, Windsor, Liverpool, Bathurst, Hobart, Port Dalrymple and Newcastle. Allen's replacement was Drennan who arrived in January 1819 but, immediately upon his arrival, he attempted to mislead Macquarie by alleging he had also been authorised to issue promissory notes in lieu of store receipts. A subsequent Commission of Inquiry into Drennan's activities did much good for there are no further accounts of corruption during the Macquarie Administration. Drennan could not explain a debt or account for missing funds of 'upwards of £6,000'[71] Brisbane had also directed D.C.G Wemyss to transmit a detailed

---

68 S.J. Butlin's Foundations of the Australian Monetary System 1788-1851'

69 SRO records NC11/5

70 HRA 1:10:116 'Macquarie to the Lord Commissioners of the Treasury (Pages 100-135)

71 HRA 1:10:629 Brisbane to Earl Bathurst 6th April 1822

and ;'certified' statement about Drennan to London, explaining the public accounts deficiency.

The next attempt to reorganise the stores was made by Governor Darling in August 1827, with the support of', and upon written instructions from, the Treasury. The Treasury requested:

> *'. . . it being desirable, with a view to a more systematic arrangement of the Accounts of the Public Expenditure of the Colony, that the expenses of articles issued from the General Store, be ascertained and classified under the following three headings:*
>
> *1. Colonial 2. Military 3. Maintenance of Convicts.*
>
> *It will be necessary that the D.C.G be furnished with separate requisitions and vouchers for each of these heads respectively.*
>
> *Under Heading 1, are to be classed all articles, issued for purposes not military or not connected with the maintenance, clothing, housing or management of convicts*
>
> *Under Heading 2, all Army, Military, hospital barrack, and quartermaster's stores and all articles for the construction or repair of buildings for the housing of the troops.*
>
> *Under Heading 3, all articles issued for the purpose of clothing, management or housing of convicts. This will also comprise all stores and supplies for the other penal settlements and for the use in government vessels and for agricultural establishments'.*

The practical arrangement for this proposal required that[72]

> *'. . . once every six months a Board comprising the Colonial Treasurer, the D.C.G, the Commissary of Accounts and*

72 HRA 1:13:698 Minute #51 Darling to Goderich

> *the Colonial Auditor was to be convened for the purpose of transferring adjustments between the colonial treasury account and the Military Chest account and in that way reimburse the store for obligations made on behalf of the colonial administration.'*

In 1827[73], 'he British Government accepted that the whole expense of police, gaols, convicts and the colonial marine was to be carried by the 'Home Treasury', although the arrangement was short-lived. Ten years later, the colonial legislature claimed Britain owed its treasury over £700,000 in reimbursements for costs expended under these categories. This 1827 plan soon caused problems for the commissariat because, at this time, the use of coinage was becoming genera. The depleted military chest could not continue to draw bills for reimbursement, so the commissariat regularly 'borrowed' funds from the colonial treasury in order to save the military chest.[74] In June 1827 D.C.G Laidley was appointed to run the commissariat but, when Darling recommended that he keep an extra set of books for the information of his superiors in London, Laidley complained about being short-staffed. An enquiry showed that 'the number of clerks employed in the commissary nearly equalled the number in all civil departments put together. A number of government orders following the enquiry were aimed at improving the efficiency in the keeping of accounts in the commissariat'.[75]

It appears that Darling listened to his small, select Board of General Purposes, which was in effect an advisory board to the governor. Darling issued an order (Government Order #1 of 1827) providing for the formation of a Board of Survey to examine the stores in each government department and recommend how best to integrate them with the commissariat store. Reports of the survey were prepared and submitted to William Lithgow, Auditor of Colonial Accounts. The eventual results of the survey were seen in 1836 when the British Government made further changes to the

---

73 HRA 1:14:332 Darling to Huskisson August 1828

74 HRA 1:16:658 Bourke to Goderich confirming loan of funds to D.C.G Laidley (June 1832)

75 HRA 1.15.745 Darling to Under-Secretary Hay–September 1830; (the number of clerks employed by the D.C.G. was 40)

operations of the commissariat by establishing within it a branch of the British Ordnance Department. This new department was given physical custody of 'the military works and buildings' and the ordnance and other stores, as well as the buildings occupied by the convicts, and the stores and clothing required in the convict establishments.[76] The result was a commissariat very much reduced in size after January 1836. With this change the physical stores had moved entirely to the Ordnance Storekeeper's department, leaving the commissariat virtually an administrative-financial branch of the British Treasury. It was still required to transport stores and this led to the growth of a transport branch of the commissariat. Under the same minute the total responsibility for gaols, police and colonial marines transferred from the Imperial to the colonial government.

The downsizing was all part of a plan in the early 1840s to stop transporting convicts to the colony. Until 1855 the NSW commissariat continued to pay for all convict establishments, including hospital and other medical expenses for convicts, although in 1850 all barracks and military buildings were handed over to the colonial government. Britain's military responsibility to the colony continued until 1870, when all imperial forces and the remaining commissariat functions (mainly payroll) were withdrawn from the Australian colonies.[77]

Macquarie's Reform of the Commissariat

In April 1817, Macquarie confirmed with the Earl of Bathurst that he intended to reform the operations of the commissary in the colony, in line with recommendations received from London. He advised Bathurst of new appointments to senior posts to replace officers engaged in insider trading and 'maladministration' and then went on to describe the 'old' and the 'new' systems.

> *'When the settlement was founded, the commissariat department was a distinct colonial entity in the charge of*

76 HRA 1:17:706 Treasury Minute dated 10 March 1835 attached to letter from Hon J. Stewart (H. M. Treasury) to Under Secretary Hay

77 Australian Encyclopaedia: 'Military'

> *a 'commissary of stores and provisions' that was directly under the control of the governor. The first commissary was Andrew Miller, who resigned in 1790 due to ill health. After the wreck of the Sirius at Norfolk Island in March 1790, the purser, John Palmer, was appointed to succeed Miller as commissary. As the colony developed, the commissary expanded, and the staffs were increased by the appointment of assistant and deputy commissaries and storekeepers. Those officials received a colonial salary, rations and allowances. In the year 1812, it was decided to alter the system and the commissariat in the colony became a branch of the army commissariat, a sub-department of the English Treasury. The change was made immediately after the arrival of deputy commissary-general David Allen in the convict ship Fortune in June 1813'.*

Macquarie's latest change was based on his perception that the operations were presently unnecessarily large and expensive. He also observed that the commissary was now subjected to internal abuse, waste and fraud. He proposed to restore government farms and make the commissariat much more self-supportive by manufacturing more of its own produce. The commissariat was also to source as much as possible from its remaining procurement from local suppliers, thus leaving private suppliers to carry large inventories and offer purchase terms. Thus, the commissariat would not have to prepay British-based suppliers with FOB bills.

The first livestock to be removed from the government herds were transferred free of charge to eligible settlers who were encouraged to use these animals for breeding purposes. There were other procedural changes; in 1813 responsibility for the military reverted back to the commissary rather than the civil authorities.[78.] This change was part of an overall revamping of the military system and a restructuring in anticipation of economic rehabilitation which would occur after the Napoleonic Wars. The change involved separation of ordnance support services, the military commissariat and a convict commissariat into three separate operations and independent stores . . .

---

78 Bathurst to Macquarie HRA 1:8: 619

As if sensitive to his wavering place in history, Macquarie assembled all his official reports for the previous ten years and wrote what he called a 'synopsis' of his administration for the Earl of Bathurst. With reference to the commissary, he commented:

> *'The system I have invariably pursued in respect of the treatment and management of the convicts is to temper justice with humanity. The value of savings to the colony and the commissary by killing wild herds of cattle for meat will be over £7,000 (using 5d per lb for the valuation). The reduction in the price of fresh meat has caused great economy to the commissary. Beef supplies are growing, and the government herds prevent monopolies of individual suppliers to the commissary. A new government farm was established at Emu Plains because of the need for fresh produce from this extremely fertile tract of land. The use of convict labour in this way means that they are usefully employed and they more than repay to the government the amount of their maintenance and all of the other expenses of the Establishment. There are over 300 convicts employed there, these being those convicts who were not required for the settlers, or for the public roads and bridges or other government purposes. The principal part of the present expense of the colony is incurred in feeding, clothing and lodging the male and female convicts. Other slightly lesser expense is incurred in the support of the civil, military and marine establishments, and in victualling, for a certain period, free settlers, their families and convict labourers. The commissary carries out the planning and support for each of these groups.'*

Although Macquarie attempted to reduce the price of wheat delivered into store to 8 shillings per bushel, the settlers convinced him that 'the grower of grain would be a loser at that price' and he restored the price to ten shillings per bushel[79]. His earlier opinions had been influenced by Commissioner Bigge and, as a result Macquarie, changed from being a supporter of government

[79] (HRA 1: X: 683 Emphasis added

farms to supporting the purchase of grains from the settlers.[80] However by 1820, after Bigge's departure, he again reported that 'there is no further economy in the measure of cultivating lands on account of the crown'.[81] This concern was later reiterated and confirmed by Major Ovens in his report on convict work practices for Governor Brisbane.[82] In addition to Macquarie's observations that government farms were uneconomic, Ovens concurred with his theory that the cost of convict labour used in clearing open pastoral land was not recovered by any increase in the sale price of the land. Ovens had calculated that eight convicts in a team or gang took one week to clear and burn one acre of land.[83]

The Macquarie 'Synopsis' also included an impressive list of the public buildings and works erected, and other useful improvements made in NSW at the expense of the crown from 1 January 1810 to 30 November 1821. He listed 67 items in Sydney, 20 in Parramatta, 15 at Windsor, twelve at Liverpool, and 52 in the outlying settlements of Richmond, Pitt Town, Penrith, Emu Plains, Spring Wood, Bathurst, Campbell Town, Pennant Hills, and Castle Hill.[84] He also drew attention to the impressive progress made in road construction, claiming 267 miles of roads around Sydney and Parramatta had been made under his direction.

In a memorial presented to Macquarie on his departure from the colony, the magistrates, clergy, merchants, landholders, free settlers and public officers wrote, 'Your Excellency's exertions for the welfare and improvement of these settlements, strongly exemplified by the rapidly increasing and

---

80 Commissioner Bigge was a former Chief Justice of the British West Indies and was appointed by Bathurst to complete an assessment of the government operations in NSW for the House of Commons

81 M.H. Ellis *Lachlan Macquarie* P.124

82 M.H. Ellis *Lachlan Macquarie* P. 132

83 M.H. Ellis *Lachlan Macquarie* P135

84 The Sydney and Parramatta buildings by Macquarie are listed in the last Chapter. The writer has computed the construction costs of each building by estimating the material content and the estimated length of construction time. Some estimates have been based on the Greenway notes found in the appendix to M.H. Ellis's biography of Francis Greenway, especially those relating to construction rates by various trades.

growing consequence of the colony, have fully evinced the judgement of your appointment and command our gratitude and affection'.[85] They were well chosen and relevant words of appreciation from a selection of grateful settlers all of whom had benefited from Macquarie's administration, as had the entire settlement.

The governor of the day demanded statistics, statistics and more statistics. In addition to the 50-80 pages in the annual 'Blue Books', the Commissary prepared reports on inventory levels, the value and source of all purchases and rations by each group, where sent, and how many were being served.[86] From these sources it is possible to track how the commissary funds were distributed between each of the banks in the colony; we know the cost of supplies as well as the quantity of grain and meat and the value of clothing and cloth supplied. We also know the contractors for all provisions and their payments, the quantity of tools provided, military and hospital rations, bills drawn each year and details of loans flowing between the commissary, military chest, colonial treasury and the London Treasury.

Between 1832 and 1842, the Military Chest was the preferred funding source for military and commissary revenue and expense. The Treasury renewed with vigour its instructions on handling funds and recording advances, loans, transfers and all expenditures. Although the working instructions provide an insight into the approved methods of operating the commissariat stores and accounts, to understand the process fully it

---

85 HRA 1:11:102

86 The 'Blue Books' Reporting System commenced in 1822 and was a compilation of internal reports of revenues and expenditures and colonial statistics. The British Treasury in London prepared its format and three copies were prepared at significant clerical time and expense. One copy was sent to the Secretary of State's office in London, one was retained by the Governor in the Office of the Colonial Secretary and the third was directed to the House of Commons. Previous to the Blue Books, the three colonial funds were the Gaol (and then renamed Police) Fund, the Orphan Fund and the Colonial Fund. After 1822 other funds emerged for revenue discretionary purposes and they were fully reported in the Blue Books; such ancillary funds included the Commissary Fund, the Land Fund, and the Immigration Fund.

is necessary to examine the inventory control procedures, purchasing and 'receiving into store' procedures, detailed accounting reports, ration levels established from time to time, and funding mechanisms. These topics are explored in detail in the following chapters.

CHAPTER 7

THE RISE OF MANUFACTURING IN NSW

In 1882 Charles Lyne wrote a book about Colonial industry of the time–*The industries of NSW.* He reviewed a total of 35 articles about Colonial Industry in the last quarter of the 19th century, for industries such as Hunter Valley Farming, Lithgow Coal, and Pottery & Brick-making. This was a landmark analysis and the first and last of such studies. Subsequent studies have been more of an overview of industrialists and their activities rather than detailed studies of specific industries.

This present study is that of tracking early manufactures and their growth over time. Innovation and growth involved entrepreneurs, privatisation and a great deal of foreign investment.

For many years, Australia was essentially a primary-producing country. Manufacturing was geared largely to supplying local domestic requirements. The discovery of minerals, a growing population and military equipping created a profitable home market and led to an expansion of this sector.

Manning Clark writes (Vol 1, *A History of Australia*–P.249) 'Up to 1810 and the time of Macquarie, neither the convict stain nor clothing, lodging, or way of life distinguished the bonded (convicts) from the free workers. Nor within the free group was it possible to distinguish the ex-bond from the native-born and the free immigrant. Tradesmen were much in demand in the building trade; others (*ex land grant owners who had failed or been turned off their land)* found employment in the small industries of the colony, in the pottery, the hat-manufactory, the tannery, the brewery, or with the shoe-maker, the tailors or the tin-smiths; others took to the sea, on coastal vessels, or a ship trading with the Islands'

The last significant study of colonial manufacturing was completed by G. J. R. Linge in *Industrial* Awakening published in 1979. In 2000 it is timely that a further review be made of the earliest industry not of 1900 but of 1800.

The reasons that early governors sponsored developing industries in the early colony are various and commence with basic survival

Of course Governor King faced his own series of challenges. He began his term of office under strained relations with Hunter and, naturally, Macarthur. Macarthur wanted to boycott this new governor and his new policies of controlling the public herds and their grazing whereabouts. However, under King, the colony made great strides in new business activities. After Macarthur was transported to England for trial, King saw that whaling was the only 'staple' and envisaged great secondary industries and huge colonial profits. An export trade in coal began from Coal Harbour (Newcastle), which received government support through a large allocation of convict labour. Coal was sent to both India and the Cape . . . Some timber was exported, but did not receive a good reception at its destination. A source of cheap salt pork was found in Tahiti. Then in August 1800, King announced 'the manufacture of linen and woollen goods has begun with some success. Tuppence a pound was paid for local wool, which was woven into blankets. The raw wool was paid for by exchange of blanket material. This could well have been the start of the flourishing future wool industry.

The Naval Officer, (Harbour master) shared his revenues between the Orphan Fund and the Police Fund. This was the start of taxation in the colony and to an extent gave the colony an imprimatur of a successful colonial trading post.

Of all the early industries, it was the timber industry that was most important. After food provision, the governor's chief role was to create housing and barracks for free immigrants, convicts, and military personnel. Not until Macquarie's arrival did any significant planning for public buildings and infrastructure begin. The timber gathering and processing by its very nature was left to convict workers, and Ralph Hawkins (The timber-getters of Pennant Hills) provides a scenario of timber–gathering in the Hornsby Shire.

Governor Phillip encouraged sealing as an entrepreneurial activity and as an alternative and supplement to his policy of independent farming and Agri-production through 30 acre land grants.

1. Sealing also supported a fledgling boat-building and provedore industry and became the first export industry. Up to 1841 whaling and sealing exports were greater than wool, coal or timber.
2. New industries such as tallow, soap, tannery, linen, hats, slops, blankets were encouraged to serve a local market (some of these were government-sponsored e.g. linen, clothing, distillery), but Macquarie saw the limitations of the size of the local market to manufacturing industries; he also saw the convict labour as a means of creating output with minimal if not competitive costs, especially where local raw materials were involved. He then built a public works program around his output until the output itself created a catalyst for new manufactures.
3. The Lumber Yard and its associated operations, in employing over 3,000 convicts had the opportunity for using any skilled labour arriving in the colony, and for making a wide-range of items in local demand, and which were encouraged as being import replacers.
4. His decision to privatise many established L/Y operations created a grass roots manufacturing industry, which although it may have been assumed by private entrepreneurs, would have been a lot longer in arriving. Entrepreneurial encouragement by Macquarie also over-rode any endeavours by Macquarie to have monopoly operations in the L.Y.
5. Thus the L.Y. was the real catalyst for growth of a manufacturing sector, mostly because of the positive policies of Macquarie and the heads of the commissariat

Thus the direct link between the commissariat L/Y and the rise of manufacturing!!

Upon his arrival, Bligh was appalled by the conditions of the colony and told Windham back in London (HRA 1:6:26) that much needed to be improved in the colony. He also wrote that of his being convinced that the immediate economic future lay in the encouragement of agriculture rather than in the development of commerce (for example the development of the wool trade) or the Bass Strait and overseas trade, for they were extremely trifling (HRA 1:6:121).

Clarke records (A History of Australia, Vol 1, P.331)

> *'by 1820 Simeon Lord had turned the profits of marriage, fishing in the south seas and trade in the Pacific Islands into a manufactory at Botany Bay where he employed convicts and from 15 to 20 colonial boys making blankets, stockings, wool hats, kangaroo hats, seal Hats, possum skin hats, all shoddy but cheaper than the imported English hats, boot leather, trousers, shirts, thread, kettles and glass tumblers. The bulk of the wool grown in NSW was shipped direct by the growers to England, and Lord was the exception to the principle that the settlers should use their great natural advantages of grass and climate to grow food and wool and import the other goods they needed'.*

Bigge reported glowingly about the future prospects for grazing and agriculture but also recorded a downside to the growth in the agricultural economy; 'between 1810 and 1820, the numbers of sheep trebled, and some settlers were finding it more profitable to sell the fleeces rather than the carcasses (J.T. Bigge: Agriculture & Trade Report–p16-18)

The Macquarie legacy was described by the retiring governor during the handing-over ceremony with Governor Brisbane. 'I found the colony in a state of rapid deterioration: threatened with famine, discord and party spirit prevailing, and the public buildings in a state of decay. I left it a very different place: the face of the country was greatly improved; agriculture flourishing, manufactories had been established and commerce revived;

roads and bridges built and inhabitants opulent and happy'. (HRA 1:12:331)

This same principle of comparative advantage was considered carefully by the Commissariat and the Macquarie Administration before the decision to expand the numerous government business enterprises which were responsible for employing convict labour was implemented and became fully operational. The colony, it was decided, needed a manufacturing and industrial base to work in conjunction with the agricultural enterprises, and to supply the government with its public works materials from local sources, rather than rely on imports from Britain.

It was a source of great delight to Macquarie that he had brought about such change, and what a difference in approach and attitude between the two governors. In fact, although Phillip, Hunter and King could have contributed little more than they did towards trade, commerce and industrial development, it was the Macquarie pro-entrepreneurial policies that brought about such great progress in both industrial and economic development

Ralph Hawkins in '*The Convict Timber-getters of Pennant Hills*' writes

> *"The Chief Engineer's department enquired after the trades of convicts after arrival and kept the most useful of them in Government employ. The Engineer's department systematised the labour of the convicts, classifying men according to their trades and instructed those unskilled and young enough or willing enough in a suitable trade. The Lumber Yard in Sydney was the centre of industrial operations in the colony. Here men practiced both timber and metal trades, preparing useful products for the government. A number of outlying gangs prepared raw materials for the public works programme. The brickmaker's gang worked At Brickfield Hill, the Shell gang gathered oyster shells for lime from the Aboriginal middens along the foreshore of the harbour and the Lane Cove River. The quarry gang prepared the stone, while further afield in the woods to the north-west of Sydney at Pennant Hills was the Timber-getting gang. This latter gang was a gang of men*

> *chosen for their skills and not a gang of men under secondary punishment. These men were mostly drawn straight from the arriving ships and worked shorter hours than most other convicts. They were of sufficient confidence to go on strike in 1819. Macquarie needed their services and they returned to work after only 3 weeks."*

In the listing of key events, certain sectors of the secondary industry economy have been selected for a time-line of progress. There are reasons for specific industries being selected.

A brief outline of events before 1810 draws attention to a number of circumstances that are of fundamental importance to an understanding of early industrial development:

i. There was a general shortage of labour
ii. Circumstances combined to prevent real income and output from small settlers from rising
iii. monopoly position of military officers buying incoming provisions from visiting ships and retailing at exorbitant prices and profits
iv. most small farmers had neither the knowledge nor the capital to improve their farming techniques or to buy stock and equipment
v. the need to take people off the store
vi. the arrival of only a few free migrants
vii. large increase in arriving convicts

References Used and Literary Review

Of particular note is that the following literature is made up of economic history writings and general history. No other economic historian has made anything of the link between the operations of the commissariat and the rise of a manufacturing sector in the colony.

This link assumes that the commissariat business enterprises under the Macquarie Administration commenced the initial manufactory before transferring operations from the public to the private sector where practical, and then allowing competition to develop, in further satisfaction of the mechanism of a market economy. This process was under the overall encouragement of free enterprise by Macquarie, and was designed to create a support sector for the already strong agri-business sector, to attract free skilled labour to the colony and to attract investment to the colonial economy as well as being an import replacement facility. Manufacturing in the Lumber Yard was intended to satisfy an artificial government market whilst transference to the private sector

1. HRA
2. HRNSW
3. Coghlan (x 3)
4. Butlin (x 2)
5. Steven
6. Blayney
7. Linge
8. Lyne
9. Hainsworth
10. Abbott & Nairn
11. Maloney: History of Australia
12. Clark: History of Australia
13. Barnard: History of Australia
14. Hawkins: The Timber-getters of Pennant Hills
15. Hainsworth: 'In search of a staple–the Sydney Sandalwood trade 1804-09'
16. Abbott, G.C. 'Staple theory and Australian economic growth 1788-1820'

These Key Events are set down by industry group as a means of demonstrating the surprising amount of originality within the economy and the potential for men of education with a flair for innovation and access to capital. They are later sorted onto a time-scale.

A. Fishing & Whaling

1. **Sealing in Bass Strait** (1797) **commenced**
2. **Boat building** for hunting seals (1798)

3. By 1804 11 privately owned sloops were engaged in Bass Strait sealing
4. Between 1800 and 1806, over 100,000 seal skins landed in Sydney
5. **Whaling began** (1802)
6. **Boat building** for hunting whales
7. By 1830, 17 ships operated from Sydney, and by 1835, 76
8. Whaling stations established in NSW (1830), Victoria (1831) and S.A.(1837)
9. In 1830, NSW exported £60,000 worth of whaling & sealing products with wool at £35,000. By 1835, wool had overtaken fishery products. By 1841 whale oil exports peaked at £150,000 p.a.; by 1850, this had declined to £28,000. The decline was accelerated by the gold rushes which caused a shortage of labour for the whaling ships. In 1851, the whaling stations in Mosman's Cove closed. By 1853, exports from NSW had fallen to £16,000
10. By 1841 there were 41 bay-whaling stations in Tasmania. In the 1840s, over 400 vessels were built in VDL boat-yards

B. Timber

1. 1788 First Fleet cuts Sydney Cove timbers as clearing of land for initial settlement.
2. Earliest tree trunks not dried and when used *in situ* warped, twisted and bowsed.
3. Phillip sent out scouts to seek better quality timber and came across the Pennant Hills Timber-getting area.
4. <u>Government Farms</u>

    i. Within the commissariat, responsibility was allocated for the supervision of convicts undertaking government work. Even after London had directed cost cutting for convict maintenance a certain number of convicts were kept for government service, and during the King, Bligh and Macquarie Administrations government farms were established in 5 rural locations, not only to provide fresh fruit vegetables and meat for use within the colony but to manage the labour and output of over 500 convicts.

C. Manufacturing

1. 1788 First bricks used for building (Darling Harbour, Brickfield Hill, St. Peters, Granville, Gore Hill, Rosehill
2. Pottery works produced plates, jars, clay pipes (1788). By 1804 several other pottery works were operating
3. 1789–first vessel built for ferrying passengers between Parramatta and Sydney
4. 1795–Sydney's first windmill had been imported and erected on Observatory Hill
5. 1795–First ale brewed at Parramatta
6. 1796–Naval Dockyard established in Sydney Cove
7. 1799–Government broom factory opened with 1 man making 6 dozen brooms each week
8. 1800 Linen manufacturing on the Hawkesbury from locally grown flax
9. 1800 House of Industry, the women's section of Parramatta Gaol and later, the Female Factory made linen and other clothing items (hats, slops, blankets)
10. 1815 Steam powered flour mill
11. 1820 Local paper mill supplying all material for publishing *Sydney Gazette*
12. 1820 carriage and harness making in Sydney
13. 1824 Sugar made from local cane for first time
14. By 1838, NSW had 2 distilleries, 7 breweries, 12 tanneries, 5 brass and iron foundries, 77 flour mills and single factories producing salt, hats, tobacco and other goods
15. In 1839, Australian Sugar Company formed in NSW

C. Mining

1. 1797 Coal found on banks of Hunter River

2. 1801 All coal and timber declared by Governor King to be property of the Crown
3. 1801 Robert Campbell shipped coal to Calcutta and Cape of Good Hope
4. 1823 Commissioner Bigge recommended Newcastle coalfields be privatised
5. 1824 AAC company opens up 1 million acres
6. 1839 Gold discovered but kept quiet
7. 1841 Silver-lead ore discovered in Adelaide and 10 ton exported to Britain
8. 1846 Tin discovered in S.A.

D. Agri-Business

1. 1788 First Fleet arrived with livestock, seeds and young plants. However, the small cattle herd and sheep mostly died; only 2 horses survived more than 2 years
2. Phillip established a 3.6 ha farm where the Botanical Gardens now stand.
3. 1789 First Government farm commenced at Rose Hill. James Ruse received one acre at Rose Hill for wheat /grain experimenting.
4. 1791 The Ruse grant was increased shortly to 30 acres.
5. 1791 First tobacco grown
6. 1792 Planting of citrus trees along Parramatta River
7. 1795 Horses imported and by 1810 there were 1134 horses in NSW
8. 1797 NSW held about 2500 sheep
9. 1797 Governor Hunter reported the first planting of grape vines; by 1802 12,000 vines had been planted around Parramatta. Original cuttings had arrived with First Fleet
10. 1807 Samuel Marsden took first cask of cross-bred wool to England for testing.
11. 1813 First crossing of Blue Mountains
12. 1816 Botanic Gardens in Sydney developed
13. 1816 First wheat grown near Bathurst
14. 1820 First dairy industry established in Illawarra district

E. Exports & Trade (202,152,177,186,221)

1. 1790 The *Sirius* under John Hunter (Phillips' intended successor), returned with a cargo of flour, seed wheat and barley, and a year's provisions. Phillip had despatched the ship to acquire rations for the colony as the second fleet had been delayed and the colony was starving. The brig *Supply* was also despatched to Batavia for a supply of rice and other provisions
2. 1792 Army officers traded in goods from visiting vessels–a pattern which was to last for many years. Dutch and Indian vessels brought further supplies for trading and officers realised huge profits. Further plans were made for ships from Cape Town, Batavia and India to bring other tradable items. Strong trading links developed between Sydney and Batavia.
3. 1798–The Commissariat's first commercial purchase of grain from local farmers–1500 bushels of wheat were purchased from Hawkesbury farms.
4. 1798 The first boiling works was opened on Cape Barren Island, where they collected over 12500 seal skins and 3000 litres of seal oil for export to China
5. 1801 Robert Campbell exported 100 tons of Hunter Coal to Calcutta and 100 tons to Cape of Good Hope.
6. Although colonial trade in sealing, whaling, sandalwood and trepang (sea slug) was well underway by 1806, export was still hindered by the British Navigation *Acts* and the East India Company monopoly.
7. In 1810, Wentworth, Riley and Blaxall signed a contract to build a new main hospital in the settlement in exchange for a monopoly on import of spirits
8. 1812, first wheat purchased by NSW from VDL
9. 1813, Scarcity forced corn prices up from 5/–a bushel to 15/–per bushel. And wheat from 6/3 to £1/8/-
10. 1814, nearly 15,000 kg of wool was exported

F. Newspapers

1. 1795 A wooden-screw press, brought with the first fleet, was used to print the first official directive by Gov. Hunter
2. 1803. First newspaper (*Sydney Gazette)* founded by Gov. King mainly for government orders and proclamations. The weekly was edited by ex-convict, George Howe.
3. 1824 The weekly *Australian* first appeared owned by W. C. Wentworth and Robert Wardell. It was published without a licence. It was printed until 1848
4. 1826. The *Monitor* was first published by E. S. Hall, who became an antagonist of Governor Darling and spent numerous times in gaol.

G. Banking

1. 1811 Macquarie considers the need for banking upon his arrival, but is directed by the Secretary of State not to proceed
2. 1817 Macquarie issues banking licence for a private investment group to start the *Bank of NSW.*
3. Bigge determines the licence is illegal but recommends the continuation of the enterprise provided directors and stockholders assume all liability for deposits. No responsibility is to fall to the Government. The licence is ratified. and
4. The Bank of Australia commences in 1826

H. Roads and Bridges

1. 1788 Governor Phillip prepared the first town plan
2. 1788 First wooden log bridge built over the tank stream
3. 1794 Timber bridge built over the Parramatta River at Parramatta
4. 1810 Macquarie introduced a toll and turnpike system for major arterial roads from Sydney
5. 1811 Engineer John O'Hearne built a stone bridge over the tank stream

6. 1813 A large span bridge built over Hawkesbury at Windsor–65 metres long
7. 1814 Old South Head Road built and Sydney–Liverpool road built
8. 1815 Road down Bulli pass built to Wollongong
9. 1818 Oxley charted what is now the Oxley Highway to Port Macquarie
10. 1826 Great North Road commenced
11. 1830 Sydney–Goulburn Road surveyed
12. 1835 Track linking Sydney–Melbourne completed

Timescale of Manufactures

1788	1. 1788 First Fleet cuts Sydney Cove timbers as clearing of land for initial settlement.
1788	2. Earliest tree trunks not dried and when used *in situ* warped, twisted and bowsed.
1788	3. Phillip sent out scouts to seek better quality timber and came across the Pennant Hills Timber-getting area.
1788	1. 1788 First bricks used for building (Darling Harbour, Brickfield Hill, St. Peters, Granville, Gore Hill, Rosehill
1788	2. Pottery works produced plates, jars, clay pipes (1788). By 1804 several other pottery works were operating
1788	1. 1788 First Fleet arrived with livestock, seeds and young plants. However, the small cattle herd and sheep mostly died; only 2 horses survived more than 2 years
1788	2. Phillip established a 3.6 ha farm where the Botanical Gardens now stand.
1789	3. 1789–first vessel built for ferrying passengers between Parramatta and Sydney
1789	3. 1789 First Government farm commenced at Rose Hill. James Ruse received one acre at Rose Hill for wheat /grain experimenting.

1790 1. 1790 The *Sirius* under John Hunter (Phillips' intended successor), returned with a cargo of flour, seed wheat and barley, and a year's provisions. Phillip had despatched the ship to acquire rations for the colony as the second fleet had been delayed and the colony was starving. The brig *Supply* was also despatched to Batavia for a supply of rice and other provisions

1791 4. 1791 The Ruse grant was increased shortly to 30 acres.

1791 5. 1791 First tobacco grown

1792 6. 1792 Planting of citrus trees along Parramatta River

1792 2. 1792 Army officers traded in goods from visiting vessels–a pattern which was to last for many years. Dutch and Indian vessels brought further supplies for trading and officers realised huge profits. Further plans were made for ships from Cape Town, Batavia and India to bring other tradable items. Strong trading links developed between Sydney and Batavia.

1795 4. 1795–Sydney's first windmill had been imported and erected on Observatory Hill

1795 5. 1795–First ale brewed at Parramatta

1795 7. 1795 Horses imported and by 1810 there were 1134 horses in NSW

1795 1. 1795 A wooden-screw press, brought with the first fleet, was used to print the first official directive by Gov. Hunter

1796 6. 1796–Naval Dockyard established in Sydney Cove

1797 **1. Sealing in Bass Strait** (1797)

1797 1. 1797 Coal found on banks of Hunter River

1797 8. 1797 NSW held about 2500 sheep

1797 9. 1797 Governor Hunter reported the first planting of grape vines; by 1802 12,000 vines had been planted around Parramatta. Original cuttings had arrived with First Fleet

1798 **2. Boat building** for hunting seals

1798 3. 1798–The Commissariat's first commercial purchase of grain from local farmers–1500 bushels of wheat were purchased from Hawkesbury farms.

1798 4. 1798 The first boiling works was opened on Cape Barren Island, where they collected over 12500 seal skins and 3000 litres of seal oil for export to China

1799 7. 1799–Government broom factory opened with 1 man making 6 dozen brooms each week

1800 8. 1800 Linen manufacturing on the Hawkesbury from locally grown flax

1800 9. 1800 House of Industry, the women's section of Parramatta Gaol and later, the Female Factory made linen and other clothing items (hats, slops, blankets)

1801 2. 1801 All coal and timber declared by Governor King to be property of the Crown

1801 3. 1801 Robert Campbell shipped coal to Calcutta and Cape of Good Hope

1801 5. 1801 Robert Campbell exported 100 tons of Hunter Coal to Calcutta and 100 tons to Cape of Good Hope.

1801 6. Although colonial trade in sealing, whaling, sandalwood and trepang (sea slug) was well underway by 1806, export was still hindered by the British Navigation *Acts* and the East India Company monopoly.

1802 **5. Whaling** (1802)

1803 **6. Boat building** for hunting whales

1803 2. 1803. First newspaper (*Sydney Gazette)* founded by Gov. King mainly for government orders and proclamations. The weekly was edited by ex-convict, George Howe.

1804 . By 1804 11 privately owned sloops were engaged in Bass Strait sealing

1806 4. Between 1800 and 1806, over 100,000 seal skins landed in Sydney

1807 10. 1807 Samuel Marsden took first cask of cross-bred wool to England for testing.

1810 7. In 1810, Wentworth, Riley and Blaxall signed a contract to build a new main hospital in the settlement in exchange for a monopoly on import of spirits

1812 8. 1812, first wheat purchased by NSW from VDL

1813 11. 1813 First crossing of Blue Mountains

1813 9. 1813, Scarcity forced corn prices up from 5/–a bushel to 15/–per bushel. And wheat from 6/3 to £1/8/-

1814 10. 1814, nearly 15,000 kg of wool was exported

1815 10. 1815 Steam powered flour mill

1816 12. 1816 Botanic Gardens in Sydney developed

1816 13. 1816 First wheat grown near Bathurst

1820 11. 1820 Local paper mill supplying all material for publishing *Sydney Gazette*

1820 12. 1820 carriage and harness making in Sydney

1820 14. 1820 First dairy industry established in Illawarra district

1823 14. 1823 Commissioner Bigge recommended Newcastle coalfields be privatised

1824 13. 1824 Sugar made from local cane for first time

1824 5. 1824 AAC company opens up 1 million acres

1824 3. 1824 The weekly *Australian* first appeared owned by W. C. Wentworth and Robert Wardell. It was published without a licence. It was printed until 1848

1826 4. 1826. The *Monitor* was first published by E. S. Hall, who became an antagonist of Governor Darling and spent numerous times in gaol.

1830 7. By 1830, 17 ships operated from Sydney, and by 1835, 76

1830 . In 1830, NSW exported £60,000 worth of whaling & sealing products with wool at £35,000. By 1835, wool had overtaken fishery products. By 1841 whale oil exports peaked at £150,000 p.a.; by 1850, this had declined to £28,000. The decline was accelerated by the gold rushes which caused a shortage of labour for the whaling ships. In 1851, the whaling stations in Mosman's Cove closed. By 1853, exports from NSW had fallen to £16,000

1831 Whaling stations established in NSW (1830), Victoria (1831) and S.A.(1837)

1838 14. By 1838, NSW had 2 distilleries, 7 breweries, 12 tanneries, 5 brass and iron foundries, 77 flour mills and single factories producing salt, hats, tobacco and other goods

1839 15. In 1839, Australian Sugar Company formed in NSW

1839 6. 1839 Gold discovered but kept quiet

1841 10. By 1841 there were 41 bay-whaling stations in Tasmania. In the 1840s, over 400 vessels were built in VDL boat-yards

1841 7. 1841 Silver-lead ore discovered in Adelaide and 10 ton exported to Britain

1846 8. 1846 Tin discovered in S.A.

CHAPTER 8

GOVERNMENT BUSINESS ENTERPRISES IN NSW 1802-1835

Government business enterprises commenced from close to day one of the settlement in 1788. We can define them as government operated, financially supported and for the direct benefit of the colony as opposed to an export facility. The very first public enterprise was that of farming to raise food, supervise the few head of livestock that had arrived alive in the colony. \Public farming kept the colony alive for the first few years before private farming based on selective land grants commenced.

The role of the commissariat in government economic planning

The commissariat had two key roles. It was an important economic driver and acted as a quasi-treasury to the colony for the first 30 years, until the B of NSW opened in 1817.

Detailing the Enterprises

The main enterprises commenced with the need for food production but shortly after moved onto the need for construction work, building materials and an export staple.

Introducing the Colonial Economy

The colonial economy was destined to grow in response to increasing population, the development of an infrastructure to underpin the colonial growth and living standards and the need for import replacing activities, in addition to the goal of creating an export market

Convict management

With few free settlers to fill the role of supervisors, and the military abdicating their duties in this respect, the job of convict supervision was left to the best behaved convicts. This was a generally unsatisfactory position. The most prominent principal convict managers were Majors Druitt and Ovens, who were the first the reform convict work practices and set goals and plan targets for the convict workers.

Manufacturing in the commissariat

From the public business enterprises and the necessity of finding export staples, a secondary industry grew in the colony. Invention really was the mother of necessity. A secondary industry commenced in export replacement areas and spread to those areas of continuing need, such as agricultural equipment as that primary industry got underway, then onto manufacturing on behalf of British industries wanting to have a presence in the colony.

Operating and managing the government farms and the public enterprises

There was continual growth in the public farming and manufacturing areas for two reasons. The number of convicts arriving in the colony increased each month, so there were more mouths to feed, and more men to put into productive work. So output increased naturally but then so did the public works program, that kept the business enterprises operating, and then diversity of manufacturing commenced which meant more technical production and output. Much of this flowed to the private sector having been first established in the Lumber Yard.

Accounting and Finance in the public enterprises

The commissariat system after 1822 attracted many convict clerical assistants, so the bookkeeping indulgences were endless. Sadly few of these records survive, but we know that orders from government departments for supplies and the public works department for materials were prepare, whilst the commissariat and lumber yard used issue dockets to account for supplies transferred. The main accounting was not the number of inventory items made or issued in the commissariat but the money it was spending. Bills drawn by the commissariat supposedly reflected the amount of value going through the commissariat as opposed to the raw materials used the convict output or the value of materials issued on account of public works.

Measuring the economic impact of the enterprises on the economy

This will be the most difficult chapter to prepare. We will have to assess the GDP annually for the colony from 1800, and try and indicate what part was generated by the business enterprises. This will have to be done on an industry by industry basis to estimate the items of output the number of convicts in use for each item of manufacture and compare it with the gross GDP. The problem with this methodology is that most items produced by the commissariat enterprises had no value due to the convicx6ts having no value as labourers and raw materials have no assigned value, thus convict output had no value.

INTRODUCTION TO GOVERNMENT BUSINESS ENTERPRISES

From its commencement in 1788, the aim of the Colony of New South Wales was self-sufficiency even though it had been set up to solve the problem of Britain's overcrowded prisons. By 1823, the British Government had decided that it would limit its direct expenditure to the transportation of the convicts and their supplies while in transit; the Colonial Administrators would be responsible for the convicts' security, food, clothing and accommodation in the Colony. Furthermore, proceeds from the sale of Crown land were to be the exclusive reserve of the British authorities rather than the colonists. The Governors were therefore forced to look for ways in which the Colony could help to support itself through working the convicts to create food, minerals (e.g. coal production), roads, housing and public buildings. Other convicts were assigned to landowners on a fully-maintained basis, thus saving the British Treasury a great deal of money.

This policy of maintenance of convicts by the Government created the need for an accounting by the Colony to the British Parliament. This led to the appointment in 1824 of a Financial Controller/Colonial Accountant to prepare monthly and annual despatches to the British Colonial Secretary. Following self-government in 1856, the procedures changed as the Colony became fully responsible for its own economic planning and fiscal management.

A Brief Overview of the Government Store

The first storekeeper arrived with Governor Phillip and the First Fleet. Andrew Miller had been appointed whilst the Fleet was preparing to sail, initially to take responsibility for the loading and recording of requisitioned stores. Upon arrival in Sydney Cove, Miller's first task was to erect a stores tent, secure it as far as possible, and commence unloading from the ships the stores that would be required during the first few weeks. These stores and provisions included such items as tents, pots and cooking utensils, blankets, hospital equipment and supplies and tools for clearing the land and erecting tents. Little was known about local conditions and Phillip's plan to have a wooden storehouse built within a few weeks could not be accomplished. He had tried to anticipate a wide range of obstacles and challenges, but encountering a difficult landscape and understanding characteristics of the local forestry proved the most difficult of all. In their various reports, Cook, Banks and Matra all praised the local timbers after only a cursory evaluation but, with no expertise amongst his crew or the convict population, Phillip's task of clearing timber and using it for construction was almost impossible.[87]

Upon their arrival, Phillip relied on Miller to operate the most basic of stores and without burdening him with limiting rations as he anticipated that the second Fleet store ships would be carrying provisions for the next full year. Miller's biggest task was the security of the provisions; the remaining items were then to be unloaded so that the ships could return to naval service. Phillip later prepared a rationing program for Miller so that the provisions would last six months, the time Phillip thought the Second Fleet was behind his own.

The stress of establishing the commissary for the new settlement and acting as private secretary to the governor eventually broke Miller's health and he wanted to return home. However, he was not to see his home again; he died during the sea voyage back to England.

Miller's successor, John Palmer, had sailed as purser aboard Phillip's flagship, *Sirius*. He had joined the Navy at the age of nine and participated in a series of voyages to many parts of the world, including North America where he married into a wealthy colonial family. After the founding of the colony, and with the expectation that he would soon return to England, Palmer sailed with the *Sirius* to the Cape Colony and Batavia on a mission to purchase food for the struggling, and hungry, colony of NSW. Whilst shipping provisions from Sydney to Norfolk Island, the ship struck an uncharted submerged rock just southeast of the Island and sunk. Palmer was saved, but the *Sirius* and its cargo was lost and Phillip found a new posting for Palmer in Sydney, replacing Miller as chief store-keeper. It was a further seven years before Palmer sailed for England, but he soon

87 Cook & Banks had written positively (and subsequently amended by Beaglehole) about the lush landscape to be found at Botany Bay, and James Matra (another Cook crewman) extended this interest in local timber to its use as a trade item between the colony & Britain, when Matra submitted his recommendation of the use of the new land as a penal settlement. Refer also Beckett: 'Reasons for the Colony' in *British Colonial Investment in the Colony 1788-1856.*

returned to the colony with his wife and sister, Sophia. The Palmer family became financially secure with a magnificent walled estate, carved from the rocky terrain of Woolloomooloo Bay, just east of Farm Cove. Sophia was to shortly marry Robert Campbell thus forming a most strategic alliance between the colony's first successful trading house (Campbell & Co, the chief supplier of stores to the colony) and the chief procurer of provisions for the colonial store (John Palmer).[88]

Governor Phillip was active in most facets of the initial colonial administration, especially the planning for the new settlement and the difficult challenge of feeding the people. He found the soil conditions around Sydney Cove were unsuitable for vegetables, grain and fruit. The vegetable patches located in the Governor's Domain failed to provide the produce desired, and Phillip was constantly looking for new, more fertile, locations. Travelling up what was to become known as the Parramatta River; he located more fertile soil, and what appeared to be a suitable clay reserve, on the south bank of the River; he named the area Rose Hill. Phillip planned a new settlement at the head of the river which he named Parramatta. Phillip recorded that, 'the soil is more suitable for cultivation than the hungry sand covering the hills near Sydney'[89]. It was imperative to grow food as quickly as possible and Parramatta offered the additional advantages of a constant supply of fresh water and a means of transporting food by boat rather than having to build building a road.

During the Palmer administration of the stores, new settlements had to be served in addition to Norfolk Island established in 1789. Settlements were developed and serviced by branch stores in areas such as Hobart (1802), Port Dalrymple (later Launceston, 1802), Liverpool (1803), Hawkesbury (Windsor, 1802) and Bathurst (1814). The role of the main store in Sydney was constantly changing as was its location. All the stores required personnel and organisation as well as a good supply of clerical assistance and many of these roles were set-aside for trusted convicts and ticket-of-leave men. The reason for the use of convicts in a sensitive and

---

88 Refer: Margaret Steven '*Merchant Campbell1769-1846*' and Beckett '*John Palmer–Commissary*'

89 HRNSW Vol 1, Part 2 p469 (Despatch by Governor Phillip to Hon W. Grenville)

secure area of government was straightforward. As Butlin has established, the cost of convict labour was a charge against the English Treasury and not included in the appropriation to the colony, so the use of convicts as workers for the government kept government civil salaries understated and artificially low. It was Commissioner Bigge who reviewed the workforce and, observing the number of convicts employed within government and thus civil service ranks, became aware of the understatement of costs in the colony. Butlin adds, 'as public employees, a great deal of convict labour was engaged on farming and public infrastructure construction and thus avoided being charged as a direct cost to the colony. It was more convenient, however, to transfer them into the labour market.

Butlin described the functions of the Commissariat in the following terms.

> *'The (British) Treasury described the commissary as one that 'keeps in the stores and issues provisions, fuel and light for the use of the service abroad'. Such a formal description fails to capture many of the crucial features of the Australian Commissariats and their subsidiaries. In addition the commissary in NSW became a source of foreign exchange and of local instruments of exchange. They were, at once, banks and credit agencies, and a springboard for banking enterprises. They were also the instruments for encouraging and reallocating productive activity for regulating staple prices and subsidies to such an extent that they have been perceived as 'staple markets'. The commissary also became the means for making supplementary allowances to officials, for compensating persons for performing public services for which no British appropriation existed or for totally funding some other public services. Through rations distribution, they effectively paid workers engaged in convict gangs on public infrastructure.'*[90]

That the commissariat operations reflected the changing needs within the colony is evidenced by its regular reorganisation. Until Macquarie's

[90] Butlin, N.G.' *What a way to run an Empire, Fiscally'* p52

arrival, there had been stability in the organisation structure and only two commissaries had been appointed: the basic operations of victualling convicts and selected settlers had remained constant, as had the provision of tools and equipment to convict work parties. Under Macquarie, the expansion of services provided by the commissariat had grown disproportionately and into relatively uncharted areas. He recognised the need for banking and financial services in the colony but, when his proposal for a chartered bank was rejected, he imposed that role on the commissariat. Likewise, the growing intake of convicts into the colony led to vast organisational limitations on government, and thus these tasks were assigned to the commissariat.

The demand on the commissariat was always significant and varied according to the number of convicts arriving in the colony, which in turn depended on the military and economic circumstances prevailing in Britain and Europe. On 1 February 1793, only five years after the First Fleet arrived in Botany Bay, Britain was at war with France, the Napoleonic Wars that dragged on until 1815. There were several important consequences: the attention of the British Government was distracted [18] away from the affairs of an insignificant and distant colony (Botany Bay); transportation of convicts more difficult and less necessary; the flow of free immigrants to the colony was reduced even further; and it enabled a small group of elite military officers stationed in the colony to create a monopoly position. In spite of the *Navigation Acts,* the war in Europe provided an excuse to develop trade between the British colony and the American colonies, although it was one-sided in favour of the American shippers.

Heavy economic commitments to the war in Europe and a downturn in the British economy from 1810-1815 led to constant pressure from the British Government to reduce expenditure in the colony. The Colonial Office in London thought this could be partly accomplished by moving people 'off the store' and reducing expenditures on public works. Both of these alternatives affected commissary operations. Apart from foodstuffs, the commissary mainly bought timber for building, leather for boots and shoes, wool (hair) for blankets and supplies such as barley for brewing beer.

The commissariat received supplies from four general sources: imports, government farms and workshops, civil and military officers and private individuals. In some matters, the commissary strongly supported private enterprise–for instance the area under grain on government farms never rose above 10% of the total farmed land in the settlement and by 1808 this was insignificant[19]. Similarly, government cattle numbers, notwithstanding the lost herd later found in the Cow Pastures at Camden, represented a decreasing proportion of total cattle numbers in the colony, falling from 70% in 1800 to 12% in 1814, whilst government sheep numbers fell from 10% to 2% of those in the colony in the same period.

The third Bigge Report provides an important insight into Commissariat activities. Commissioner John Thomas Bigge, a former Chief Justice of the West Indies colony of Jamaica, was appointed by Lord Bathurst to visit the Colony and assess progress and to evaluate the growing expenditures of Governor Macquarie. The instruction to Commissioner Bigge read in part: 'you will inquire into the courts of justice, the judicial establishments and the police regulations of the colony[91]. You will also turn your attention to the question of education and religious instruction. The agricultural and commercial interests of the colony will further require your attentive consideration. With respect to them you will report to me their actual state and the means by which they can be promoted.' Bathurst added:

> *I would more particularly refer to the authority, which the governor has hitherto exercised, of fixing the prices of staple commodities in the market, and of selecting the individuals, which shall be permitted to supply meat to the government stores. With respect to these regulations, you will investigate how far their repeal is likely to lead to any general inconvenience, or to any public loss. I am aware that when the colony was first established the necessity of husbanding the scanty means of supply and of regulating its issue, might justify an interference on behalf of the government; but now*

---

[91] The first two paragraphs of Earl Bathurst's letter of 6th January 1819 to J.T. Bigge have been summarised for purposes of expediency
The full instructions from Bathurst to Bigge and the correspondence from Bathurst to Sidmouth are printed

> *that the quantity of land in cultivation is so much increased, and the number of cultivators enlarged, I confess I have great reason to doubt the expediency of these regulations; at the same time I feel unwilling to recommend so material an alteration without some examination on the spot as to its probable effects.*

A second letter of the same date and also from Earl Bathurst directed J.T. Bigge to consider the suitability of Sydney town as the main recipient of convicts and the opportunity of:

> *'forming on other parts of the coasts, or in the interior of the country, distinct establishments exclusively for the reception and proper employment of the convicts, who may hereafter be sent out. From such a measure, it is obvious that many advantages must result. It would effectively separate the convict from the free population, and the labour of forming a new settlement would afford constant means of employment, including that of a severe description. By forming more than one of such separate establishments, the means of classifying the offenders, according to the degree of crime, could be facilitated. But on the other hand, you will have to consider, what would in the first instance, be the expense of the measures, and what may be the probable annual charge which may result from their adoption.'*

Earl Bathurst, in a separate note[92] to Viscount Sidmouth dated April 1817, set out his concerns of the mixing of convicts with free settlers and the problems resulting from ever increasing numbers of convicts being transported[93]. He wrote:

> *'Another evil resulting from the increased number (of convicts transported), is the great difficulty of subjecting any of the convicts to constant superintendence, either during the hours*

---

92 *with the third report by Bigge to Westminster, as presented to the House of Commons in February 1823*

93 Ritchie, John *Punishment and Profit*

> *of work or relaxation; and the necessity of leaving a large proportion of them to the care of providing their own lodgings during the night, from the inadequacy of public buildings allotted to their reception, forms one of the most formidable objections to the current system. I intend to place the settlement on a footing that shall render it possible to enforce strict discipline, regular labour and constant superintendence, or the system of unlimited transportation to New South Wales must be abandoned. I propose the appointment of commissioners with full powers to investigate all the complaints which have been made, both with respect to the treatment of the convicts and the general administration of the government'.*

In his instructions to Commissioner Bigge, Bathurst had recognised the impact of over-regulation and enforced pricing of goods sold to the government stores. However, the commissariat (or Government store) relied on imports for its grain and meat supplies and, until 1800, to a lesser extent on the private sector. From 1804, grain was in reasonable supply, except in periods of drought, floods and disease, and was grown mainly by the small settlers. Cattle and sheep raising tended to be in the hands of the military and civil officers and other settlers with larger holdings. The government set basic prices for commodity purchases by the Stores, but these were often exceeded because of the general shortage of labour[94]. The governor set fixed prices for the commissariat for grain but the settlers found they had to sell at lower rates to influential middlemen, who then obtained the fixed price. This group had influence over what supplies the stores would buy and from whom. According to Linge[95], a similar clique 'was able to buy up ships' cargoes and resell them at ten times the price and more' After 1800 Governor King tried to break the monopoly position of these groups (mainly officers) but his efforts brought only temporary relief to small settlers, many of whom were in debt.

The difficulty of changing the role and activities of small farmers was that the vast majority was ex-convicts with little literacy and certainly neither

---

94 Fletcher, B.H 'The Development of Small-scale farming in NSW under Governor Hunter' JPRAHS, 50 pp 1-8

95 G. J.R. Linge 'Industrial Awakening'

the knowledge nor capital to improve their farming techniques or buy stock and equipment. In Van Diemen's Land, Lt-Governor Sorrell lent small operators a bull or ram from the government herds and flocks for breeding purposes in an endeavour to improve the herd and provide some small assistance so these operators could acquire breeding livestock. Such arrangements was not extended to or followed in the colony of NSW although Samuel Marsden, a leading practitioner of flock improvement in the colony, did loan some special rams to neighbours and parishioners around Parramatta. The record shows Governor Darling loaned 'cows' to small farmers although this was a strange way of increasing the private herds rather than the public herds.

Commissioner Bigge[96] reported:

> *'Clerks in the Commissariat department generally consist of persons who have been convicts, and also of persons who are still in that position, but who have received tickets of leave. They receive pay, differing in amounts from 1s 6d to 5s per day, and 'lodging' money; they likewise receive the full ration, and a weekly allowance of spirits. A system must be installed that reduces the perpetual temptation to plunder from the necessary exposure of public property. It is for this reason recommended that public rations of bread should be baked by contract (at a potential savings of 1/6th of the flour used); Private contracts (let under the tender process) to supply the hospitals with bread, meat and vegetables have proven to be of advantage to those establishments; both changes result in considerable savings to government'.*

The report confirms that in 1820, those victualled in NSW numbered 5,135 to whom 7,027 rations were issued daily (some convicts were on 1½ regular ration because they were considered to be in heavy manual labour). In total, the numbers victualled, including military and civil officers, rose from 8,716 in August 1820 to 9,326 in December 1820. Bigge reported 'I see no reason for not applying the former rule by which the rations of those officers whose salaries exceeded £90 per annum were taken away. I

96 Bigge, J.T. Report # 3 Agriculture & Trade in NSW (1823)-p.132

recommend that they be taken off the stores and a compensating amount be paid to them from the Colonial Police Fund.'[97]

The British Government constantly reminded colonial governors of the growing cost of running the colony and the need to take people 'off the stores'. During 1800-1803 more than 2000 convicts were transported, adding to the number dependent on the store: there was also a significant increase in the number of small farms allotted, mainly to the growing number of convicts whose sentences had expired. At that time, a small 30-acre land grant, achieved at least three benefits for the new owners: they generally improved his social status (and therefore their mindset towards crime and property ownership); they were taken off the stores and told to be self-sufficient; and they became eligible to sell produce to the store thus becoming an important cog in the colony's food chain.[98]

In his 'Working Paper', Butlin offers some interesting numbers with respect to the growth in farming activity, for the period 1800-1810. 'Excluding the holdings of civil and military officers, the number of farms grew from 400 in 1800 to 600 in 1804 and 700 in 1807. Thus, even though grain production had reached a reasonably satisfactory level by 1804 and 40 new farms were coming into production each year; the number of mouths to feed was increasing by only a few hundred annually at this time. However, meat remained scarce. Cattle were preferred to sheep because they were less prone to attack by wild dogs, thrived better in the wet and humid climate and were more suitable for salting down; whereas in 1801 the ratio was 6 to 1 in favour of sheep, by 1809 the ration was reduced to only 3 to 1'[98] The 'Epitome of the Official History of NSW' suggests the numbers of livestock in 1800 was 1,044 cattle and 6,124 sheep; in 1810 the number had increased to 12,442 cattle and 25,888 sheep; by 1821 cattle numbers had grown to 102,939 and sheep to 290,158[99].

---

97 Bigge, J.T. Report # 3 Agriculture & Trade in NSW (1823)-p.149

98 Butlin, N.G 'What a way to run an Empire, fiscally' (Working Papers in Economic History (ANU)

99 'An Epitome of the Official History of NSW' compiled from the Official and Parliamentary Records of the Colony in 1883, under the direction of the Government Printer, Thomas Richards.

This series of events before 1810 set the foundation for the future direction of the pastoral industry in the colony. Although there were troubling but isolated incidences of military officer domination of trade and profiteering, the colonial economy was growing and settling into a pattern of life suitable for self-sufficiency and growing independence and local governance. From 1811 to 1815, the pattern changed and turned into a commercial depression in the colony, brought about by a number of internal and external factors. 'Sealing vessels were having to sail further to find grounds not already picked bare by Colonial, British and American gangs, and in 1810, news reached Sydney that the British Government had imposed a duty of £20 per ton on oil caught in the Colonial waters.'[100] Further, in England the price for sealskins fell from 30/–to between 3/–and 8/-. Between 1810 and 1812 the British economy suffered a downturn and the financial troubles, brought on by a long drawn-out war in Europe, were soon transmitted to NSW. Indian and English merchant houses called up debts and refused to underwrite further speculations and the British Government pressed the colonial administration to further reduce running costs[101]. Locally, the Commissariat's venture into money operations helped intensify the shortage of money in the settlement and, to add to these distractions; in 1813 local duties were imposed on sandalwood, sperm oil, skins and timber, whether intended for home consumption or export. The English Government weighed in with another cost cutting exercise by reducing the military numbers in the colony from 1600 in 1813 to 900 in 1815. Steven concludes that by 1815, 'Sydney's commerce had almost totally collapsed'[102.] She also suggests that one side benefit of the commercial downturn was that, because individuals and partnerships could no longer see easy openings in trade, commerce, land and livestock, they may have turned their attention to industrial activity, establishing a profitable base for further local production of manufactured items and import-replacement industries.[103]

---

100 Linge 'Industrial Awakening' *op cit*

101 To these circumstances, Briggs and Jordan, writing the 'Economic History of England' adds the Malthus observations on a rising population (8% between 1808 and 1812) and the effects of the industrial revolution.

102 M. Steven 'Merchant Campbell 1869-1846' p.136

103 Steven *ibid* p.142

In summary, one of the supplies carried by Governor Phillip on the First Fleet was a 'forge'. Such an item would have been considered necessary to make or shape a metal object by heating and hammering e.g. for use by farriers and vets, but for the First Fleeters' there were no horses and very little metal objects, so Phillip must have had a repair use in mind for broken axes, adzes, hammers etc. However, the forges were to come in handy later during the Phillip administration when, first Phillip then Hunter and finally King required small metal items specifically adapted to colonial conditions. The local environment was much harsher than originally anticipated by Phillip when ordering supplies for the first voyage, and few items adapted well to the new surroundings. Thus it was time thought King to put the forges to good use. Ordering new supplies took at least twelve months before receipt, and the quality, of even the most expensive items was inadequate, so the decision was made to save time, to be in receipt of suitable items by making them locally. Obviously there were side benefits–'no direct cost' and thus a saving of foreign exchange; developing a local secondary industry and developing local skills.

This was the beginning of the network of government-owned and sponsored industries, other than public farming. The novel concept of government owned and operated farms, (as opposed to full privatisation) had been a bi-product of necessity undertaken by Phillip. Without public farming of grain, vegetables livestock and fruit trees, private settlers would not have been able to support the settlement's needs for many years. However it was not long before having gotten the basics of food production for the settlement, Phillip commenced the privatising approach, by making land grants to suitably enterprising emancipists and military officers who wanted an alternative to trading in speculative cargoes. Thus the scenario became one of a ***directed economy***, the acceptance of prisoners as unpaid but supported labour, and the usage of that labour to underpin private and public farming. But farming also needed access to roads and public infrastructure, so some of the convict labour had to be set aside to make roads (really cart tracks, build barracks, build a water supply system and develop a system of public buildings as hospitals, churches, commissariat store and wharves, bulkheads around Sydney Cove, gardens etc. All this need stretched the usage of the few prison labourers, and Hunter appealed for further transfers.

A small settlement, struggling to feed itself, receiving significant number of prisoners, and being watched for every penny it spends, and therefore struggling to find an export commodity. Such an export can't be manufactured, but instead must be a primary or basic industry. Meat is not exportable, nor grain, since both are in limited supply, but natural resources are a possibility. The items that come to mind are timber and coal. These are always in demand in Britain, and Britain is the only available export market. Fisheries are explored but a local market exists for fish; however, seals are a multiple product source and their by-products of skins and oil are much in demand. Finally a staple capable of being exported from the settlement–an industry that is not too labour intensive and capable of employing a number of skills and of being associated with other industries. The shipbuilding and provisioning industries are young and in need of support. Visiting ships will also be supportive of these two industries. The commissariat can't get involved in these commercial type businesses, other than by providing financial services in the absence of a treasury. What the commissariat needs is some basic routine industry that is capable of employing a growing number of convicts and of producing a relevant product for the settlement. If the commissariat can't directly contribute to generating export income, it can contribute in another important way and that is to save on import expenditures, and that is exactly what operation is available. Instead of importing many standard items, why not produce them locally. If man hours were valued, and if raw materials were priced, then these items may well be more expensive that their importation, but the system does not work this way. In the mind of the British Treasury officials who make the rules, prison labour is not costed nor is extracted resources priced. So if other needs are identified, such as timber frames for housing, doors, windows, trusses for roofs, etc, then by matching supply and demand, the commissariat can meet production needs of all types of building products. This in turn will require a great deal of labour, up-skilling of many trades, a lot of supervision but most of all, a public works program can be got underway for little cost.

CHAPTER 9

THE STORY OF THE VAN DIEMEN'S LAND COMPANY

A well-thumbed book in my collection of Australiana is a volume by Henry Gullet, published in 1914, and with an introduction by Lord Chelmsford, Governor of Queensland (at that time) and then of NSW in the first decade of the 20th Century. Gullet writes in this volume, which he entitled *The Opportunity in Australia* 'When my memory begins, the worst of the pioneering was finished on the selection. Our block, like the rest of agricultural land in northern Victoria was taken up from the Crown at 20s an acre, payable in twenty years. That was in the early seventies.' There are remarkable similarities between Gullet's story and our story of the VDL Company.

Amongst the numerous writings in support of 'opportunities in VDL in the 1810-1820 period', is one by an Edward Curr, who presented (as an opportunity for future settlers and investors) 'the great country of VDL' from which he had achieved wealth and land ownership. The text by Curr was written during his boat trip home to England, for a short visit, following his father's death, and as a means of protecting his interest in his Father's estate from a greedy brother. Little did Curr realise what fortuitous events would follow the text's publication in the London of 1824. It was used by a group of 'investors' (active in the wool industry and milling in England) as a means of establishing a reliable source of wool for their mills, as well as the means of becoming involved in the great speculative atmosphere of the day. That Curr would be accepted by this group of wool merchants, who were starry eyed about prospects for producing wool in the VDL, is indicative of both his persuasive abilities and his greed. But the similarities between Gullet's story and the story of the VDL Company diverge from that point. These profiteers led by Curr did not want to pay 20s per acre for their selection. They wanted to follow the Australian Agricultural Company who had applied for and received (from Lord Bathurst–Secretary for State of the Colonies) one million acres of land grant in NSW in exchange for agreeing to develop the land, grow wool (Bathurst demanded the growing of 'fine' wool), and take on as many convicts as required and thus relieve the government of the expense of holding and working these convicts. Another side benefit to Britain was the opening up and development of new farming country and settlements, thus diversifying peoples and towns far and wide in the new colony. The Curr group named themselves tentatively the VDL Company, because their plan was to compete with the AAC not in NSW but in the VDL) and they applied for 500,000 acres in the Van Diemen's Land Colony, and then offered to capitalise the company at half a million pound and grow fine wool–not so much for the general market, but for their own use within the woollen mills owned by the company promoters. These promoters were drawn from the ranks of woollen mill owners, merchants, bankers and investors.

The origins of the VDL Company

Edward Curr, a young Englishman attracted to and by the colonies, had returned to England from VDL following his father's death when he was invited to attend a gathering of the proposed VDL Company planning group in London. The publication of Curr's booklet on conditions and opportunities in VDL had drawn attention to the fact that he was in England. A group of wealthy woollen mill owners, wool merchants, bankers and investors had planned to invest in a pastoral operation in the new colonies shortly after learning of the apparent success of the Australian Agricultural Company (AAC) which, following its charter by the Westminster Parliament and being appropriately capitalised, had received a grant of one million acres in the Port Stephens region of the NSW mid coast.

Curr, having spent only a few years in the Colony, had returned from NSW and VDL, having received a small grant of land in VDL. Curr was a promoter and, while returning to England by sailing ship, he had written a booklet for publication with the intention of promoting the VDL Colony. *An Account of the Colony of Van Diemen's Land* was published in London in 1824 and, together with a collection of other similar publications of about the same time (refer list on previous page), became influential in awakening interest in the new Colonies of NSW and VDL, especially as havens for making money through absentee land ownership and emigration. In one of his more uncharitable moments, Jorge Jorgenson suggested Curr wrote his short story, during a moment of boredom, whilst becalmed near Mauritius on his way to England.

The 'syndicate' of influential merchants and mill owners applied to Lord Bathurst for 500,000 acres of land in the VDL Colony. Bathurst at first disapproved of the idea but he was willing to give it lengthy consideration and to receive frequent representations from syndicate leaders. He finally agreed to sponsor an Act through the British Parliament, under which a charter of incorporation would be issued and stamped with the Great Seal, through which the regulation, land selection and grant approval would be incorporated. In November 1825 the Act passed both Houses and, by this means, the company was required to issue One million pound in shares and employ their capital in cultivation and sheep farming; to lend money on mortgage and to persons engaged in fisheries; to undertake public works on security of tolls, but they were barred from engaging in banking and commerce. In return, the company would receive a grant (subject only to quit-rents) of 250,000 acres in VDL.

Bathurst had liaised with Sorell (who had returned to England following his recall), and Sorell offered support for the concept, but warned Bathurst that no large blocks of fertile land remained locatable. Bathurst decided to limit the grant to 250,000 acres, to be taken on the northwest coast in one square block, bounded by Bass Strait to the north and the ocean to the west. Negotiations followed between Bathurst and Curr, who had originally been appointed secretary of the company, but was then appointed chief agent and manager of the company in the colony. Curr's conflict of interest commenced when he subscribed to a large block of shares, as well as being an employee of the company. The Managing Director, based in London, remained responsible to the Governor and Court of the company (also based in London) whilst the land granted was to be valued to the company at 2/6 per acre, and the whole 'quit-rent' charged was 'four hundred and sixty-eight pounds, sixteen shillings' per annum. This quit-rent was redeemable at twenty years in the lump sum of £9,575, although one-fourth could be offset for 'useless' land. The employment and full maintenance of convicts would entitle the company to a further remission of quit-rent, up to £16 per male per annum, and £20 per female. The terms of the Charter, and the Instructions from Bathurst signed off on by the Company are included in Chapter 4.

Curr sailed to VDL, arriving in Hobart in 1825, with handpicked officers of the company, Stephen Adey, livestock superintendent; Alexander Goldie, agriculturalist; Henry Hellyer, architect and surveyor; Joseph Fossey and C.P. Lorymer, assistant surveyors. Curr was so anxious to select the land; he made little preparation to determine an outline of the parcel from which selection could be made. He was so confident of his success at selecting suitable land for grazing and raising sheep for wool that a boat, loaded with sheep collected from Spain, was only months behind their arrival in Hobart. In the Colony, not all was well for Curr's exploration plans. Because of constant bickering between Lt-Gov. Arthur, and Curr, the selection of land was not completed until 1830, and then only by Bathurst using a veiled threat to cancel the agreement unless speedy progress was made.

Our knowledge and understanding of those early years of the VDL Company come from a variety of sources. For instance, we learn of the bickering and disputes between Arthur and Curr; Bathurst and Inglis (VDL Coy Managing Director in London) from their voluminous exchange of correspondence, reported in Series III of the *Historic Records of Australia*. This offers us the thoughts, plans and desires of the governments and the Company but we need to look at the semi-official writings of the Company's directors to learn if rational planning took place in moving it forward.

That there was a frequent and almost alarming redirection of business strategic policy within the company is apparent from the annual reports of the company and the failure of consistency to pursue any one of these subsidiary business operations for any period of time. Today's corporations could not afford to be as shallow as to pursue turnarounds and turnabouts of planning and policies at the same rate as the VDL Coy did between 1830 and 1850. However, dealing with this superficial pursuit of profits without any apparent planning or strategic analysis is for another chapter. What we do need to point out here is that the company failed to plan and changed direction as often as was necessary to offer hope to the shareholders who year after year faced calls on the shares, and learned of no dividend again this year, and, in fact, in many years faced a technical insolvency, that today would have been an invitation to the liquidators and administrators to move in 'en masse' and close the operation down. However, for all the company records that are available in the National Library of Australia (NLA) and the Tasmanian Archives (TA), there are no minutes of meetings where a 'business plan' or strategic plan was unveiled and adopted. Instead we have these regular visits of the directors from London, who arrive in Hobart to visit the 'estate', (although sometimes not even leaving the domesticity of Hobart) and in return for the all expenses paid trip write a favourable report of how well everything is going, whilst the figures and statistics indicate the opposite is the case. Bischoff, the Managing Director after Inglis visited and wrote in 1832. Sir Edward Poole, representing the general directors of the Court during his visit in 1859, was the first to report in a practical fashion of what the company had by way of useful assets and what it could profitably do with them. This 'business plan' prepared very independently of the local manager James Gibson, who Poole declined to meet with during his visit was the first 'road map' of future operations and was followed for the next 40 year with success. Such a step some 30 years earlier could well have put the company on a sound financial footing. In the interim, the annual reports of the Agent-in-chief and Manager in Tasmania (as it became in 1826) was attached to the Company's Annual Reports as the means of keeping the demoralized stakeholders informed.

Before we return to the establishment of the VDL Company, it is timely to ask–Did the VDL Company fail in its objectives or mission, or just fail financially? The short answer must be 'no'. The two-fold main objectives were to produce a reliable source of wool for its merchant-owners in England, and upgrade the quality of local sheep flocks (hopefully through livestock sales). An amazing quantity of wool was exported from this small island over the years, and this story is told in Chapter Four, on gathering and interpreting the company's statistics. That this was a potentially reliable source of wool exports is not questioned either, nor is the upgrade to the company's sheep flocks which grew in numbers as well as quantities year after year, especially as the tenant farmers were encouraged to produce more and areas of fertile land held by the company was opened up to production.

However, the company did fail, not only financially, but also in a moral way, for nothing it started seemed to be given longer term support, and nothing the company started seemed to ever reach its optimum goal. For instance, the company in 1849, after having worked its lands for 20 years, was still only running 6,519 sheep on 325,000 acres *(Return of Livestock for the year ending 31st December 1849*). The company return for 1850 shows sheep on hand to be 6873, whilst only 1966 sheep were sold for an income of £708. Those figures suggest that the flock was not being managed for reproduction or growth, and so neither income nor gain was received.

In the same vein, unable to show major gains in the pastoral operations, the company turned to tenant farmer development (by leasing out farmland to immigrant farmers), and the development of a Port at Circular Head. Tenant farming peaked at 843 in 1850, at the same time company-employed workers were in decline. Company income from a third income area was only £1764 in livestock sales. The point here is that the company seemed to have no clear predetermined sense of direction, nor any particular goal. Even if cash flow had not been in annual crisis, the company could have optimised its flocks to cover the 350,000 acres granted; or optimised its tenant farming operation to a degree greater than having 800 odd farmers yielding poor results such as to put both them and the company at risk every year.

There is a need, at this point, to make a brief observation on the financial side of the VDL Company between 1826 and 1850. It would be thought that a company of VDL stature and capitalisation would have an attractive set of financial statements–should they be optimistic in order to attract new capital and stockholders? Should they be less than honest in order to justify further capital calls on existing stockholders or should they be minimalist but honest in order to show that the managers are performing, even if at less that desired levels? Well, the 1850 Balance Sheet, which is unlike any we could observe today, shows 'investment in livestock at £28,186.17.9 (even for a pastoral company of VDL Company's standing, this was remarkably low–sheep averaged about £4 per head); debts of £7241 for unpaid wages, commissions, obligations and promissory notes; and accepting that the 360,000 acres of land granted to the company came at nil cost, the balance sheet states 'investment in land' at £108,054. Of this sum, £35,471 was the value of the Circular Head 'head office', which merely reflects that the company had invested in office buildings, houses, ports, wharves etc rather than the pastoral arm of the company. Losses for the year of 1850 reached £23097, although the cumulative losses are not recorded in the Balance Sheet at this time. Cash on hand was less than £1,000, but bills receivable were listed at £6977.

Later chapters will pursue this analysis of the company operations, but it is sufficient at this point to say that the company failed in every way except for the self-serving production of quality wool for its merchant stockholders, which occurred in ever decreasing quantity.

Although Curr's writings on the condition of the country in VDL were clear and precise, the first selection of land around Circular head was not encouraging. Nor was the opinion of Adey and Hellyer on the worth of the land between Circular Head and Cape Grim. Opinions on the initial selection possibilities were poor as was the land itself. Curr would not accept any responsibility for such selection criteria, required of him, but wanted to keep an argument running with Arthur over what Bathurst intended in his written instructions to the company–where was the north-west region, why couldn't the grant be in separate parcels; was the 250,000 acres granted to be of 'quality or fertile, arable lands' and exclusive of waste-lands?

In the end Curr achieved better than he deserved by mere bent of the other side being exhausted through this continual stream of questions, complaints and misinterpretations. In 1830 Curr accepted the grant of six parcels in the northwest region, amounting to over 350,000 acres, indicating that at the equation of less than 70% arable land in each parcel, the productive land would net to the originally intended 250,000 acres.

One side benefit of these numbers was that the average value per acre reduced from 2/6 to about 1/6.

The land grants were as follows:

• 'Woolnorth'	150,000 acres
• Circular Head	20,000 acres
• Hampshire Hills	10,000 acres
• Middlesex Plains	10,000 acres
• Surrey Hills	150,000 acres
• Coastal Islands	10,000 acres
Total Acreage	350,000 acres

An indication that Curr was perhaps under growing pressure to take up the offered land was that the high lands towards the westward of the region were found to be barren and cold, and unsuitable for the imported breed of sheep. As a result, in the years 1831-1833 the company lost its entire flock to climate and disease problems, and psychologically, probably never recovered from this near-fatal blow. The essence of the conflict between Curr and Arthur was that because of the barren land and unfavourable climate, Curr wanted to move his region as far north towards the sun, but Arthur held him to the literal agreement. So in the end, Curr was granted 350,000 acres of land but much of it was in unacceptable locations (unacceptable only to Curr, for it suited the VDL governor to open up new regions of lesser quality land). The whole scheme of granting the VDL Company such a huge parcel of land was distasteful to Arthur–he was aware of the potential risk to and challenge of his authority from a large company, headquartered in London and unable to be reined in without political brinkmanship. An oversight by Bathurst had failed to place the raising of capital in the covenant between Government and the company. Bathurst could only delay the issuing of the charter until satisfactory assurance was received of the subscription to the capital. The public works undertaken by the company were far from what Lt-Gov Arthur had envisaged, even with the assignment of convicts specific to building roads and connecting tracks between each of the properties. The instructions by Bathurst to the Company were largely ignored, even though they appear to be clear, to be commercially viable and in the end result, performable to the benefit of the company, its employees and its subsidiary operations.

Gullet records in his book:

> *'I did not then know what it was to have missed the pioneering; to have come too late to see the selection covered with a green eucalyptus forest untouched by the axe, too late to ride in shadow over the 320 acres and choose the site for the homestead on the little sand hill in the north-east corner, or to set about the ring-barking and the clearing, and all the rest of the work which is the most satisfying in the world–the carving of a home out of wilderness.'*

Curr had faced these problems with his selection, 70 years before the pioneering Gullet wrote his tome, but Curr did not miss the tall trees, or the ringbarking or the sand. By 1824, he was ready to be a 'manager' and guide the fortunes of a well-capitalised company with access to lots of workers–even if they were going to be convicts–from behind a desk. Curr had had enough being poor and doing all the hard work. Lord Bathurst had restricted the land grant to 250,000 acres of wool growing land (not forest area, Curr argued), to be selected from the north-west corner of the Island–an unexplored and largely wilderness area, whose productive value was untested but Curr shrank away from forest land as being too costly to develop, but on the other hand he could not find sufficient open 'quality' land. Curr's associates held very different opinions of 'quality' land, which somewhat signalled the start of the failure of the VDL Company over the next 180 years.

The way Gullet spins his story is certainly an inducement or enticement for migrants from Britain to realise the opportunity awaiting them in colonial Australia. However, Curr's story is anything but the realisation of an opportunity. Rather it is the tale of wasted opportunities, of fiscal failure, poor management and ego-driven actions that brought disappointment to the London directors and the stockholders, and disrepute to the company within Van Diemen's Land itself. We do find an explanation, of sorts, for the eventual disinterest, by the English directors, in the company operations in the colony. Their reliance on European wool was over, and there was a virtual glut of colonial wool arriving in England, both from elsewhere in VDL and from the colony of NSW. Within 20 years of VDL Company finally selecting its land grants (which activity took almost five years), England was receiving half its wool imports from the Colony. No longer was their wool supply the by-product of a political will and the result of tenuous, if not temporary, peace negotiations in Europe.

In the early years, VDL (as a new Colony) enjoyed greater prosperity than NSW. Marjorie Barnard writes in *History of Australia* 'The mainland's needs were her (VDL) opportunity. By 1820, sixteen years after the foundation, VDL was exporting wheat and salt meat to NSW. She had a population of about 5,500, of which 2,588 were convicts and 2880 free men, of whom all but 712 were ex-convicts.'

It is estimated that in 1820 there were 30,000 cattle and 180,000 sheep on the Island. The wool industry commenced when Governor Sorell (the third VDL Governor) imported merinos bought from Macarthur in NSW. Earlier, Governor King had already sent eight merinos to VDL to try to revert the breeding of sheep for meat to a breed more suitable for wool production. The early wool, if used at all, was restricted to the stuffing mattresses and it was this type of fleece that sold in NSW in 1820 for 4p per pound–for manufacturing of rough woollen clothing for convicts, if not entirely satisfactory for mattresses. Sorell tidied up the wool industry in VDL and improved its methods. Besides the Macarthur rams from NSW, he bought in English and Saxon Merinos. Of the first 300 rams brought from NSW, 119 died on the journey. The rest he distributed to deserving farmers and by 1830, over 1 million pounds of wool was being shipped from VDL. Wool had replaced sealing and whaling as the major export product and meat and grain markets were shrinking, as NSW became self-supporting. In 1826, the common opinion was that VDL was better suited to the wool industry than NSW, the pastures were better, disease less frequent and methods better. Pastures were improved and runs were fenced in VDL long before they were on the mainland. Other industries suitable to the VDL climate and landscape were being developed. Potatoes were exported to NSW in 1817, hops for beer in 1820 and the apple industry would begin in earnest in 1827. The Island was thought of as a fertile garden; only the markets were lacking. When the Commissariat stores in both VDL and NSW were full, there was no other outlet for produce. Agriculture declined whilst wool thrived.

This was the setting and background which the VDL Company agents reached in 1826. The company had great potential but a lot to prove. It would all depend on what initial steps were taken. The next five years are largely taken up with arguments between the company and the governments of VDL and Britain and this in itself became a recipe for failure.

Curr was not the last British manager of the VDL Company who did not succeed in that role. Following his dismissal by the Directors in 1842, a further succession of ill-equipped, untrained and ego-driven managers, appointed in London, tried to understand and conquer the colonial territory, but none came close, until 1850 when the colonial manager, James Gibson, recommended the company be liquidated. A special committee of one director and four stockholders was appointed to advise the directors on further steps but the committee's report was that the company's assets were less than its liabilities. Thus the directors were once again misled on the true value of the company's assets. For some reason, the committee fell for an accounting trick and accepted the capitalised expense of the company's properties in Tasmania as being the current book value of the property assets, even though current land and livestock sales and leases could not support the book values being used. The assets were overvalued in the books, probably as a way of convincing the directors that the capital had been spent wisely and to show the Government that the required development works (committed to under the original grant terms) had been carried out by the Company.

From 1850 there was a period of consolidation and liquidation, although again not in any rational way. What was showing itself to be the company's best, biggest and most valuable asset was being sold for a trifle. The forestry lands, which by the late 1850's were beginning to show some market interest and worth, were being offered for a fraction of their real value and on terms too generous to be of commercial intent.

The committee that handled the company's break-up must have realised it was a hopeless assignment, since they recommended delaying further action as they awaited a detailed assessment of the mineral worth of the company's lands. A mineralogist from the mainland examined all the properties, looking for gold and ores (tin etc) but found nothing within the company's boundaries. Running out of luck again, a new discovery of tin ore (like an earlier tin discovery) was made just outside the company's boundaries. The directors decided that, if they could not extract the minerals, they would handle their transfer from the remote mountain location to the company port of Emu Bay (Burnie) by a company-built railroad mainly over company lands. The thinking was sound–protect the company's main town and port, before the Government stepped in to open up a competitive port. Unfortunately the assessment was again uncommercial. Gibson, the manager who had blown the whistle on being able to keep the company alive in 1851, recommended the railway project. He suggested the rails should be built out of wood in order to keep the costs down and projected the cost to be £800 per mile. The actual cost came in close to £100,000, or £1,400 per mile, but the government, thinking it could do better, re-routed the line to its own port.

As with most VDL Company business enterprises, success was illusive. Activities undertaken, including such diverse programs as tenant farming (with the company offering lessee farmers a guaranteed buy-back of all produce), commercial livestock sales, timber sales, port operations, township land sales, wool production, railway operation and land development, almost always fell short of expectations. The tenant farming concept, of leasing land to immigrant farmers and then buying their produce at commercial prices, resulted in a company loss of over £30,000 when the produce could not be sold and was dumped in the Emu Bay Harbour. Not one of the business enterprises that commenced resulted in a direct company gain, even though the directors and stockholders were annually promised–'this next year is the one', 'success is just around the corner'.

It took until the 1900s for a rational plan from an Australian manager to emerge. However, the first 75 years had taken its toll on the company's finances and little was developed and ready to sell off, or even make productive. The 20th Century realised further consolidations and small progress, although concentration had returned to the Company's core focus, as set down in Bathurst's original instructions to Curr–growing (fine) wool, developing, and making the land productive, and improving the quality of the livestock.

Today, the first signs of success can be seen. Carrying over 40,000 sheep, 2,000 cattle and agisting a large dairy herd, the company's sole remaining property, 'Woolnorth', is profitable and productive. This 50,000-acre property is all that remains of the original 350,000 acre grant but, during its 175 years of operation, the stockholders made numerous capital contributions and received one large return of capital when property sales showed a windfall gain greater than the directors could spend.

It has taken 175 years, numerous controlling stockholders and many managers for the Van Dieman's Land Company to realise its original mission. Not many companies can experience such failure and remain in business. The shareholders carried the company, meeting many 'calls' on the capital obligations, waiving dividends, seeing profits ebb and flow and receiving little accurate information on which to base firm business decisions.

This then is the story of a company, historic in formation, whose history is largely the history of the north-west region of Tasmania. Its failure to realise its opportunities and potential is the failure of managers (mostly British) to understand Colonial conditions whose personal shortcomings almost ended the company's existence.

Of course, this outline will need to be fleshed out with events, plans and results over the whole period of the company between its beginnings in 1824, until a suitable stopping point is found in 1900. It will include some of the less pretty episodes of its existence–dealing with the assigned servant problem, the aboriginal problem and the hiatus that existed for so many years between the company and the local VDL government. The policy conflict between Bathurst and Lt-Gov Arthur over the use of government land grants, convicts and scarce local funds in support of a corporate giant, based in London, weaves through the tale like a spat between spoilt boys that is never resolved. Being principally an economic history, the financial changes to the company are given special attention and treatment, but the overall story is simply one of missed opportunities and wasted advantages.

At this point, an assessment should be made about 'sources'. If not in profits, the company is rich in records, and the official records are replete with the correspondence between company representatives, the Secretary of State in London and the VDL Government in Hobart. Sources are scarcely under abundant and the challenge becomes mainly one of sorting through voluminous handwritten records in order to determine what is relevant and important and in what context.

Unlike much of our early history, there remains some original property to help put the challenges and opportunities of the VDL Company into perspective. The house built by Curr in 1826 still stands and reminds us of the lifestyle pursued by 'gentrified' folk. Most of the original maps, plans and diaries, as well as the original 1826 exploration records, also remain to offer a basis for assembling an economic analysis of the Van Diemen's Land Company between 1824 and 1900.

The first settlers

The history of VDL is much aligned with the history of the VDL Company so a brief outline of the origins of the settlement may be of interest.

West, in the *History of Tasmania* introduces his section on the first settlers by pointing out:

> '*. . . the establishment of a settlement in VDL, perhaps thus hastened by a jealousy of a rival power, was at first chiefly intended to relieve Port Jackson. Fifteen years had elapsed since its foundation, and from six to seven thousand prisoners had been transported to Botany Bay–dispersion became necessary to security–to repress alike, the vices of the convicts or places of punishment, and the indolent and intemperance of emancipist settlers, both of which endangered authority.*' (John West: *The History of Tasmania*–1852 Part 2 Section II)

Thus VDL was colonised–'a place of exile for the most felonious of felons–the Botany Bay of Botany Bay'. (West Part 2 Section I p.30)

The first settlement was also encouraged by another motivation, the 400 rebels who led 'the Irish riots (uprising)' which, broke out at Castle Hill, seven miles from Parramatta in March 1804. The remoteness of VDL, its comparatively small size and insular form made it well fitted for the purposes of penal restraint–'a place where its most turbulent and rapacious could find no scope for their passions. Its ports could be closed against commerce, and thus afford few means of escape'. (Barnard: *A History of Australia*)

In '*A Statistical, Historical and Political Description of New South Wales* (London 1830–p.210*)*, Wentworth writes: 'In the great south land, labour and produce were redundant, wherein overwhelming harvests reduced the price of grain so low, that it was rejected by the merchants; goods could not be obtained in exchange; and the convicts at the disposal of government were a burden on its hands–almost in a condition to defy its authority.'

David Collins, the first Lt-Governor of VDL had long held the posting of judge advocate general in Sydney and was the recorder of the Botany Bay settlement in *Account of the English Colony in New South Wales* (London 1798)–the second volume of which was dedicated to Lord Hobart in 1802. Collins' first attempt at establishing a new settlement south of Botany Bay had been at Port Phillip but he had been unable to construct the basics of an on-going settlement there. Collins, following a survey, preferred the west side of the Derwent (named after a stream in Cumberland, England, immortalised in prose by the poet Wordsworth). He arrived at Sullivan's Cove with his party of marines and male prisoners on 30 January 1804. Collins named this new location Hobart Town however by any standards; the settlement grew slowly and uneventfully.

In all, the administration of David Collins brought little progress. By 1810, the total population was still only 1,321 persons, even though the 410 persons had originally landed at Sullivan's Bay. There were no roads into the interior, no public buildings and Government House was a simple cottage. Only a few acres of land had been cultivated by convicts; cattle had arrived from Bengal and sheep from Port Jackson. Under his closed ports policy, even the most necessary articles had unavailable in the settlement. The earliest settlers purchased their clothing of prisoners, being preferable to the skins of animals in which they were often clad. This early failure was attended with disastrous results and in all; the administration of David Collins brought little progress. He died in Hobart in March 1810 at the age of 56 and is buried there.

The northern settlements were not brought under the governance of Hobart until 1812, for at the same time as Collins was naming Hobart Town, Colonel Patterson named the northern settlement (on the west bank of the Tamar) York Town, later to be renamed Port Dalrymple. Bass had noted this area as suitable for agriculture and pasture, whilst Flinders had simply noted the difficulty in obtaining local fresh water. The next important event in the settlement of VDL was the removal of the settlers from Norfolk Island (first settled in 1788). In 1803 Lord Hobart had issued the first direction to relocate all settlers but only four people had responded by 1805. The order was renewed in 1808 and enforced by Captain Bligh, with 254 arriving in October 1808 in Port Dalrymple. These new settlers were welcomed with unconditional grants of land (double their allocation on Norfolk Island) as well as support from the public store, loans of livestock and the establishment of a barter system whereby a keg of rum was worth more than a common farm.

Colonel Davey was appointed the second Lieutenant Governor in February 1812. He opened the ports for general commerce in June 1813, and local traders, Messrs Lord and Reibey supplied the colony with English goods, following their arrival in 1816. Encouraged by Davey, the resources of the Colony were developed and a military officer discovered a new species of pine, highly valued by artificers–the Huon pine. Birch, a local merchant, built a vessel to survey the western coast and discovered Macquarie Harbour in 1816. He was given a one-year monopoly over the fishing trade. The whale fishery was enlarged, corn was exported, the plough introduced, a mill erected, and the foundations of St. David's were church laid. A passenger Ferry connected both sides of the Derwent River and a civil court was established. The first local newspaper, the *Hobart Town Gazette* was published in June 1816.

Despite this marvellous progress, the welfare of VDL was retarded by the 'number, the daring, and the depredations of bushrangers' (Hobart *Gazette,* August 1816*)*. In response, Davey placed the whole Colony under martial law and encouraged flogging for those (free or bonded) that broke the evening curfew. Davey's term expired in 1817. The development of VDL was following the pattern of development in NSW but with a different accent. The land grant system was the same, so were the land sale regulations. English law ruled. Progress towards self-government was parallel, and the same economic depressions affected both colonies.

William Sorrell, the third Lt-Governor, landed in Hobart in April 1817. He set out to restore safety in the Colony and, armed with individual pledges, he offered large rewards which were sufficient to persuade the military, constables and private settlers to identify the culprits. This was successful and the greater portions of the bushrangers were captured within three months of his arrival. Whaling and sealing were bringing business and money to the town. Sorrell had commenced the practice of an annual muster of all settlers, and thus accounted for each family and their livestock and the name, residence and civil condition of every inhabitant became known. Sorell's progress in building population and livestock numbers was now well documented by the Governor's despatches of July 1821. Sorell's initiative in attracting free families with capital was applauded by Macquarie, who in his despatch during his visit to Hobart, writes, 'recent influx of several respectable free settlers with considerable property will not fail to hasten the period at which VDL will hold a high rank among the settlements of the British Empire'. (Governor's despatches July 1821)

This transfer of settlers from Britain was an important event: their efforts were experimental and their achievements prophetic. The arrival of so many emigrants led to the exploration of the inland of the island and the opening of many new opportunities–the VDL Company grew from such rich resources. To provide a settlement for strangers, Sorell explored the region lying between the Shannon and the Clyde Rivers to their junction with the Derwent: which area was free from timber and within 20 miles of navigable waters and this district welcomed several distinguished settlers. Expansion followed development and by 1820, £20,000 of wheat had been exported to Sydney. This prolific result came from the farming on the more fertile and open plains, already free of timber and scrub.

Vessels commenced arriving directly from Britain and in 1822 600 new settlers arrived bringing their capital–already a new tone was prevalent in the society. Much praise was being heaped on VDL in books published by explorers and colonists–'the fertility of the soil, and the beauty of the climate . . .' These publications also generally contained a theory of pastoral increase–'geometrical progression towards wealth.' (Godwin) and include the books by W.C. Wentworth, Edward Curr, Commissioner Bigge, James Dixon, George Evans, Charles Jeffrey and Godwin's *Emigrant's Guide to VDL*. The results were impressive. Between 1810 and 1822, the population grew fifty-fold, whilst wool exports to Hamburg helped promote flock improvement.

However, the greatest landmark in the population growth of the early settlements was a decision by the British Government in 1831 that the principle of assisting the payment of emigrants' passages was accepted, and officials were appointed to supervise emigration. Australia was now seen, not merely as a solution to prison overcrowding, but as a relief for unemployment and poverty among law-abiding citizens. In the next 20 years 200,000 assisted emigrants entered Australia in addition to the almost 160,000 convicts transported to the country.

The position of VDL favoured its settlement and advantages offered to settlers included land grants, loans of livestock and seed: the price for wheat remained at an attractive 10s. Per bushel and meat at 6p per pound. By 1821, there were 7,400 residents, possessing 15,000 cultivated acres, 35,000 cattle, 170,000 sheep, 550 horses and 5000 swine. Scarcity in NSW led the Crown to buy £10,000 of meat in Hobart for transfer to Sydney. Land grants, between 1818 and 1821, rose from 25,000 acres to 250,000, whilst cultivated land tripled to 15,000 acres. Macquarie's final visit in 1821 was a great success, which was dutifully recorded in the *Sydney Gazette*: 'the architectural taste of the private buildings; the handsome church; the commodious military barracks; the strong gaol; the well constructed hospital' were all impressive and a welcome improvement over the Collins-style settlement. Macquarie also commented on the enterprise and industry of the people, the spacious harbour, the pier, the battery and the signal post.

It was the spectre of wealth creation and the prospect of large quantities of good wool that appealed to a group of wealthy merchants and gathered them into the VDL pastoral holding club, to which Curr and Sorell sowed the seed of new investment in cheap land and control of pastoral activities.

It was surely a fitting salutation to a Colony, in which the wealthy merchant group in London (the VDL Company stockholders) was planning to invest. All they required of the Government, facilitated by Lord Bathurst, was a grant of 500,000 acres.

Towards the end of Sorell's administration, circumstances favoured commerce and development by English merchants in overseas colonies. The motivation was not only wealth; it was often the securing of regular supplies of commodities in an otherwise troubled Empire–the Napoleonic Wars had left Europe torn and withdrawn. All England's wool was imported from Germany and Spain, two countries interested in using strategic supplies to advance their own position against Britain. The commerce of the VDL Colony was assisted through the enterprise of some such merchants.

Following his visit to VDL in 1820, Captain Dixon, commander of the *Shelton* published a volume (*Narrative of a Voyage to NSW & VDL–1822)* on the capabilities of the colony. He suggested the formation of a pastoral company, having shares with a face value of £100, as a wealth creating opportunity. A speculative spirit was awakened amongst the merchants and investors in England, and they were willing to subscribe to such opportunities with enthusiasm, including the Van Diemen's Land Company. One object of this latest speculation would be to relieve Britain from dependence on foreign wool, and to improve the quality of the Australian flocks.

In 1823 a company was formed at Leith (Scotland), with a capital of £100,000, professing 'to promote the welfare of the colonies, by taking their produce in exchange for merchandise' (West p74) A succession of vessels was despatched, which transferred many families from Scotland. Their position and capital made them amongst the best in the land.

Sorell received his recall in 1823, and decided to return to London for a debriefing program. His successor, Colonel George Arthur, arrived as the fourth Lt Governor of VDL in May 1824.

Narratives on VDL

As described above, there were numerous books published 1800-1825 in support of VDL. Listed below are some that can still be tracked.

- W.C. Wentworth: *A Statistical, Historical and Political Account of the Colony of New South Wales and its dependent settlement of VDL* (1820)
- Edward Curr: *An Account of the Colony of Van Diemen's Land* (1824)
- John Thomas Bigge: Reports 1, II and III on various aspects–State, Judiciary and Trade and Agriculture–of the Colony of NSW (inc. VDL) (1821-1823)
- James Dixon: *Narrative of a Voyage to NSW and VDL* (1822)
- J.K. Tuckey: *An Account of a Voyage to Establish a Colony at Port Phillip* (1805)
- David Collins: *An Account of the English Colony in NSW* (1796)–Vol I
- David Collins Vol II of his account deals with his stay in VDL (1802)
- George Evans: *A Geographical, Historical and Topographical Description of VD*' (1822)
- Charles Jeffreys: *Van Diemen's Land Geographical and Descriptive Delineations of the Island* (1820)
- T. Godwin: *Emigrants Guide to VDL (1823)*

TABLE 1: EXPORTS OF WHEAT AND MEAT FROM VDL 1816-1820

	Wheat	Meat	Total Exports
1816	13,135 bu	10,000 lbs	£21,054
1819	24,768 bu		
1820	47,131 bu	36,000 lbs	£33,225

West offers us a fairly 'grim' look at the company operations before 1850 (p. 91).

"The operations of the company were conducted on a liberal scale: artisans were sent out. The proprietors had been promised a remission of £16 for men, against the quit-rent. This was the first encouragement of free immigration, except for employers, to this quarter of the world. A road was opened to Launceston, chiefly useful to absconders.

The importation of sheep and horses was of great value to the country. The value of the grazing flock to the company was £30,000 when the value of wool exports from those sheep was only £2,000. The servants of the company left them on the expiration of their engagements: many before. The company supporters, claimed no police, no prisons, and none required. Those statements vary from the facts. The company provided no religious teaching for its people, although it had built a church, at some expense in Circular Head as a token gesture. The losses incurred by the company were great: the cold and disease had destroyed the livestock; and their crops often perished from moisture, in many forms. Sometimes the season never afforded the chance to use the sickle: in the morning the crop was laden with frost; at noon it was drenched with thaw and in the evening it was covered by dews; and thus rotted on the ground." (West: *A History of Tasmania)*

Although Curr had numerous staff at his disposal, his attitude and demeanour drove him to fulfil his nickname of 'potentate of the north'. His demagogic style left his subordinates–an agriculturalist, an architect and surveyors usually without firm or useful guidance. Servants, engaged in England at low wages, often escaped upon their arrival and after a short survey of life in the region. In 1834, the population on the company estates was about 400, half of whom were prisoners of the crown. However the company remained unprofitable for many years.

Having set the scene for economic development based on discovery, exploration, trade and history, it is timely to summarize the VDL Company-formation, land grant and convict disputes.

The VDL Company could not have begun on a worst footing that it did. Challenges to the Secretary of State for the Colonies (Lord Bathurst), and to the Lieutenant–Governor of the Colony, were frequent and acrimonious. Nothing positive could be achieved out of such friction and nothing was! The beginning of the end had been realised before the beginning could be fully fleshed out.

Whether for self-preservation purposes, or self-protection, company sponsored recordings and reports of the foundation and progress of the VDL company are the most numerous and reliable. Curr's own diary and then the writings of Bischoff, Poole, Hellyer, Jorgenson and Adler provide an interesting insight into company operations, especially since planning was not recorded, if it took place at all. An early researcher into the origins of the company, Meston, did not paint a very encouraging or positive picture of the actions taken by management or of the prospects for company success. The exchange of correspondence is reliability reported within series III of the HRA, and is unexpurgated and uncensored in this form. The formation of the company had taken place in 1824. In the initial stages some opposition was received from the Australian Agricultural Company. The AAC was authorised by 5 Geo.IV, cap. Lxxxvi, and was incorporated by letters patent, dated 1st November 1825.

Although the operations of the two companies were restricted to NSW (the AAC) and Tasmania (the VDL Company), the directors of the AAC thought their interests might be adversely affected by competition between the two colonies and by a rise in the value of sheep in Europe. Macarthur (an advisor to the AAC) expressed the opinion that the introduction of a large amount of capital into each colony would have an evil influence on that colony. After negotiations, the AAC proposed (1) that the VDL Company not purchase any sheep in NSW, or any sheep imported from NSW within VDL for a period of twelve years, and (2) that VDL should not purchase sheep in Europe for a three-year period. At a meeting in February 1825, point (1) was accepted but (2) was declined. Bathurst wrote with this resolution to Curr, in Hobart dated April 1825. The statute 6 Geo IV, cap xxxix, was passed in June 1825 authorising the granting of the charter to the VDL Company and the charter received the great seal in November 1825. Bathurst had restricted the sale or issue of shares to the public until the charter was granted. In consequence, no prospectus was ever issued.

Bathurst advised Arthur of the formation of the VDL Company on 2nd June 1825. He wrote "The establishment of a company for the cultivation and improvement of waste lands in VDL is deserving of the support of H.M. Government. A company has been formed under the title of 'The Van Diemen's Land Company' and offers the immediate advantage of introducing a large amount of capital for investment in agricultural operations, but more especially to the rearing of flocks of sheep of the purest and finest breed. You will also note, (writes Bathurst to Arthur), from the Bill that the Company has certain limitations. You should also note that the land grant will be contained by the Basse's Strait to the north, by the ocean to the west and on the east and south by lines drawn from either shore, and these lands should be reserved until the Company selection has been finally made.

He also asked Arthur to 'afford every facility to the Company officials, who will be carrying out survey and valuation of the lands to be conceded to the Company'. A month earlier (April 1825) Bathurst had written to Edward Curr, the then Secretary of the company, setting out the terms for the formation of the Company.

Its main paragraphs contained information as follows:

a. The formation is to be encouraged because of the advantages of new capital being transferred to the colony of VDL. 'It is our conviction that the judicious introduction of capital into the colony cannot fail to produce the most beneficial results'.
b. 'The essential basis of any agreement for the formation of the company must be the subscription of the nominal capital and putting the avowed designs of the company into effect'. (Bathurst had accepted the plans of the company to improve the sheep flock in the colony and export wool from the colony to the woollen mills in England).
c. 'Before I can introduce any bill into the Parliament I need to see 4/5ths the nominal capital subscribed, and I need to be assured that the subscribers are men of substance and honour in relation to payment for their shares'.
d. 'Before the charter is issued, the subscribers must actually pay 5% of their initial subscription in cash to the company. I would like to also render the shares inalienable for a few years, or else I will accept that the nominal value of each share shall be £50, as set down on the share certificate. The Government may from time to time authorise the issue of additional capital. These shares shall

be preferred to existing shareholders as a second set up to the number of first shares taken up'.

e. 'Conditions of a resolution of a general meeting will precede the government approval of additional capital, as will evidence that the original capital was put to good use (especially as to Public Works and Improvement of the Lands)
f. 'The original subscription of capital will be for £500,000 in £50 parcels. Each director and auditor will be required to have 50 qualification shares'.
g. 'Any variation to the employment of this capital other than as specified will be deemed a violation of the charter'.
h. 'Upon the issuance of the charter I shall direct His Majesty to approve a grant of 250,000 acres of land in the Island of Van Diemen's Land. One of the primary objects of the use of company capital shall be the clearing, improvement and cultivation of this tract of land. Improvement will include the construction of roads, drains, bridges, erection of houses, mills and other works and machinery necessary for the occupation, or cultivation of the soil and or the depasturing of sheep or cattle.
i. 'Another primary use of original capital will be the sponsorship of emigration of persons intending to settle upon any part of the company's estates. Full assistance will be provided to these people.
j. 'A third primary purpose of capital will be the encouragement of mining. The crown will reserve mining rights to itself; however, permission will be given to the company for leasing rights for mining. Mining can only take place on land the subject of these grants.
k. 'Capital may be used to make loans to settlers, provided they are publicly recorded with a limit of £50,000 to any one settler. The company will not be permitted to lend money on mortgage other than to settlers on company owned estates. I do not intend to limit in any way the amount advanced to settlers using company owned lands for production.'
l. 'The company may not enter into any banking operations, nor lend money on interest'.

m. 'Regarding public works, there will be a limitation of £50,000 in any one undertaking. This restriction will cease ten years after the date of the charter'.
n. 'The company may loan up to £100,000 to the governor or treasury at any one time. This limitation will expire after ten years'.
o. 'Whaling and fishing investments, because of the risk and management time demands must be limited to £20,000'.
p. 'The company is not to engage in any species of general trade, which shall include barter or sale of the product of the company's lands'.
q. 'Further land purchases will not be permitted without the authorisation of the Governor. However some capital may be invested in the purchase or erection of housing, wharves in company townships. The limit of such investment will be £20,000'.
r. 'The following rules will apply to the selection. The company will receive its grant in the northwest district of the island, bounded by Bass Strait, the Ocean and on the east and south by lines drawn from either shore. The company will have discretion in selecting land within that specified region, but all lands must be contiguous and approximating a square'.
s. 'The whole quantity of useful land, that is land capable of tillage, is to be 250,000 acres. Whatever useless or unprofitable land may be accepted will be granted to the company gratuitously, as an addition to the 250,000 tillable acres'.

    1. 'The survey and valuation of the selected land will be carried out to the mutual satisfaction of the company and the Governor, and the parties shall share its cost equally'.
    2. 'The report of the surveyors and valuers (to the Lt-Gov) shall be binding and unanimous, and will be the formal accounting of the limits of the grants and operational area of the company'.
    3. 'Quit rent shall be charged at the rate of 30s for every £100 of land value, and will become payable at the expiration of five years from the date of the grant. The company will be able to offset the quit rent by fully maintaining convict labour for 15

> years, provided it can be verified that the company has saved the governor an expenditure of at least £25,000, using the rate of £16 per convict for a whole year'.

Bathurst confirmed to Arthur on the 12th September 1825 that the Charter had received the great Seal. Bathurst again urged the cooperation of the governor towards the VDL Company, by assigning convicts, offering a military guard to surveyors whilst carrying out their surveying duties, and meeting equally the costs of the survey and the valuation process. He suggested, where practical, the utilisation of natural boundaries, and the early issuance of any licence of occupation of lands to assist the company. Bathurst extended flexibility for the governor to negotiate the location of the grants with the company's agent reserving to the government any stands of valuable timber suitable for naval purposes, and also any lands near harbours suitable for naval or military purposes. He was further authorised to waive quit rents under certain conditions. Bathurst ordered any mining on Company lands to be approved.

On 26th January 1826, Arthur replied to Bathurst's communications and assured Bathurst of his loyal support for the company, with the reservation that Macquarie harbour penal settlement may be impacted by the selection of Company grants. He was most concerned that company lands may be used to hide or harbour escaped convicts. "Every countenance and support, wrote Arthur, which your Lordship has desired to afford to the company in England, would be zealously and cheerfully continued by this local government."

Arthur added that there was a scarcity of convict labour and the company's request for convicts could not be met–'the applications by settlers for convict labour already exceeds the present capacity of the government to supply.'

I expect you will increase the number of transportees to meet the new needs and the demands of all. Public works has slowed due to the shortage of mechanics, and I urge your consideration of free settlers to provide additional labour.

Arthur advised Bathurst that military protection for company officials was unnecessary. "If a good system is introduced and order and regularity follow, the prisoners will generally behave well; if the arrangements of the company are defective, a whole Regiment will not insure harmony". I have promised Mr Curr and Mr Adey that a few soldiers would be available to accompany them on their travels.

Arthur had already seen evidence of Curr being difficulty to deal with and he advised Bathurst "Your instructions will be carefully observed, although a question has arisen concerning ambiguity in the instructions. Arthur was merely covering himself in the event Curr challenged the instructions. Arthur stated 'I fear a difficulty will arise in determining what land is considered available to the company and what may be rejected'. Again Arthur was putting Bathurst on notice of future complications, which may arise and be the responsibility of Bathurst and not Arthur.

Arthur reiterated again that Macquarie Harbour penal settlement might have to be abandoned if the company selected land adjacent to Cape Grim.

On November 14 1826, Arthur once again appealed to Bathurst to withdraw his offer of convict labour for the company. 'I venture to state, writes Arthur, that between Mr. Curr's arrival in the colony and this very hour, I have received requests for over 800 prisoners by free settlers, who are most anxious and pressing to obtain their services, and without seeking the slightest gratuity would esteem the assignment of a prisoner as a great favour. It would seem most contradictory to draft the prisoners off to VDL Company with the concession of 16 pound per head per annum.'

Arthur points out that Curr's position is simple–the Home Government made a bargain and must be made to meet it, otherwise compensation will be sought from the government. In response 'My decision has been to grant the company the convicts they desire, as I would on no account be the means of their suspending operations, or give them occasion to ascribe their failure to measures taken by this local government, but to notify their Agent that I have taken action purely from the desire to relieve government from any liability or damages'.

Arthur is demonstrating to Bathurst that it is really Bathurst's inept action that is causing these problems; that he (Arthur) does not really agree with the commitment by the British government to the Company but he wants to remove any disloyalty or claim or charge of inaction from against himself.

This was *mea culpa* by any other name. Arthur finishes his letter with a gentle rebuke to Bathurst 'I read from Mr Undersecretary Hay's letter to Curr, that Your Lordship has promised the Company further support and assistance in the prosecution of their *ulterior views so far as they may not be injurious to the general interests of the settlers, or as may not on other accounts be objectionable*'

Arthur is once again appealing to Bathurst to cease making commitments against the colony of VDL without reaching some consensus with the governor (who has to implements these policies made on the run) first.

Arthur, in stating he was responding to an application from Curr, was acceding to Curr's request of 5th October 1826 when he wrote to Arthur's office 'I have to request that 25 men be assigned to the VDL Company. I need labourers, tree fellers, gardeners and timber splitters'

Arthur responded to Curr's letter advising that 25 men would reluctantly be made available but that Lord Bathurst, when making the arrangement for convict labour with the company 'laboured under a misapprehension as to the State of the colony, and that instead of a pecuniary allowance being made to the company, a charge should have been made for using convict labour'.

Arthur reminded Curr "There would be an apparent injustice if the Company were to obtain servants on more advantageous terms than other settlers."

Arthur further informed Curr that any future convicts could only be assigned conditionally, and that is because convict labour can only be used to complete public works required of the company.

Arthur then referred these 'delicate' points to Bathurst for adjudication, and raised the question of another settler having been granted 2,000 acres of land within the reserved area for the VDL Company. From the tone of the Arthur letter and the Bathurst reply, it is apparent that both parties were getting very tired of Mr. Curr's inability to work with the system, instead of against it. Arthur again points out that most of these disputes arise because of the difficulty of understanding the original Bathurst instructions on the location of the land grant, as well as the impracticality of offering a grant of so large an area on this Island. "Your Lordship should have raised a doubt as to whether so large a tract as the company required could be found available in this colony, and the company expectation of getting 3 to 5 hundred thousand acres (Curr suggests it may take one-quarter of the whole island) should not have been accepted by Your Lordship without the benefit of discussion, survey, long consideration, and checking with the VDL administration". Curr writing to the Colonial Secretary on 27th July 1826 finally reveals his plan: "The current discussions are founded upon an erroneous view of the subject. Lord Bathurst never indicated any intention of excluding certain areas (e.g. Port Sorell) from our consideration. Although Lord Bathurst did not clearly define what he intended by the Northwest district, yet his words, taken by themselves admit only the construction placed on them by myself".

In response Arthur accepts Curr's interpretation and gives permission for selection of the grant to include port Sorell. Furthermore Arthur apologises for having made a mistake with the 2,000-acre grant, which is the subject of much correspondence. Arthur does not apologise lightly not allow his judgement to be easily swayed. The sting is to come. Arthur advises Curr that: Lord Bathurst originally gave instructions that "the Company will receive their grant in the northwest district of the Island, that district for present purposes being the square thus drawn from seashore to seashore which shall be the only area considered for the grant. I consider Colonel Sorell's letter to Lord Bathurst as not being in disagreement with the above. Therefore, I have determined:

- *Some* latitude of selection should be allowed to the company, and
- It is equally evident that no selection can take place unless the district is larger than the land to be selected, therefore

- Lord Bathurst's intention was that 'within the district I have directed their lands should be received, they may select any ungranted lands at their own discretion'.

I urge you to act, without loss of time, on completing the survey and measurement according to Lord Bathurst's directions."

This ultimatum would not be pleasurable to Curr and he would have to decide if he had taken his fight to the full.

Curr decided to continue his fight, and turned back to Bathurst with an argument for concessions on quit-rents. One can only conclude that Curr had a lot of excess time and little inclination to finalise his land selection and move the property into production. More and more letters and more and more arguments were produced in this voluminous exchange of correspondence. On 30th October 1826, Curr claimed to Colonial Secretary Hamilton that unless the Government gave in to his demands, there would be 'possible injury to the company's interests and he would be making a tentative claim for compensation from the Government on behalf of the company'. By 15th November 1826, Arthur was telling Bathurst "I have not permitted any interruption to take place in the good understanding that has hitherto existed between Mr Curr and me. My arguments with Mr Curr have been founded entirely upon the reasonableness of the objections; and although he is very anxious to remove them to the interest of the company, he is, I believe, sensible that they are brought forward and naturally arise out of circumstances not fully anticipated at home'.

Arthur again was covering his rear. He was not fully privy to correspondence between the company and Bathurst, and if there was any such correspondence, Arthur was sure that it would be critical of Arthur's threat to cancel the agreement, so Arthur was getting in first with Bathurst. 'My discussions with Curr, implies Arthur, have been cordial and I could only commit to carrying out your intentions, and not making a revised deal'.

Lord Bathurst was being pressured by Arthur on one hand, who was opposed to the great concessions being made to the Company, and by Curr and Inglis (the London-based Managing Director), on the other hand. Curr and Inglis had different strategies, however Bathurst shot at both of them.

"If Curr went to VDL suffering a misapprehension (as implied by Inglis) he has taken three years to produce his arguments and maps. This should have been divulged earlier. Bathurst then argued that there was a dichotomy between the company's wish to use their map to base the area for selection, and the company's intention to obtain the best grazing land. Bathurst says that the Crown Surveyor opines the map coverage is not good grazing areas. However, Bathurst concedes, 'go ahead and select from within the lines on your map. I will instruct the Governor of this change." Two days later, Inglis responds to Bathurst and argues about the quit rent concessions, admits his map has been misunderstood and withdraws any threat against the government for compensation. This may now be the turning point for offering concessions to Bathurst so as not to lose out altogether.

Another red herring arrived from Curr. He wants the governor to give him grazing rights over 10,000 acres whilst the land grants are being finalised. He does not wish to pay for them. Bathurst decides he can have the grazing rights but only at the same cost as would be the case in NSW, which is a rent of one pound for every hundred acres. This charge may well decide the company's future, as Curr has already made his report to the Court of VDL Company in London that if 250,000 acres is accepted on the northwest point, it will cost £13 to improve each acre of land in order to make it finally worth only 2 pound per acre. The Court offers a concession by claiming that one continuous parcel of land is not possible, but a number of parcels would be acceptable. "The court, writes Inglis, have no wish to avail themselves of a literal interpretation of the agreement, to press for an area of territory which could be of no advantage to their undertaking, and are therefore content to take detached portions of useful land, in any part of the Northwest Territory.

These concessions were to enable the disagreement to reach settlement although a further two years would elapse before the surveys were completed and the company made plans for various settlements on their land. Of course, we have only observed the relationship between the company and the government from the written word and without the benefit of a company representative offering an interpretation for their confused and beleaguered approach.

A variation on the correspondence can be found from the writings of Bischoff and Curr (to be found in the Appendix to this volume).

The Annual Reports

We learn from the writing of the annual reports that Curr's reports were not always included, and that Bischoff misstated the quality of the land grant in order to ensure 'calls' were paid, and in order to allow the stock to trade at a reasonable value on the London Stock Exchange. What we don't read very much about is how the company performed financially.

So we can work within certain parameters in order to better understand the company's performance.

The company's fiscal year was the calendar year–January to December. Two separate sets of books were kept (one in London to cover 'Head Office' expenses, and one in Circular Head to reflect VDL expenditures) but they were not fully reconciled, and even though they were officially audited, the 'advances to' Circular Head in the London accounts, never quite balanced to 'advances received from Head Office' in the Circular head books. There is an explanation for this but not one that was ever brought to stockholder's notice in the audited accounts, nor was the audit report ever included (before 1901) with the Annual Report, as is the case today.

So the observations that can be made from the published accounts are done so without the benefit of seeing the comments made to the Directors by the Auditor.

a. The first observation we can make is as to the Organisation structure. The Company had a fully supported office in London (it started at 31 Finsbury Circus, before moving to 6 Great Winchester Street, and then moving again to the final registered offices at Blomfield House on London Wall.

b. We learn that nepotism abounded. In 1857 the chairman was John Cattley, whilst the Company secretary was Henry Cattley. Two Pearse family members (Brice and Charles) sat on the Board at the same time.
c. In 1856, the shareholders were advised in the annual Report 'The funds in London are not sufficient to admit of an immediate distribution of (i.e. a return of capital) ten shillings per share (par was £100)", however, the report concludes with the statement "The directors consider there is nothing in the present circumstances of the company to lessen the confidence of those who have hitherto been disposed to think favourably of its future prospects". This statement in spite of the 'Liquidation Committee' reporting only two years earlier.
d. The 1873 report states, "There are 9,000 effective shares, limited to £30 each, and of which £28.10.0 has been paid".
e. New auditors appointed in 1871 again revalued the company's assets, and recapitalised the land grant properties with accrued expenditures for improvements at £255,796, an increase of £138,156. The cash position was worsening with only £23 pound in cash in the colony and receivables of £4,225. Cash in London was little better with only £1171 on hand, which include petty cash of 5/7 (five shillings and seven pence). Receivables in London were 100 pound. Revenues in the colony for 1871 were well down on previous years at £2,528, including land sale instalments of only 45 pound. The company had been floundering now for over 20 years, and obviously a new approach was overdue.
f. What is surprising is that even with revenues down; expenses were down even further and in line with plans to re-build the cash reserves. So the year 1872 ended with an increase in reserves of £755. The support, on the board, for increases in Head Office expenses was apparently nil. They lived off accumulated reserves and received no fee income from the colony, or from the efforts made by Directors towards operating the company. Cash on hand in London had declined by about £1,200 to the unhealthy £1,171. Deferring the dividend was obviously not the answer. For its whole life, dividends had been paid out of capital and not out of profits. Any profits declared were merely book profits and derived from revaluations of land and livestock assets in the colony.

Auditor emoluments for 1871 were set at £6.6.0, which was the same amount actually paid (according to the annual report) for a 'small iron safe and stand'.

g. From the 1856 accounts we learn of two new operating areas. The mining and extraction of slate, which ran out at a depth of 12 feet, but in addition was of poor quality, and not suitable for roofing as had been planned. The accounts for the year showed a healthy increase in port activities through the Company Port at Emu Bay (Burnie). Between 1853 and 1856 tonnage processed had increased from 433 to 892, whilst value of processing rose from £3487 to £14353.

h. An observation of interest but without adequate explanation is that the auditors appointed were individuals rather than a firm (which would have provided continuity) and those individuals usually lasted not longer than two years. We know not the reason for this continuous change but could conjecture that:

- The emoluments at 6 guineas were not attractive (especially for the work required to be performed); or
- The accounts were in such a bad condition that no auditor could risk his reputation by being associated with the company; or
- The auditors demanded accounting changes, which were not acceptable to the directors and new auditors, were then selected (when questions began to be asked).

i. From statistics included with the annual report of 1849, we know the extent of livestock in the colony, owned by the Company. Sheep numbers ('in the company's possession') were 6,519, but were recorded in the Balance Sheet at only £7979. Cattle numbers were 2282 but were not separately valued in the accounts. 185 horses were valued at £4948, whilst deer numbered 76 with a value of £133. Valuations from year to year showed no rationale. Sheep killed for food in 1849, numbered 316 but there is no write off in the accounts for this 'personnel' expense. Similarly, the various properties were all 'valued' but there is no relationship to a value per acre. There was no 'unimproved value' with improvements being identified and capitalised. The accounts for 1851, although audited are not in balance, and no explanation is offered for this situation. The total assets are made up of Land, livestock, machinery and stores and sundries (including cash of £164) and amount to£223,330, but liabilities total £255,900.The difference is not accounted for against 'shareholders' equity'.

CHAPTER 10

INTRODUCTION

The colonial economy started on the assumption that the settlement would be operated as a penal community. The colony required no currency and therefore had no treasury. Bills of Exchange would be drawn on the London Treasury for any essentials, but where would any purchases be made? This was a closed economy except for the supplies transferred directly from Britain. The centre of the penal settlement had to be the commissariat–the government store that was obliged to issue food rations for every soul in the colony; to have on hand tools required for land clearing, planting vegetables, fruit trees and small areas of grain; tools and supplies for erecting tents, building make-shift buildings from local trees, building a wharf, bridges and cart tracks.

The Store was the only means to an end. That end was the survival and well being of the settlement and its inhabitants

The economy was very reliant on Britain for supplies, convict migrants, and items that could improve the quality of life in this distant land.

Immigrants and population growth were essential to even the penal colony meeting its goals.

This story will review the factors that grew the colonial economy between 1802 (the year when the first local taxes were imposed and the first direct revenues were available for the governors' pleasure.

This study will review the factors; free migration, convict transfer, local revenues, British Government expenditures on the colony, and the foreign investment that came in the form of private capital and public infrastructure capital.

On the 26th January 1788, there were approximately 1030 Europeans and probably about one million aborigines in Australia. Until 1830, the majority of white immigrants to Australia arrived in the country as convicts (63,000 arrived as convicts out of the 77,000 total arrivals) but after 1830 the colonial government encouraged free immigration by using Crown Land sales revenue for those wanting to come under private resources. By 1850, about 187000 free settlers had arrived and 1460000 convicts, being some 333000 immigrants in all. Then came the gold rushes of the 1850s, which attracted free settlers from all over the world, but the colonial government because of prosperity and a severe shortage of labour (both agricultural and industrial) continued the assisted passage schemes. The result of these policies saw the arrival of 230000 assisted people between 1851 and 1860 and during the same period, 372000 arrived unassisted, in all 602000 additions to the population for the decade. Since Victoria had uncovered the best goldfields, that colony received the most new immigrants.

ESTIMATED FREE ARRIVALS 1788-1860

Colony	Assisted	Unassisted	Total
NSW[104]	157000	79000	236000
Vic	98000	236000	334000
SA	68000	9000	77000
WA	6000	11000	17000
Tas	81000	12000	93000
TOTALS	410000	347000	757000

By 1856, Victoria overtook NSW as the most populous colony. Fluctuations started to occur after 1858 in immigration movements–the periods of high intake were associated with good seasons, widespread economic prosperity, heavy borrowing of funds in London and other

[104] Queensland was part of NSW until 1859

money-markets, large-scale railway building and other developmental projects. The periods of low immigration were usually associated with war, or bad seasons, economic recession, a rundown of economic projects and the reduction of assisted migration.

The following statistics reveal several important trends. Victoria, SA and Tasmania gained relatively little through migration. Queensland was the most active colony recruiting migrants through offering assisted passage. NSW gradually regained its number one population position over Victoria

IMMIGRATION 1861-1900

Colony	Assisted	Net Migration
NSW	77400	330900
Vic	52100	28100
Qld	200200	256300
SA	46400	18200
WA	7100	133800
Tas	5100	-1300

Convicts Arrivals

Between 1788 and 1810, over 31,000 convicts arrived in the penal colony of Botany Bay.

Despite Macquarie's attempts to convert the colony to a transitional one and encourage more free settlers, the British authorities sent as many as 66,000 convicts to the colony during Macquarie's administration. The greatest increase arrived after the end of the Napoleonic wars in 1815, owing mainly to the reduction in the needs of the English dockyards for convict labour and the increase in crime arising from the post-war depression.[105] Macquarie used the increase to implement a plan for utilising the convict labour that was available in the colony. He built the Hyde Park Barracks to house them; he expanded the government farms to feed them; he expanded the Lumberyard, the Timber yard, the Female

105 A.G.L. Shaw *Convicts & Colonies*

Factory to employ them; he established road gangs to build public roads and bridges to improve internal communication; he assigned many for the private workforce and encouraged many to be self-sufficient so as to keep them off the store and the public ration program. The other part of the Macquarie policy for convicts was to bring him much criticism from key local settlers. Macquarie believed 'Long-tried good conduct should lead a man back to that rank in society which he had forfeited'. Bigge recommended major changes to the Transportation program after Macquarie's departure.

Commissioner J.T. Bigge was in the colony from September 1819 to February 1821. He found that many of the criticisms of Macquarie by the leading settlers and citizens were unjustified, but his recommendations in his three reports were in favour of tightening-up the transportation system. No ex-convicts should be should made a magistrate; grants of land should no longer be given automatically to emancipists; pardons should be granted only for especially meritorious service; the number of convicts employed by the government on public works should be reduced, both in the interests of economy and because it was argued that their productivity was really low and many were idle during the day and prone to misbehaviour in the townships. Macquarie's policy was also that 'where possible convicts should be assigned to public service in the interior'.

Macquarie had encouraged the use of convicts as public servants, more especially as clerks in government service. This practice after 1822 was gradually reduced apart from the Marine and Survey departments, the hospitals, the constabulary and domestic service for government officials (all of which positions granted a reward for good conduct). Shaw records that "government employment tended to be arduous and convicts were often returned to government service for breaches of discipline or failure to work effectively for private masters.[106] After Macquarie's departure, by far the majority of convicts were assigned to private employment. For a long time they provided the bulk of the labour force of the colony. This proved economical to the government in that the number of persons 'on the store' (receiving rations from the commissariat) did not rise as dramatically as

---

[106] Shaw *Convicts & Colonies (2nd Edition*-1971)

the growth in population. However, the assigned convicts were clothed. Fed and housed by their masters, in exchange for their free labour.

The scales of rations and clothing for all convicts were prescribed by the Government, and in 1838, according to Shaw, a little more than 5 kilograms of wheat, 3 kilograms of mutton or beef or 2 kilograms of salt pork, 56 grams salt, and 56 grams soap were allotted to each convict per week. Annually they were entitled to two jackets, three shirts, and two pair of trousers, three pairs of shoes and a hat or cap.[107] Many masters supplemented these approved rations with 'indulgences' such as tea, sugar or tobacco, as an incentive to good conduct or as a reward for it. They were not allowed to pay wages to convicts and rarely did so

Punishment of miscreant convicts was arbitrary and quite capricious. Most punishment was by flogging. For this interfered less than imprisonment with the ability of the convict to work. In 1833, in NSW, 5800 out of the 23500 convicts was sentenced to be flogged and the magistrates ordered 233,000 lashes. More severe punishments were hard labour on the roads, with or without irons or transportation to a penal settlement such as Port Macquarie (NSW), Moreton Bay (Queensland), Macquarie Harbour (Tasmania) or Norfolk Island (a British protectorate).[108]

More than 160000 convicts were transported to Australia between 1788 and 1868. Of these, nearly 80000 were sent to the colony of NSW and 32000 to VDL. Between 1841 and 1852, Tasmania received a further 37000 bringing its total to 69000.

Great Britain viewed the system as punishment but in effect, it had many advantages to Britain. The need for more and larger penitentiaries was obviated and 160000 convicts were transported to the colonies at an average cost of less than £15 per head. They were maintained in the colonies at less than £30 per head per annum, less than half the cost of maintaining them in Britain. The work they carried out in the colonies was productive and they were self-supporting.

---

107 Shaw *ibid*

108 Shaw *ibid*

It is estimated that, at the rate of 3/–per head per day for convict labour and costing materials utilised, the public building program adopted by Macquarie had an opportunity cost of nearly £2,000,000. The actual cash cost was probably less than £350,000. Assuming that a proportion of the public infrastructure and building program was not absolutely essential, Britain still saved itself a great deal of expense by adopting the transportation program. Even if 160,000 prisoners could not be housed in Britain, the social cost of a higher crime rate and the cost of social disobedience would have more than been saved by the public expenditure of having these misfits living in a far-off land.

From the Australian point of view, the great value of the system lay in its provision of a supply of labour. It may not have been good labour but it was better than none and it would have been very difficult to develop a settlement depending only on free immigrants. This was shown to be the case in Western Australia.

Shaw claims that the evil of the system was seen when the number of convicts transported were far in excess of the labour needs of the colony (Shaw quotes the Tasmanian situation after 1841)[109].

One may have thought that the real evil in the system was the transfer of vice and crime to the colonies, but Shaw concludes "many settled down after their sentences expired, to regular work and the slums of Sydney and Hobart seem to have been little worse than that of London or other cities in Great Britain".[110]

A conclusion to the convict saga and the transportation story should be that the men and women who came to the colonies as compulsory pioneers rendered a very considerable service to the colony and although the disproportionately small number of women in the community (less than 10 % of the total transported were women) meant that their offspring were relatively few, they founded a number of families which have taken useful parts in the affairs of the nation.

---

109 Shaw *ibid*

110 Shaw *ibid*

The Importance of Convict Labour

In terms of using convicts as part of the labour market, two approaches were in evidence. Britain sought punishment for those transported and hopefully, reformation. Colonial official were most concerned about using convicts for economic purposes. British fiscal policy and spending restraints imposed a clearly defined pattern for utilising convicts as labourers. Between 1810 and 1840 convicts labour was a highly significant proportion of the adult population in the colony. The 1806 muster suggests that convicts accounted for about 40% of the adult population. Between 1806 and 1810, this proportion fell because of the low intake of new convicts and the high level of expiring sentences taking place. However after 1813, convict arrivals rose rapidly and Macquarie selected the most suitable of the arrivals for government service. The proportion of convicts rose to about 50% and remained at that level until the 1830s.

The choice of developing a public market in the colony of NSW similar to the one developed by the British in North America was only one option. Other options suited the transportation program better. The 'assignment' program was meant to relieve the government of having to financially support the convicts whilst using a few to complete a public infrastructure program. This allocation of convict labour to the public sector for the building of roads, wharves, buildings, exploration etc, fluctuated but at all times until Governor Brisbane arrived with instructions to cut the allocation, it was a significant feature of the transportation program. One feature of the cost cutting exercises imposed on the governors by the British Treasury was to exchange the major public roads with toll roads, using the theory that the tolls would cover the cost of maintenance on the roads, but in fact it went into general revenue without any plans to limit maintenance work, to the amount of tolls collected. Another feature of the transportation program and its use of convict labour for public works construction was that most works were, for strategic reasons (security, ease of supervision, and ease of servicing the convict work gangs by the Commissariat) within proximity to the townships of Sydney, Parramatta, Liverpool, and Hawkesbury. The effect of this policy was that little work was done in the newer and more remote settlements, and little was done to sustain the expansion of natural resource exploitation.

Convicts as Human Capital

Butlin points to two interesting features of convicts as human capital. The first is that the relatively young age of arrival in the colony and the longer life span expected her over that expected in Britain provides a long and potentially more productive working life in the colony than in Britain.

Secondly, there are certain aspects of the lack of skilled labour arriving in the colony that deserves consideration[111]

John Cobley in his series on the early colony has analysed the occupations of male convicts[112]

OCCUPATIONS OF MALE CONVICTS 1788-1816

Skill	1788	1800	1813	1814	1815	1816	Ave
Unskilled	56.4	30.6	22.3	34.3	34.9	35.1	34.3
Timber /bldg	7.9	11.6	17.0	14.	15.	11.3	13.3
Textiles	6.7	19.1	13.8	9.6	10.9	10.	10.8
Services	9.1	1.7	16.2	12.2	12.3	14.6	12.8
Other	19.9	37.	30.7	29.9	26.9	29.	28.9

This table does not suggest that skills were wasted. There are four observations to be made.

Firstly, the ability to acquire skills in Britain may have pointed to a level of intelligence that could have a general value in Australian conditions

Secondly, pioneering conditions in the colony, imposed the need for many skills and the possession of any one by each member of the workforce could mean the ability to employ that skill in the colonial convict workforce

Thirdly, convict labour in lieu of working from dusk til dawn on six days each week, was allowed 'free' time in which to work for private reward, or grow a garden for their own use and benefit.

---

111 Butlin, N.G. *Forming a Colonial Economy* p.51

112 Cobley, John *Sydney Cove* Vols 1-4

Fourthly, colonial conditions differed greatly from those in Britain and created an opportunity for multi-functional activity.

It should be remembered also that in spite of pleadings for certain skills to be transferred to the colony via the transportation program (Phillip, Hunter and Bligh all made such an appeal to the Colonial Office), neither the criminal justice system nor the courts could be perverted to a made-to-order program. The convicted were not hand-chosen for their skills but rather for their crimes.

The Land Market

By 1810, the principle of private ownership of land was established although it was subject to British Crown claims as 'waste lands'. Transfer of title to private individuals was accepted as policy from 1810. The abundance of 'crown lands' implied low prices in transfer from the government, although public sales did not commence until 1832. The principles of land grants were initially to establish private farming for food, and supply of any surplus to the Commissariat. Shortly thereafter, land grants were used as a supplemental arrangement for military and civil officers instead of cash remuneration.

A number of problems arose after the arrival of Macquarie in 1810. How was he to handle too many grants of land made by the military cabal after the overthrow of Bligh? How could Macquarie keep the administrative processes up with the level of grants made? At the end of the Macquarie Administration, there was over 500,000 acres of land grants, untransformed because of the shortage of surveyors. How could the boundaries of settlement continued to be expanded if the government could not provide the administrative backing? In response, Brisbane established the *Land Board,* whose role it was to survey all land grants, to regularise crown land sales and create a policy of integrated expansion of settlement and land surveys.

When did Economic Development get under way in the Colony?

K. Dallas in an article on *Transportation and Colonial Income* writes, "The history of economic development in Australia is concerned with the transplanting of British economic life into a unique and novel environment. All colonial societies resemble each other in the problems of transplanting, but only in Australia was there no indigenous communal life vigorous enough to influence the course of future development"[113]

Dallas in the same article declares, 'The economic effects of the transportation system are usually misunderstood. The real development of Australia begins with the pastoral industry and the export of wool in the 1820s. Until then, penal settlements were a base for whalers, and made the pastoral possibilities known to English capitalist sheep farmers earlier than they would otherwise have known."[114]

Since this is such a major point on which much disagreement exists, an analysis of its merits is required. No less authority than N.G. Butlin, J.Ginswick and Pamela Statham disagree and they record in their introduction to 'The economy before 1850 'the history books are preoccupied with the pastoral expansion in NSW. It is reasonably certain from the musters that a great many complex activities developed and Sydney soon became not merely a port town but a community providing many craft products and services to the expanding settlement".[115]

The next section of this study outlines the remarkable contribution of Governor Macquarie between 1810 and 1821, most of the physical development taking place before the arrival of Commissioner J.T. Bigge in 1819. The table of infrastructure and public building development below confirms that the greatest period of economic development in the colonial economy took place under the Macquarie Administration and did not wait until the spread of settlement and the rise in the pastoral industry

[113] Dallas, Keith *Transportation & Colonial Income* Historical Studies ANZ Vol 3 October 1944-February 1949

[114] Dallas *ibid*

[115] The Australians: Statistics Chapter 7 'The economy before 1850'

(which brought with it so many economic problems) in the late 1820s and 1830s.

The Macquarie Administration

Governor Macquarie arrived in the colony in December 1809 and commenced his administration on 1st January 1810

In 1812 a select committee of the House of Commons was appointed to enquire into the colony of NSW. The circumstances related mainly to the disposition of former Governor Bligh and the many complaints received in England regarding the hardships caused by the monopoly of the favoured class".[1] A new Charter of Justice was conferred on the colony as a result of the committee report in 1813[2]. The Governor's Court was a 'modification of the previously existing tribunal'[3]. The Supreme Court was to consist of a judge, appointed by the Governor–the first Judge Jeffrey Hart Bent arrived in July 1814 but following a dispute with Governor Macquarie, Bent was recalled by Earl Bathurst and replaced by Mr. Barron Field, an English Barrister who arrived in 1817.

Macquarie oversaw a period of agricultural expansion and a series of explorations in order to open up new grazing areas in the inland

In 1813, the first crossing of the Blue Mountains took place and the Bathurst Plains were discovered. This search for new, more fertile land was made necessary because of the repeated droughts and the unsuitability of the coastal plains for agriculture or pastoral purposes. The three explorers Wentworth, Blaxland and Lawson 'effected a passage across a chain of mountains clothed with dense timber and brushwood, and intersected by a succession of ravines, which presented extraordinary difficulties–not so much from their height as from their precipitous character".[4] Within fifteen months from the discovery, Governor Macquarie ('with characteristic promptitude'[5]) caused a road to be made; sand many new settlers quickly transferred their flocks and herds to the newly discovered country.

In 1817, Captain P.P. King (son of former governor King) sailed from Sydney to survey the east coast to Cape York. In the same year Surveyor-general

John Oxley explored the Lachlan River following it for more than 400 miles. During his return he came across an extensive and fine pastoral country, which he named Wellington Plains and he finally reached the Macquarie River. The following year Oxley traced the Macquarie River and reached the Liverpool Plains and discovered the Hastings and Manning Rivers.

In 1818 Hume discovered the pastoral district of the Monaro of which Goulburn is now the centre. In the following year Hume traced the Murrumbidgee River, and the Riverina district.

With these discoveries, the known area of the colony grew by twenty times its former extent, and "the new sources of wealth, of incalculable amount, were thrown open to the industry and enterprise of its inhabitants".[6]

With the new agricultural lands had to come a new agricultural policy and this came in the form of minimum prices for produce purchased by the Commissariat. But the colony was experiencing a new lease of life as was expressed by a correspondent to the *Morning Chronicle*, printed in September 1825. The nom-de-plume of 'Austral-Asiaticus' supposedly belonged to Lt. G.T.W.B. Boyes, who had been appointed during the Macquarie administration to head up the Commissary accounting and audit systems.

The letter was a response to printed criticisms of Macquarie policies, and the incredible deterioration since the resignation of Macquarie and read in part "Under Macquarie's judicious administration, commerce and agriculture flourished, because they received from the Executive Government that fostering protection and encouragement which, in turn, in the infant state of the colony, were indispensable for their growth. The farmer received for his corn, the grazier for his cattle, such a fair equitable price from the Commissariat, for the large purchases made on account of government (namely 10/–per bushel for wheat and seven-pence per pound for beef) as enabled them respectively to support a state of decent mediocrity, suitable to their sphere of life and encouraged increasing industry and perseverance in their pursuits. The merchant was not embarrassed in his commercial speculations by the difficulty of making his remittances, but could, at all times obtain Treasury Bills for that purpose without paying, as at present, a premium of from £15 to £20 per centum for the accommodation. Under the change of system, introduced on the accession of the present governor, an entire and distressing alteration of affairs took place . . ."[7]

However successful Macquarie was with his encouragement of exploration and his agricultural policy, the most remarkable feature of Governor Macquarie's administration was the number of public buildings erected, the total reaching 250. His roads policy almost must also be noted for the benefits it produced.

Commissioner Bigge had been directed by Earl Bathurst to "examine all the laws, regulations and usages of the territory and its dependencies, and into every other matter or thing in any way connected to the administration of the civil government, the state of the judicial, civil, and ecclesiastical establishments, revenue, trade and resources".[8]

Macquarie did little to defend his administration other than writing an extremely long letter to Bathurst which commenced" I found the colony barely emerging from infantile imbecility and suffering from various privations and disabilities; the country was impenetrable beyond 40 miles from Sydney; agriculture was in a languishing state; commerce in its early dawn; revenue unknown; threatened with famine; distracted by faction; the public buildings in a state of dilapidation and mouldering to decay; the population in general depressed by poverty; no public credit nor private confidence; the morals of the great mass of the population in the lowest state of debasement and the religious worship almost totally neglected–Such was the state of the colony when I took charge in 1810. When I left the colony it had reaped incalculable advantage from my extensive and important discoveries. In all directions, including the supposed insurmountable barrier called the Blue Mountains to the westward of which are situated the fertile plains of Bathurst; and in all respects enjoying a state of private comfort and public prosperity"[9]

GENERAL STATISTICS 1810-1821

	March 1810	October 1821
Population	11,590	38,778
Cattle	12,442	102,939
Sheep	25,888	290,158
Hogs	9,544	33,906
Horses	1,134	4,564
Acres cleared and in tillage	7,615	32,267
No. of buildings	523	1,084

Local Colonial Revenues 1810-1820

The summary financial statements[10] show that Macquarie used a significant proportion of local revenues for road making and maintenance and public building construction and their maintenance. Although there was a 'tacit' agreement between Bathurst and Macquarie that the British government would fund military and the main church buildings, the colonial revenue would be used for infrastructure and most 'public' use buildings

The point being made here is that although the British Treasury was burdened with nearly £100,000 of colonial expenditure per annum[11], the local community, by having to pay higher prices for its imports was carrying about 50% of the British expenditures which include much that rightly should have been paid by the home government. In addition to British ownership of the public buildings, colonial government departments and divisions were paying 'rent' for the use of those buildings. The local commissary was paying £200 per annum rent for the use of the 'bonded' store–a building that cost only three times that when it was built in 1818 by convict labour and local materials. A loan by the Colonial Fund to the Commissary account of £19,000 is never shown as being repaid, so the British government was being directly subsidised by the people of Sydney Town.

It was left to Brisbane (Macquarie's successor) to recommend construction only through the tender process. It had been Macquarie's submission to Bathurst that the tender process would be expensive to the colony and add unnecessary costs to buildings. As Lithgow was to later recommend that no building under an outlay of £200 should need any British approval, thus obviating the time-consuming preparation of plans, estimates and waiting 18 months for project approval. (HRA 1:11:386)

The Report of Major Ovens and William Lithgow[12] in reform of convict work organisation offers a principled insight into the obligation of convicts to work for the government and the various trade's roles entered into by convicts. A sub-enclosure to the report lays out the expenditures on maintaining convicts, being £12. 8. 2 on rations per annum, plus an amount of £7.8.3 for 'indulgences' to convicts, offset by 'contra' of the value of 'production' or output per convict. Ovens concludes that convicts 'pay their way' provided they are made to work and be productive. Thus if each convict were only paid 3/–per day, the cost would be £54. 15.0 Per annum. Against this is the cost of £20 for their maintenance, justifying the loss of 50% productivity that Oven's envisages by convicts not committed to their work.

A wide range of Macquarie era statistics is available to demonstrate economic growth during the period 1810-1821

Macquarie encouraged exploration in a practical way, by using government funds and government stores to support a practical program of exploration. By 1815, cattle were being moved across the Nepean, Bathurst was a settlement, grain and vegetables were being grown on the Bathurst Plains, Blaxland, Lawson and Wentworth were enjoying the governor's plaudits while each were receiving a thousand acres of land, but only Lawson chose to have his land across the ranges. The road to Bathurst of 191 miles in length was completed and travellers were using it daily, together with bushrangers, and aboriginals. The Lachlan River and the Liverpool Plains region were being opened up and Oxley was exploring north to Morton Bay. Even Bathurst was amazed when he heard of the discovery of the Macquarie River–he did not expect 'after the fruitless attempt by Captain Flinders to discover any considerable river, to expect that such a river as the Macquarie would be found in the interior of the continent flowing so far westward'. Bathurst ordered further exploration along the stream to verify if 'a few hundred miles beyond the penetration of the continent, the Lachlan and Macquarie Rivers ran into the western sea'.

Macquarie took to heart the need for town planning, improved roads and a better image for the still young colony. New roads, even before the major 191-mile road over the Mountains to Bathurst, were being built by soldier labour to South Head and the colony's first turnpike to Green Hills on the Hawkesbury had reached Parramatta. The two bridges in Sydney had been widened at the cost of much good liquor currency. Everywhere were to be seen the evidence of the Macquarie ability to contribute to the 'ornament and regularity of the town of Sydney, as well as to the convenience and safety of the inhabitants thereof'[116]; these monuments included the new stone wharf at Sydney Cove, the improved wastes of Brickfield Hill, the completion of Macquarie Place and the houses of Sydney not to be built unless approved by the governor; they were not to encroach on the street, less they be forced to move back into line. Each house was to be numbered at the cost of 6d to the owner. Neat frontal palings of 4 feet high must guard all dwellings; wood must not be cut in the public parks, and shirts were no longer to be washed in the Tank Stream.

Macquarie needed to convince the majority of settlers in both the towns and the rural areas of the need for 'ornamental' improvement in the colony. These were the poor, uneducated people, many emancipists and ticket of leave people, married or de facto with children to protect and look after. Already under previous administrations, differences of opinions between these people and the propertied segment had developed, and the local newspapers even with their small circulation were quite influential and persuasive not only of government but have public opinion as well.

---

[116] HRA 1:7:427 Macquarie to Bathurst

SUMMARY REVENUE OF THE POLICE FUND 1810-1821[117]

Year	Beckett's figures[118]	Ginswick figures[119]
1810	6489	3272
1811	11359	10939
1812	11347	13494
1813	23109	14621

117 The Police Fund was originally commenced in 1802, under the name the Gaol Fund. Governor King intended to replace the original Sydney Town Gaol constructed of woods but which burnt in 1801 with a new gaol, built with British Government funds; the British Treasury declined to approve the funding so the governor sought voluntary community funding to finance the building but this appeal fell short so he used Treasury funding with the understanding it would be replaced by local revenues. He imposed a duty on spirits and liquor coming into the colony, until Macquarie decided in 1810 to use this source as discretionary revenue to supplement the funding for his building program. The revenue growth within the colony was embarrassing to Macquarie's predecessors and King decided to introduce an Orphan Fund and share the revenue, initially 3:1 but then changed the role of each fund and shared the revenue 7/8 ths to 1/8th. The Police fund paid for road repairs, fencing, wood for heating public buildings, building repairs and often civil salaries, when other funds were not available. The quarterly results for both funds were published in the *Sydney Gazette,* after 'auditing by the Lt-governor. Darcy Wentworth was treasurer of the Police Fund and Samuel Marsden was Treasurer of the Orphan Fund, whose monies were used for building the Female Orphanage in Parramatta and sponsoring schools and teachers in the colony.

118 The author has prepared his own financial summary of both the Orphan and Police Funds from quarterly reports in the *Sydney Gazette.* The purpose of reporting these figures is to highlight the unexplainable differences between the Beckett figures and the Ginswick figures. No trace can be made of the Ginswick figures since no copy of the MS remains in the public domain, so the Ginswick source cannot be verified for accuracy.

119 Jules Ginswick was an economic historian who specialised in statistics from the pre-1850 period and whose Ms was quoted extensively by N.G. Butlin

1814	8378	13325
1815	16544	17994
1816	18076	17782
1817	23709	24706
1818	28996	31006
1819	38684	40844
1820	40389	42968
1821	45338	44507
Total	**272418**	**275460**

MAJOR PUBLIC WORKS IN NSW 1817-1821

Roads
Sydney to Botany Bay
Sydney to South Head
Parramatta to Richmond
Liverpool to Bringelly, the Nepean and Appin
Buildings
Sydney
A military hospital; military barracks; convict barracks; carters barracks; Hyde Park
Toll-house; residences for the Supreme Court Judge, the Chaplain and the
Superintendent of Police; an asylum; a fort and powder magazines; stables for
Government House; a market house; a market wharf; a burial ground; St. James
Church
Parramatta
All Saint's church spire; a hospital; a parsonage; military and convict barracks; a
Factory; stables and coach-house at Government House; a reservoir
Windsor
St. Matthew's Church; military barracks; convict barracks
Liverpool
St. Luke's church; a gaol; a wharf; convict barracks

PRIVATE FARMING IN NSW 1810-1821[120]

Year	Wheat	Maize	Fallow	Pasture	Total acres	Cattle	Sheep	Hogs
1810	Na	6360	12795	74509	95637	7767	32034	8992
1811	Na	4437	15061	75669	96059	9454	37540	11753
1812	9429	4783	6654	127136	149633	14016	58307	15710
1813	7386	5415	Na	Na	159857	21543	65121	14856
1814	8613	5917	18416	157469	192057	23273	73299	11009
1815	10712	6089	8769	180324	208527	23013	60944	10106
1816	13028	7590	Na	Na	221657	22244	54014	16554
1817	14446	11714	Na	Na	230331	33637	66684	15654
1818	14928	8445	Na	Na	284853	40094	73364	22630
1819	17957	9175	Na	Na	336375	42624	96715	26748
1820	16641	11211	Na	Na	389217	49974	97078	24853
1821	17356	11068	Na	Na	381467	67949	119777	29042

IMPORTS INTO THE COLONY BY SOURCE 1816-1821 IN £ STERLING[121]

Year	From Great Britain	From China, India	Total
1816	45982	95787	141769
1817	65157	91559	156716
1818	47056	72137	119193
1819	57291	76927	134218
1820	93338	148007	241345
1821	131309	64827	195136

TREASURY BILLS DRAWN IN NSW 1788-1820[122]

Year	£	Year	£	Year	£
1788	891	1799	43448	1810	75805
1789	1341	1800	50707	1811	92128

120 Sourced from HRA 1:7-10: various pages. The accuracy of some of these statistics are questionable but they were evidence to the Bigge enquiry and no other source is available

121 Sourced from Bigge Report on Agriculture and Trade 1823

122 Sourced from Bigge Report on Agriculture and Trade 1823

1790	13064	1801	18267	1812	91019
1791	2114	1802	17837	1813	57948
1792	13451	1803	21465	1814	74174
1793	10099	1804	19298	1815	86021
1794	11771	1805	32351	1816	109117
1795	37240	1806	13972	1817	101163
1796	28619	1807	31264	1818	141310
1797	14909	1808	23222	1819	153956
1798	26407	1809	49921	1820	181273
1821					
1822					

CONVICTS ARRIVING IN NSW[123]

Year	Total from Britain	Year	Total from Britain
1802	669	1812	324
1803	842	1813	591
1804	332	1814	1171
1805	0	1815	1073
1806	575	1816	1424
1807	303	1817	1830
1808	294	1818	2717
1809	334	1819	2371
1810	510	1820	2574

During the Macquarie years in the colony of NSW, the British Government expended £3,104,875; colonial revenues were in excess of £100,000; and the number of convicts in the colony averaged 10423. The value of Macquarie sponsored buildings in materials consumed was just over £2,000,000[124]. The value of trade shipped to Britain in 1817 was £255,000, and the amount of imports was £246,000.

The economic growth for the ten years 1810-1820 was considerable and far outweighed the benefits accrued during any other period between 1788 and 1856.

---

123 Sourced from Australians Historical Statistics: The Economy before 1815

124 This author's costing–refer appendix

Colonial Economic Drivers 1788-1856

- Population growth including immigration of convicts & free settlers
- Foreign Private Investment
- British Public Funding transfers
- Local Government Revenue & Expenditure
- The Land Board
- The Commissariat
- The Financial Institutions

POPULATION STATISTICS 1810-1821 AND 'OFF-STORE' FIGURES[125]

Year	Total popln	No on Store	Convicts Total nos
1810	10452	6225	4766
1811	10025	6429	4801
1812	10521	6445	4938
1813	12173	8367	5019
1814	12116	8318	5234
1815	12911	8828	5377
1816	15175	11136	5490
1817	17265	11878	5795
1818	Na	Na	6082
1819	26026	Na	12749
1820	29963	Na	10873

FREE IMMIGRANTS TO NSW 1788-1850[126]

1788-89	0
1790-1800	47
1800-1809	304
1810-1819	237
1820-1829	1202

125 Sourced from various musters, recorded in the HRA. These original figures appear faulty but have been reported as set out in the original documents

126 The Australians: Statistics *The Economy before 1850*

1830-1839	31626
1840-1849	85399

CONVICT ARRIVALS 1788-1850[127]

Year	Convict Arrivals	Year	Convict Arrivals
1788	717	1824	
1789	1665	1825	16233
1790	3384	1826	16413
1791	3439	1827	217164
1792	3499	1828	15668
1793	3367	1833	24543
1794	3358	1834	27251
1795	2934	1835	29182
1796	2492	1836	27831
1797	2017	1837	36109
1804	2837	1838	38562
1805	2077	1839	38035
1816	5490	1840	38415
1817	5795	1841	26977
1818	6082	1842	24948
1819	12749	1843	21426
1820	10873	1844	19175
1821	13814	1845	16843
1822	11801	1846	10838
1823	11110	1847	6664
		1848	4015
1850	2364	1849	3517

BRITISH OUTLAYS ON NSW 1810-1822[128]

Year	Convict Transportn	Victuals	Stores	Bills	Civil Salaries	Military	Marine	Total
1810	40767	18136	2134	78805	12269	25357	1232	178700
1811	5637	55114	20748	92128	13309	24312	3449	214697
1812	31115	17911	1296	91019	11701	31257	1248	185547
1813	79348	31760	829	57948	13295	33792	1763	218735
1814	55536	23009	34651	74174	13298	20893	3525	225086
1815	39041	18833	557	86021	12788	24350	na	181590

127 The Australians: Statistics *'The economy before 1850*

128 Sourced from Ginswick MS as reported by N.G. Butlin

1816	36504	24613	16513	109118	12423	17121	na	216292
1817	54094	31821	21927	101163	12815	10765	na	232585
1818	77856	50382	5290	145520	12605	33478	na	325132
1819	78496	42619	2343	163465	16825	24097	na	327845
1820	81234	48296	17391	174110	17081	35204	na	373316
1821	73569	39892	52647	207050	17081	35111	na	425350
1822	65260	35689	47760	162677	13347			40996

Local Revenue Collections & Expenditures

Orphan & Police Fund

SUMMARY OF TOTAL REVENUE 1811-1818

Import duties	17649
Farm supplies sold	998
Work by orphans	310
Licenses sold	21422
Road tolls collected	2530
Court fines collected	583
Market fees collected	2568
Auction licenses and fees	301
Naval officer net collections	73442
TOTAL	£120,286

Orphan & Police Fund

SUMMARY OF TOTAL EXPENDITURES 1811-1818

Bridge Repairs	9404
Contract Construction	15778
Gov't buildings; churches	9920
New wharves	2002
New roads	6080
Sundry charges	56836
Public schools	2480
Orphanage and other	12589
Cash on hand at end	5515
TOTAL	£120,286

CHAPTER 11

THE ECONOMIC GROWTH OF NSW BETWEEN 1788 AND 1850

Abstract

This essay will track the growth of the colonial economy between 1788 and 1850, and will attempt to explain the events and initiatives that underpinned the economic growth–the 'how' of growth, and then why these events occurred.

The overall philosophy promoting the colonial economic development is defined as being two influences converging to structure create and sustain the growth. Hartwell[129] puts it in this way: "there was a complex confusion of dependence and synergism"[130]. This can be restated in more modern terminology–'planning, infrastructure, and sustainability'[131]. Firstly, we see that the concept of planning for the colonial economy includes both social policies and fiscal policies. The social policy, in turn, includes population growth, education and transportation, whilst fiscal policy includes the commissary operations, building and infrastructure and the treasury support payments. The concept of sustainability is that the economy continued to grow from this foundation through policy

129 Hartwell, Ronald Max (1921-) sometime Lecturer in Economics at UNSW, & Professor of Economics at Nuffield College, U.K

130 Hartwell 'Economic Growth of VDL'

131 Beckett 'The economics of Colonial NSW 1788-1850' (colonial press 2003)

formation, including trade measures, migration, financial institutions and a regular 'pattern' of economic development Each of these inputs converged and confluenced to create and sustain growth. The concept of infrastructure is simply creating the colonial 'foundation'–of an economic variety to be the linkage between the planning and the events, which comprise the sustaining facets of period.

A new concept of the 'pattern of growth' [132](as distinct from the 'sequence of growth') will be incorporated into this essay, a concept, which is different in style and content to the traditional explanation of the colonial economy.

There are a variety of forces at work

The definition of economic growth we can adopt for our present purposes is 'A process whereby a country's people exploit more fully the resources available to them, including the reorganisation of economic life by the use of new economic productive techniques with emphasis on capital formation and increasing the exploitation of new resources"[133].

Hartwell suggests that "the growth of the VDL economy between 1820 and 1850[134], makes for a success story" incorporating the following ingredients for this success–a colony rich in land; opportunities creating free trade and free enterprise and an economy delivered from the house of bondage by wool and whale oil. There were common patterns of growth and development in both the NSW and VDL economies, at least until 1826–both regions were reliant upon convict labour, both locations were of a strategic nature to the British, and trade was important in each colony Although VDL trade statistics showed great gains, much of it was 'exports' to NSW, especially in terms of meat and food transfers. Wool production in VDL grew rapidly, especially under the guidance of Governor Sorrell, who acquired breeding stock (on behalf of government) and loaned the

132 Beckett ibid

133 Based on a definition by Hartwell in 'Economic Growth of VDL'

134 Hartwell-ibid, p5

animals to small farmers as a means of upgrading and improving the quality of their livestock.

The (Hartwell ascribed) attributes that were forces in the VDL economy can be applied equally to the NSW colonial economy. However, along with the successes came setbacks, which included competing interests–sealing and whale oil was traded at the expense of general agriculture (limitations of the market and of available labour, made either whale oil or farming the area of concentration); cruelty to aborigines was a sad reflection on the indifference of government and the ruthlessness of the colonists; convicts were often badly treated. These factors were merely reflections of an imperfect economy rather than a policy failure.

In an economy torn between free enterprise (capitalism) and government enterprise (of a Marxist strain[135]), there was little attraction for investors. Potential for investment was one of the attractions of the colony in the original planning by the British Government, pre-1788. However, there were no obvious raw materials, no bullion, and no cheap labour to attract British investment into the colony. There was no market or outlet for British manufacturers, and no mutual advantage in a commercial sense. Government enterprise related only to the bare necessities and did not flourish and another ingredient was likewise missing–the relationship between the British Government and the colony was more social and political than economic[136].

Early Intentions, Policies & Plans

It was British policy to retain the concept of a prison settlement but only if the colony could pay its own way. Such dual desires were in conflict. Autocracy (as in being necessary to operate a prison) would destroy any freedom of enterprise, which in any other circumstances was essential to the growth of colonial income. Would social and political progress come with economic advances?

---

135 Suggested by Hartwell–'Economic Growth of VDL'

136 Abbott–Economic Growth of Australia

Wealth would increase continuously between 1802 and 1850, not due to any industrialisation, but due to an entry into a cycle of investment in pastures and sheep–'the golden age'. Wealth was measured in purely tangible forms–Coghlan in '*The Wealth & Progress of NSW*–1886', computed the wealth of the colony at that time, in terms of the value of rural holdings, the value of residential town developments, the value of government buildings, of roads and other infrastructure, plus the value of all usable plant and equipment. Needless to say, this measurement got unwieldy and did not last as a statistical guide to the success of the colony. Probably Coghlan was being forced to compare the colony of NSW with other colonies in Australia as well as with similar countries overseas, for political purposes. Coghlan produces a table comparing the NSW wealth per head with that of numerous overseas countries, with little point except to comment that measuring standards were different elsewhere.

The cycle rolled forward–opening up new land, adding the grazing of sheep, adding to 'national income' followed by more investment–and the cycle rolls around again. Diversification of the economy soon followed and led to an ever-increasing standard of living, which, in itself sustained further growth.

Capital formation followed, mostly in agriculture but increasingly in manufactures[137]. Such steps usually relied on borrowing externally, but such borrowing must have been accompanied by development of financial institutions.

A society, which cannot by its own savings finance the progress it desires, must strive, in the alternative, to make itself credit worthy and will only succeed if it follows market opportunities and adopts comparative advantage.

Because future prospects depend so much on present imports, the colony must look for profitable export industries[138]. It must also offer prospects of gain to people of enterprise.

---

[137] Butlin–Forming the Colonial economy

[138] Based on Hainsworth–The Sydney Traders

Let me restate the salient points of the above synopsis.

The main characteristics of the colonial economy in transition [139](before 1832) are

- The Colonial Government adopted the policy of free enterprise and free trade, during and following the administration of Lachlan Macquarie.
- Out of necessity there was a dominance of agriculture in the economy–this was a social phenomenon because of the needs and availability of convict labour.
- Social problems with bad treatment of aborigines and convicts curbed the otherwise 'clean' image of a successful economy.
- Lack of catalysts for British private investment prevailed until Macquarie converted the colonial image in the 1810-1820 period with new buildings, cleaning up the slums of the 'Rocks' area, and encouraging new enterprise.
- Wealth creation was taking place through capital investment and speculation.
- The growing need for financial institutions came with the commencement of borrowing and capital migration.
- The need for private borrowing overseas occurred because of the lack of savings, wealth and financial institutions in the economy before 1830.

On the other hand the key factors of the (gradually) maturing colonial economy changed slightly (after 1832)

- Transportation and the convict labour program was the catalyst for growth until growth plateaued and transportation became more of an economic burden that could not continue to be tolerated
- The importance of the on-going British treasury support payments was that there was a steady flow of funds arriving in the colony, not only as support payments for the convicts, but they also had a flow-on effect through the commissary into the pockets of small farmers, pastoralists and vegetable growers as well

---

139 Beckett, G 'The economics of Colonial NSW' (colonial press 2003)

as to the numerous cottage industries springing up throughout the settled areas of Sydney, Parramatta, Liverpool, Newcastle and the Hawkesbury.

- The role of free immigration and the accompanying capital contributions was essential to the constant demand for labour, enterprising operators and the capital formation within the colony. They brought capital goods, capital ideas and just plain capital to the colony.
- The role of land sales[140] was that it provided the colony with the funding boost it required to diversify the colony. Land revenues provided the direct funding for immigrants, aboriginal support, and a small amount of supplemental discretionary funding for the governor.
- The rise of the pastoral industry was crucial for trade, attracting immigrants, British investment and then to the attracting of manufacturers associated with the agricultural industries, including the extraction industries.
- The growth of manufactures[141] closely followed the growth of the agricultural sector and attracted another source and variety of capital and direct investment
- British capital investment and speculation was encouraged by the creditworthiness of the colonies, by direct investment of landowners from Britain and by migrant flow. British newspapers gave many column inches to events in the colony and there was a constant stream of books being written about life and exploits and successes in the colony.
- Population growth[142] was constant and fast and was supported by emancipated convicts, and convicts whose sentences had expired, by free immigrants and even by British ex-Military personnel attracted to the colony from India and post-Napoleonic Europe.
- The importance of education cannot be overstated. The illiteracy rate between 1788 and 1802 was high, but Marsden led the

---

140 Butlin 'Forming the colonial economy'

141 Hainsworth 'The Sydney Traders'

142 Hartwell 'Economic Development of VDL'

movement for schooling young people as well as creating literacy programs for the mature aged worker[143].

- Statistics collected for the period come from a variety of sources such as 'The blue books' original records held by the (NSW) State Records Office, from the HRNSW and the HRA. Some of the pre-1822 statistics are questionable but with nothing better, they offer a limited picture of life in the colony. Coghlan was the official collector of statistics for over 30 years and his 'Wealth & Progress' provides a vital contribution to our understanding of fiscal events, trends and achievements within the colony as well as a graphic comparison of the six colonies.

Each of these elements contributes to the growth of the colonial economy.

Thus, this is 'how' the economy grew[144], the 'why' is another matter. The why was, in reality, to further the goals of British colonial policy–to create a strategic base for defence and foreign policy rationales, as an investment outlet, as a source of trade, both with raw materials being exported to Britain and British goods being imported–a Navigation Act scenario, and mostly, in practice as a transference of some of the worst social ills in Britain to a colony' out of sight'. Wrapping all these aspects together was the goal of self-sufficiency and self-support.

As in any modern economy, the colonial economy had practical and physical limitations[145].

- The trade and economic cycles in the colony were influenced by events overseas, as well as local.
- Droughts and floods, insect plagues and livestock disease.
- Grazing land had limited availability until explorers found a way across the Blue Mountains in 1816.

---

143 Abbott–Chapter 3 in Economic Development of Australia

144 Beckett 'The Economics of Colonial NSW' Chapter 3–Policies & Planning

145 Based on Beckett, G 'The Public Finance of Colonial NSW' (colonial press 2002)

- The Depressions of 1827 and 1841-1843 were manmade and largely the result of British speculators, but the negative effects were largely offset by the boom times which attracted the investors and speculators, improved the trading between the two countries and improved the overall standard of living at a rate far greater than if there had been no cycles.

To offset these limitations[146], there were a number of positive aspects within the economy

- There was a continuous and growing flow of convicts between 1820 and 1842. In all over 160,000 convicted souls found their way to the colonies in Australia.
- Ever increasing physical and fiscal resources were provided by Britain to the colonial economy.
- There followed the creation of basic capital accumulation by individuals.
- Sustained higher living standards were underpinned by British fiscal support.
- The growing population was underpinned by the progressive freeing of prisoners, as well as by sponsored immigration, which in turn brought a constant social change.

Other commentators and writers comment on the source of growth in the colonial economy. Abbott and Nairn[147] introduce a number of specialist economic historians in their edited version of '*The economic Growth of Australia 1788-1820*', Hartwell[148] writes of the Economic Development of VDL 1820-1859, and Fitzpatrick[149] offers another opinion in 'The British Empire in Australia'.

---

146 Based on Butlin, S.J. 'Foundations of the Australian Monetary System 1788-1851'

147 Abbott & Nairn (Eds) Economic Development of Australia

148 Hartwell 'Economic Development of VDL'

149 Fitzpatrick 'The British Empire in Australia'

Butlin, N.G. [150] suggests his own formula of economic growth factors in 'Forming the Colonial Economy'.

However, Abbott in his Introduction[151] points out the dearth of any written treatment of the early phases of Australian economic development in publication between 1939(Fitzpatrick) and Shaw's Convicts and Colonies[152] in 1966. Abbott & Nairn try to fill that gap through a collection of short papers, usually an abbreviated version of the author's full account elsewhere in print. They believe (as stated in their Introduction) that the 'economic advantages to the colony included the resources made available by Britain, although the convicts provided merely the means, not the end of settlement'[153]. They also insist that the economic and strategic motives ascribed to Britain in the settlement of the colony must include the 'examination of the decision to transport convicts to Botany Bay in terms of British colonial policy before 1786, and of the prevailing social and economic conditions in Britain and their possible relation to crime[154]'.

Having considered the how of the equation seeking to determine the contribution to growth of the colonial economy, now we need to consider the reasons why.

The economic growth of the colony was but one of the considerations necessary to meet the defence, foreign policy, economic and social goals of the British settlement plan. An undeveloped colony did not gain the British any credibility in meeting their goals, and it was the transfer of the convicts to this alternative penal settlement that provided the workhorses of development to meet their full objectives. In addition, at least in Governor Phillip's settlement implementation plan, the convicts would be used to develop the infrastructure whilst at the same time encouraging the extraction and utilisation of available raw materials ready for shipping back to Britain.

---

150 Butlin, N.G. 'Forming the Colonial Economy'

151 Abbott & Nairn 'The Economic Growth of Australia'

152 Shaw, A.G.L. 'Convicts & Colonies'

153 Introduction to Economic Development of Australia 1788-1821

154 Abbott & Nairn (Eds) 'The economic Growth of Australia 1788-1821'

We will now consider the key factors set down above, within the space constraints of this exercise. Each one would be the subject of a broad study in chapter length[155], under a number of category headings viz. Colonial Economic Statistics; Capital Formation in the Colonial Economy; Sequencing the Growth (an Abbott concept); The Patterns of Growth and The Cottage Industries.

A. Statistics

The statistical[156] summaries[157] show numerous highlights of the colonial economy and can be listed as follows:

- The population growth[158] was regular and challenging, although the surplus of males over females was disparate and potentially detrimental. We should be mindful of the number of children and their specific needs. The nexus between total population and those 'on the store' was broken and reduced year by year. This progress affected the role, influence and operation of the commissary. Two other observations on the population growth can be made. Firstly, the growth rates in the Town of Sydney followed similar trends to those later found in Parramatta, Liverpool and Windsor. This means that selected decentralisation locations were attractive to new settlers and met the needs of these settlers. Secondly, as the earliest settlement outgrew its natural boundaries (of the Blue Mountains, the Hawkesbury to the north and the Nepean to the south), the new expansion settlements of Bathurst (ten (10) small land grants were initially made 1815-1818) and Newcastle (twenty-three (23) small agricultural grants were made in 1821) supported Lord Bathurst's policy of large-scale land grants to be a catalyst to growth.

155 Refer Beckett who includes chapter length discussions in 'The Economics of Colonial NSW'

156 Sourced from Beckett, G 'Handbook of Colonial Statistics' (colonial press–2003)

157 Reproduced in the appendix to this study

158 Source HRA, *passim*

- o The number of convicts[159] arriving in New South Wales made a big difference to the colony in transition
- o The volume of treasury bills[160] drawn by the colony, especially in those first important 30 years, reflected two facts–the amazingly low cost to the British Treasury of operating the colony (that Treasury goal was being achieved) and of just where the 'capital formation' in those early years was coming from.
- o The return of livestock[161] shows the successful pasturing of sheep and cattle and the quality of management, climate and husbandry proffered this burgeoning industry.
- o Trade statistics[162] (imports) shows the source of such imports and the need for securing the Asian trade routes, for the majority of imports arrived from India and China and only in 1821 were the majority of imports from Britain.
- o From as early as 1810, private farming[163], based on evidence to the Bigge enquiry as contained in his subsequent report, was dominant, successful and essential to the needs of the colony. The accuracy of some of the statistics is questionable but they are the only statistics available. The total acres appear to be well balanced between grazing (sheep, cattle and hogs all grew rapidly with little sign of breeding loss or slaughter for food) and grain, with wheat and maize sharing the farming land.
- o By reviewing the prices obtained at the London auctions of NSW Wool between 1818 and 1821[164], we can understand Bathurst's goal of growing 'fine' wool, which he thought would have averaged 12s. Per pound rather than the 2s 10p it actually achieved.
- o Wool shipments[165] soared between 1807 and 1821 and grew from 13,616 lb to 175,433 lb annually during that time.

---

159 Shaw, A.G.L. *Convicts & the Colonies* pp363-8

160 Bigge, J.T.–Appendix to Report III (1823)

161 Source: Select Committee of the House of Commons on Transportation 1838

162 Wentworth, W. C. 'History of NSW '

163 Bigge evidence

164 Macarthur Papers Vol 69

165 ibid

- An early 1821 map of Sydney[166] shows the location of the emerging manufactures of the colony. The second slaughterhouse had opened, a sixth mill was opened and we find the locations of boat-building, tanneries, salt works, furniture, candles, earthenware, tea and tobacco and a brewery, all serving the colony. Manufacturing was not the largest employer but in terms of import replacement goods, was the most important employer. Agriculture won the export stakes and supported the colonial local revenue base by allowing imports to match exports, and supporting a duty and tariff on all imports. This local discretionary revenue started off small and convenient, but grew rapidly into a major government source of revenues to cover every expenditure apart from the direct costs of the convict system.
- A listing of major Public Works[167] helps us understand the benefits to the colony of the free settlers, the convicts, the contractors and the entrepreneurs. In summary, the period between 1817 and 1821 witnessed the development of 6 main roads, of major government buildings, of churches, of military barracks and growing infrastructure. Mostly the period witnessed the success of the Macquarie administration and his major contribution to the colonial economic growth.
- This writer's assembling of raw colonial economic statistics[168] (refer appendix) suggests a positive balance of payments growth during the 1826-1834 period with growth, but sometimes negative balance of payments at other times. Imports took a dip in the depression years of 1827 and 1828 but grew dramatically until the next depression of 1842-1844. Local revenues, which the British treasury relied upon to replace contributions from Britain, also grew as a reflection of the burgeoning colonial economy. If we use 1826 as a base year then growth to 1834 became a cumulative factor of 280% over those 8 years or a remarkable 4% per annum.

---

166 NLA Map Collection–Sydney Map published 1822

167 Cathcart, L–Public Works of NSW

168 Beckett 'Handbook of Colonial Statistics (colonial press 2003)

All in all, the statistics acquaint the reader with a fairly comprehensive picture of 'how' (much) the colony was growing, especially during those important formative years. The colonial establishment had laid the basis for a successful colony and for supporting the future rounds of convict transfers.

B. Capital Formation[169]

If the statistical summary shows how progress was made in the colonial economy then a brief study of the mechanics of 'capital formation' will evidence the fiscal factors underpinning that progress.

Capital formation in the colony during these early years can be focused on the massive building and construction program. In the new colony, there was a demand for convict and military barracks, housing and government buildings, storehouses for the commissary, docks, wharfs, draining programs, fresh water, and so on. The support services required a supply of bricks, tiles, timber, furniture, roads, boats, agriculture and farming for food production. *The core of government practical economic management between 1788 and 1830 was The Lumber Yard*[170]*, which included The Dockyard, the Stone Quarries, the Female Factory, and various timber harvesting, land clearing and road making enterprises.*

The capital for these government enterprises had been provided by the British Treasury, and certainly in greater quantities than originally estimated. Matra, in his 1776 submission to the British Government estimated an outlay of £3,500 for the first year and from then on self-sufficiency and no further cost to the British Treasury.[171] This estimate was not only optimistic but did not allow for adequate infrastructure once the colony

169 This section acknowledges the Butlin publication: Butlin, N.G. 'Private Capital Formation' ANU Dept of Economics–Social Science Monographs

170 Refer Beckett' The Public Finance of NSW' where a full discussion is made of the Commissary and convict management including the various enterprises of the commissary operations.

171 HRNSW–Copy of Matra's letter to the British Colonial Secretary detailing the costs of establishing the new colony

was settled. Matra's plan was for a small convict contingent by the shore of the deep water mooring, with a fresh water stream close by, level ground for building log barracks and store buildings. No weather disturbances, no wild animals, no deleterious convicts, and a plentiful supply of wild animals and fruit and vegetables, good soils, and no interference from any natives. Matra's dream world was far from realistic and practical but his projections suited the senior government and parliamentary officials who approved a small impractical budget for the expedition.

The basic economic problem within the growing economy, and thus one of the early limitations to solid or speedy growth, was the provision of savings to sustain the army of unskilled and semi-skilled workers engaged in this construction and development work–this in turn, hindered private construction for other than settlers who had ready money to invest in such work, and thus most early residences were supplied and furnished by the government. However, in the absence of an adequate local supply, the greatest part of these 'investment' funds was to be drawn from outside Australia, in the form of imported British capital. This flow of British capital helps our understanding of the aggregate capital formation in the colony. British capital was important in inducing the smooth expansion during the first four decades of the colony, and it was a key factor in the subsequent economic declines in 1827 and in 1842-1844. For most of this period, prices and wages rose slowly if not persistently and inflation was imported on the back of speculative activities.

Obviously public authorities played an important role in capital formation[172] and the public sector seems to have contributed a declining portion of the aggregate from 100% to approx 50% during these first four decades. Four components dominated overall aggregate capital formation. These are ranked in terms of volume: Infrastructure such as roads, buildings, barracks etc; agriculture such as government farms, grain growing and livestock grazing; residential construction, and finally manufacturing. In broad terms, we can see that manufacturing investment in workshops and offices matched each other, and it is interesting to note that manufacturing investment did contribute to what was perceived as a dominant agricultural, pastoral and farming economy. It is also noteworthy

172 Based on Hartwell 'Economic Growth of VDL'

that the British Government continued to pay for and thus contribute the convict and transportation system, the colonial defence and the 'civil list' for the colonial use.

C. The Role of the State[173]

If capital formation reflected the engine of growth and the statistics reflected the multifarious facets of growth, then the State became the conduit for growth[174]. Competent government policies, capable administration and sound conditions for enterprise were the essential ingredients for colonial economic growth, and even the dichotomy within the colony of 'free enterprise' or 'government enterprise' could not slow the clamour for better living conditions, jobs and a controlled haven for entrepreneurs.

Fitzpatrick in *The British Empire in Australia* reminds us of the transition in 1834 from the point 'where the earliest community was primarily a state-supported establishment to the next point (after 1834) when imported capital applied to wool growing and associated or derivative industries rapidly endowed the community with the character of British private enterprise instead of public enterprise, and appointed the pastoral sector as a field for investment into a profitable colonial territory'[175]. The Forbes Act (by the Legislative Council) in 1834 offered inducements to British capitalists to invest in New South Wales, and as a result the colony of NSW, with three million people, had received twice as much British capital as the Dominion of Canada, with a population of nearly 4.5 million. There are obviously two distinct stages of state intervention in reaching out to overseas investors. Before 1834 the role of the state was to provide British capitalists with free land and labour in the colony, then came the development of sheep-raising of fine wool, and the sequel was, having facilitated the importation of capital for investment, its role was to provide services which would facilitate the earning of dividends on the capital invested. However, even though initial dividends were sent

173 Based on Fitzpatrick 'The British Empire in Australia

174 Based on Beckett–Chapter 5–'William Lithgow' where capital formation and the role of government is discussed

175 Fitzpatrick 'The British Empire in Australia

'home' in ever-increasing quantities, the time came when local people and institutions were the recipients of these dividends and great enterprises were part owned within the colony.

The state had, according to Fitzpatrick[176], four main functions:

- Firstly, to take the responsibility for adjusting claims when the economic system reached crisis, as in 1827 and 1842, although Governor Gibbs acted reluctantly and belatedly in the latter crisis.
- Secondly, the state is to administer essential services, in the operation of which private investors could not derive normal profits.
- Thirdly, the state must nurture enterprise, including well-capitalised undertakings, by means of tariffs, bounties and other concessions.
- Fourthly the State is to take responsibility for restoring to private capital, power, which has been taken away from it.

Fitzpatrick can be challenged on, at least, this last point. It surely cannot be the role of the state to supplant, supplement or fiscally support private capital lost within the colonial economy. If private investment criteria is invalid or faulty, then within a free enterprise economy, even one adopting an extended use of government enterprise, private capital must be supported by or subjected to market forces and not 'restored' by the state.

The introduction of the railways, just outside our time-line is such an example. The British were strongly urging private operators to install and operate in-town rail services. The *Sydney Railway Company* was empowered by the Legislative Council to build a private line with the support of 'government guarantees', with the right of the government to resume operations with minimal compensation to shareholders if the enterprise collapsed. The enterprise did collapse, was taken over by government planners, financially restored to health and the railway system

176 ibid Page 347

moved on to be become a successful government enterprise[177]. The role of the State, in this typical case, was not to guarantee speculators, but to protect the suppliers and contractors who placed their trust and faith in the free enterprise system. Fitzpatrick is confusing a touch of Marxist policy with a shackled government enterprise.

We can deduce that the state had an important role in the development[178] of the colonial economy and filled this role with supportive mechanisms and policies–especially guidance for financial institutions following overseas borrowing, overseas investment and land speculation.

D. Sequencing Economic Growth[179]

I come now to a brief study of 'in what sequence' did the economy grow, and as N.G. Butlin, in the Preface to *Investment in Australian Economic Development* writes 'I have found no guidance on this question from the few essays which examine the early economy in identifying the sequence of economic growth in terms of both aggregate behaviour and the performance of major investment components".

One must fear to tread where Butlin finds weakness or gaps. This essay may still not fully satisfy the larger Butlin type questions but the immediate concern is about the 'hows' and the 'whys' of the colonial economic growth between 1788 and 1850 and as such there is an obligation, albeit ritualistic, to outline the main sectors of investment contributing to that growth. Since this study may cover many areas, methodology and circumstances of sequential development may not matter as much as first thought.

Some facts should perhaps be stated first as the basis for future conclusions:

177 Beckett 'The Public Finance of the Colony of NSW' (colonial press 2002)

178 See also Butlin, N.G. 'Forming the Colonial Economy' for a discussion of these factors leading to changes in financial institutions

179 Based on Butlin, N.G. 'Investment in Australian Economic Development

- o Government enterprise towered above private enterprise[180] at least between 1788 and 1821 because the government had the sole access to capital, land and labour, and government enterprise met the needs of the colony and its community of free settlers.
- o Government enterprise was based on two facts–survival and self-sufficiency of the colony. From Phillip's livestock and building materials imported with the first fleet (including his 'portable' government house), government had undertaken to be the planner, the contractor, the financier and the provider of all labour and material resources in this new penal colony. That essentially was the nature of a penal settlement[181]. Then King decided he wanted a little 'spending money' outside the purview of the British Treasury, and this was a development unknown in normal prison or penal colonies but became the first step in the transition to a semi-autocratic free settlement. If this is an anachronism, then substitute 'planned economy' into any government encouragement of free enterprise. Then add Governor Macquarie, who as a free spirit, developer extraordinaire and ego driven creator of entrepreneurship[182]. Macquarie's contribution is in itself extraordinary. He applied, wisely, firm private enterprise principals to planning and development and set his sights on bettering the colonists' standard of living, changing the reliance on government hand-outs (the colony had to stand on its own feet, which is subtly different to being entirely self-sufficient, but is a good first step to self-sufficiency) and encouraging entrepreneurship in the colony. In Macquarie's mind, the role of his administration was to reduce British Treasury support payments, increase discretionary local revenues, build desirable government buildings and infrastructure, and create the atmosphere for manufacturing in the colony.
- o Obviously agriculture was the main objective of economic planning. It could use most of the convicts arriving in the colony[183]; it was minimalist in skills requirements, and relied more on natural events than most other colonial activities, but

180 A concept of Marjorie Barnard in 'Macquarie's World'

181 Based on Ellis Chapter 11 'Lachlan Macquarie'

182 Concept from Barnard 'Macquarie's World'

183 Refer Shaw 'Convicts & Colonies'

was mainly the most important of labour intensive undertakings. Agricultural operations would be extended to government farming, land clearing, timber harvesting and much of the work of the Lumber Yard. Its success was essential to maintaining the colony and making it self-sufficient As was pointed out above, agriculture contributed to more capital formation in the colony than did manufacturing but the rise of manufacturing mostly during and following the Macquarie administration created balance within the economy and created a support structure internally and an import replacement opportunity

- o The growth of government enterprises such as the government farms, the Lumber Yard,[184] which in turn included the stone quarries, and the timber forests, the Female Factory and the Dockyard, encouraged rather than damaged any move to free enterprise operations. The earliest private enterprises, other than pastoral establishments, were government contractors. Little capital was required, only limited skills (other than a nose for making money) were necessary, and there was plenty of work available and not a lot of competition.
- o British private capital was uncertain and untried in the colonial context; investment within Britain or in the tropical colonies was considered more profitable and safer; of the hundreds of companies floated in the United Kingdom between 1820 and 1850, only five important companies were formed for investment in Australia. The Land Grant Companies–these were the three (3), plus two banks, within the Australian context–The Australian Agricultural Company (AA Coy), The Van Diemen's Land Company[185] (VDL Coy), The South Australia Coy (SA Coy), Bank of Australasia and The Union Bank of Australia–filled a role as catalyst for attracting new investment and even offered some official sanctioning and support parameters for colonial investing[186].

---

184 Refer Beckett 'The Economics of Colonial NSW'

185 Refer Beckett, G. 'The economic circumstances of the Van Diemen's Land Company (colonial press 2003)

186 Hartwell refers to similar factors in 'The VDL Government 'Historical Studies ANZ, Nov 1950

- o A question should be posed, at this point, as assistance for understanding the sequence of development. Was the colonial NSW economy in 1830 a capitalist economy[187]? It was, as we learnt earlier, an economy in transition before and after that date. In so far as capitalism implies a rational, and acquisitive society, then NSW had been capitalist (urged along by Macquarie) ever since it had broken the bonds of being the self-contained prison promulgated in 1788. Capitalist techniques, as opposed to traditional techniques of economic planning, assisted with the transition from a penal to a free economic society. The transition included the organisation of production by the capitalistic entrepreneur for profit, by the combining of labour and materials into a marketable product. The capitalist enterprise portrayed itself in the banks, the insurance companies, merchant houses and the large-scale pastoral farms–all institutions, which were rationally organised for the pursuit of profits. The most important means of production–land–had fallen by the 1830s into relatively few hands–trade and finance were highly concentrated, most of the population were without ownership of property, and worked for a wage determined by the market. West, in *A History of Tasmania*[188], offers us a quotable insight into the settlement progression 'The dignity and independence of landed wealth is Whatever his rank, he dreams of the day when he shall dwell in a mansion planned by himself, survey a wide and verdant landscape called after his name and sit beneath the vineyard planted by his own hands"
- o Another brief quote may also be in order. Hartwell, writing in *The Economic Development of VDL 1820-1850* thinks "it is impossible to study the trade cycles without reference to general economic development, and the existing economic histories of Australia did not answer the kind of questions I was asking"[189]. His point is that he offered, in his work, a specialist account of economic development, as will this account try to be in relation to the growth of the colonial economy in New South Wales.

---

187 Butlin, N.G. in 'Forming the Colonial Economy states that the colonial economy was 'capitalistic' This portion of the essay is examining this claim

188 West,' History of Tasmania–edited by Shaw in one volume

189 Hartwell 'Economic History of VDL' P.251

E. Patterns of Economic Growth[190]

Although Butlin raised an interesting question on sequences of growth, any reference to sequences can also be raised in terms of 'patterns'.

The highlights of any 'pattern' can be traced to the foundation of the colony. This will also serve to identify some of the 'whys' in the essay topic.

The colony was founded for the multiple purposes of creating an intermediate stopping point for British ships travelling to India and China, of provisioning them, offering some form of back loading for the return trip to Britain, after unloading goods at this Port of Botany Bay. It was also considered to be of strategic value in limiting the expansion of Portuguese and Dutch interests in the sub-Asian region. Bonus reasons were considered to be that the East Coast region could be a source of raw materials for British industry[191], which was at that time coming to the implementation stage of the industrial revolution, and that any future colony would utilise British shipping and be an outlet for future investment and finally but almost as an after-thought any colony in so isolated a region could be a suitable location for a penal settlement.

Thus the growth in the colony followed first the formation of capital, then the importation preferences of capital, then the needs of the colony and finally the desires and preferences of the entrepreneurs and traders. This cycle continued right up to the discovery of gold, but it was not the traditional boom and bust cycle. It was a trade and investment cycle of designating an investment opportunity, bringing together the capital required, filling the opportunity and recommencing the cycle by starting all over.

The pattern changed somewhat in the mid-1830s (the colony was by now almost a mature 50 years of age) when the pattern of growth suddenly had a new spoke–local wealth, local ownership, locally retained dividends and the need for reinvestment. This change in pattern broke into the

---

[190] A Beckett concept developed in The Economics of Colonial NSW

[191] Proposed by Sir Joseph Banks (HRNSW–Vol 1)

overseas raising of capital, and the overseas distribution of dividends and the overseas domination of manufacturing in the colony.

Local traders were gaining prominence in sealing, whaling, exporting and importing, merchant financing and the commencement of local auctioneering. Traditionally the Sydney markets had favoured enterprising practitioners who had surplus livestock or cottage industry manufactures, and these pursuits often led to more than the public markets as their distribution point. Simeon Lord, the master trader, bought a hat manufacturer in Botany whose rise had been exactly along those lines, cottage industry production, public markets distribution, rented premises, paid labourers, advertising, then buy-out and take-over.

Government policy fitted largely into this pattern and we have covered already the encouragement of business enterprise, however, the main role of government was to create the climate and the environment for entrepreneurs, borrowers, lenders and a satisfactory circumstance for making a profit and the return of capital. This came by way of successful business ventures, in both the agricultural and industrial enterprises. Because the skill levels within the colony were only gradually expanding and refining, there was official encouragement of British industry expanding with branch operations. Agricultural enterprise was encouraged by offers of land grants and then the cheap sale of land, and later the provision of either cleared land or convict labour.

Abbott[192] discusses the 'constituents' of the New South Wales colonial economy, and lists six. Agriculture; The Pastoral industry; Manufacturing; Trade within the colony; Exports other than wool; Government Works and Services.

Let me turn to some 'constraints' on the growth of the colonial economy; these include[193] Government policy; land, labour and capital.

There was an implied constraint to local colonial growth imposed by the Westminster parliament. The last of the series of Navigation Acts was

192 Abbott & Nairn 'The Economic Growth of Australia

193 Abbott & Nairn 'The Economic Growth of Australia

in 1696 but stood unchanged until after the recognition of American Independence in 1783[194]. In general, until the legislation was passed,

British colonists had been free to trade with any country and to use ships of any nationality, and accept the cheapest freights. Following the passage of the legislation and the numerous amendments, they were obliged to use only British (including colonial) ships, to send all their exports direct to Britain and to import all their overseas goods direct from Britain. In this way, writes Abbott in *Economic Growth of Australia 1788-1821*, the colonists were virtually insulated from direct contact with the world economy.

F. Cottage Industries

Hainsworth in his Chapter Twelve 'Dawn of Industry' from *The Sydney Traders*[195] guides us in a review of the growth of manufactures before 1825.

'Thanks to the initiative of Sydney traders, manufacturing and processing industries emerged very early and helped to transform NSW from penal settlement to colony'.

The traders supplemented government activity, often by carrying out similar activities, and sometimes launched various types of manufacturing in which the government was not concerned. It was natural that the government should play a dominant role at this early stage, for it had the responsibility of clothing, housing, feeding and working the convicts, both male and female. The government role was as the chief employer of the convicts, the chief provider of capital and the chief consumer of their output. In a limited way, the government was prepared to foster industrial enterprise, though this encouragement was haphazard, capricious and oftentimes playing favourites. The government, itself, launched brewing, salt-making, milling and basic textiles, and operated a number of crude industrial processes before allowing them to be taken over by enterprising

194 Discussed in Hainsworth 'The Sydney Traders'

195 Hainsworth, D.R. The Sydney Traders

colonists on favourable terms. Privatisation was not a deliberate policy, one more so of convenience.

Sealing[196] by 1800 was dominating the trading calendar. The official return for that year showed over 118,000 skins had passed through Sydney with Simeon Lord and his fellow ex-convicts, Kable and Underwood handling over 72,000 from just one source–Antipodes Island. By 1815, the *Sydney Gazette* was reporting the sealing industry was in decline. The intense harvesting of the seals had lowered their natural numbers, but the British Government was influenced by the 'whale lobby' to raise discriminatory duties against colonial oil, seal and whale. Spermaceti oil was to bear a duty of 15s 9d per ton for British ships but £24. 18. 9 if obtained by colonial ships. Duties of £8 8s a ton were imposed on Black Whale oil from the Derwent estuary. Thus through these discriminatory tariffs, colonial oil was virtually barred from London.

Cottage industries were not only the preserve of the small home-based manufacturers. Coghlan[197] points out 'those who had the enterprise and industry to devote land to gardening were amply repaid'. The broad acre crops raised were chiefly wheat and maize, with a little oats and barley, some potatoes and other vegetables.

Excellent opportunities, for fresh fruit and vegetables, were provided by the weather, the climate and the generally good soil around Sydney, but gardening was not undertaken other than by the few conscious of home grown vegetables. They were able, says Coghlan, 'to grow almost all ordinary English vegetables, all the English fruits and some fruits, such as grapes, grew in abundance. Macquarie described his garden at Parramatta as 'full of vines and fruit trees and abounding in the most excellent vegetables'

Stock-raising was given impetus when, in 1805, the two Blaxland brothers arrived in the colony, bringing a considerable amount of capital and more than a little acquaintance with husbandry of cattle. In 1810, horned cattle numbers stood at 12,442. Ten years later, when Macquarie left, the herds

196 Based on Hainsworth 'The Sydney Traders Ch12 'The Dawn of Industry'

197 Coghlan, T.A. 'Labour & Industry in Australia' (Page 117–Vol I)

numbered 102,939, so that the annual increase was at the rate of 20.5%. The numbers were carefully guarded and there was no undue slaughtering, and salt beef was still being imported in 1814. Even so, the records show that beef was cheap with a herd selling at £8 per head. Horses, says Coghlan, 'throve[198] in the settlement from the beginning although their numbers increased very slowly. In 1800 there were only 203 horses, but by 1810 the numbers had grown to 1134 and by 1821, the numbers totalled 4564.

Coghlan recognises the importance of the timber industry and writes "the export of timber became fairly considerable and in 1803, Governor King spoke of it as the only staple of the colony"–the inland forests could not be exploited because of the lack of any means of transport, and as a result 'numerous saw-pits were established on the inlets of Port Jackson, along the banks of the Hawkesbury, and later at Newcastle on the Hunter, where convicts were engaged cutting timber as well as in mining coal"

Occasionally cargoes were shipped to India, and in 1809 timber to the value of £1500 was sent to that country in part payment for a return shipment of rice. "The presence of so much valuable timber would in ordinary circumstances have led to the establishment of shipbuilding yards. Vessels were built for sealing purposes as early as 1791, but the presence of craft capable of going to sea was considered a menace to the safe-keeping of the convicts and the governor directed no boats were to be built of greater length than 14 feet". Hunter removed this restriction in 1798, and in fact encouraged the shipbuilding industry by permitting a vessel of 'thirty tons to be built to procure seal skins and oil in Bass Straits'.[199] Campbell then built a vessel of 130 tons launched in 1805[200].

There was considerable activity mostly through the *Dockyard* (attached to the Commissary) in boat-repairs, refurbishing and provisioning, but the stoppage of the fishery in 1810 was a serious blow to the industry.

---

198 This is an editor's change–the Coghlan text states 'shrove'

199 Coghlan, Labour & Industry Vol 1 Page 121-2

200 Steven, Margaret 'Merchant Campbell 1769-1846'

Immigration to the colony was mostly by way of assigned servants between 1821 and 1826, but the difficulty experienced in collecting the payments for the servants made the whole notion difficult. Coghlan tells "in the matter of indentured service many employers, principally those in the country districts were willing to advance £8-10 towards the cost of each immigrant labourer obtained by them and in February 1832 Governor Bourke despatched a list of 803 labourers who might be sent out on these terms. It was on immigration at the cost of land revenue that the colonial authorities placed their confidence. They offered to set aside £10,000 from the land fund for emigration purposes; of this sum they desired that about two-thirds be devoted to promoting the emigration of unmarried women, as the proportion of men in the colony was excessive and that one-third should be used in loans for the emigration of mechanics".

After 1836, it was decided that the whole of the rapidly increasing land revenue of NSW should be devoted to immigration[201] and in 1837 over 3090 immigrants were brought to the colony of whom 2688 were sponsored through the Emigration Commissioners in London and 405 were under the bounty scheme by colonial employers.

Summary

The question is: "How and why did the NSW economy grow between 1788 and 1850".

The simple answer to 'how' is in the words of Hartwell 'there was a complex confusion of dependence and synergism'. However, assuming that this trite phase does not do justice to the question and further explanation is necessary, then the following pattern of how growth took place should complete the answer. Notes prepared by Dr. D. Meredith make clear that 'institutions matter in explaining growth, and it is not what resources any particular economy has that matters, but what it does with them'[202]

201 Coghlan 'Labour & Industry in Australia–Vol I Page 178

202 Meredith, D. Notes on economic Growth in Australia–March 2003

The pattern of growth has been explained previously, but in summary, development using government enterprises commenced with the foundation of the colony in 1788, and followed the sequence of building government accommodation, government residential housing, storehouses, buildings, roads, wharves, boats, ship repair yards, ship provisioning areas, but mainly agriculture for food supply. Then followed the development of private industry and during the Macquarie administration, the rise of entrepreneurs and the growth of free enterprise. Agriculture still dominated the economy through 1850, but the manufacturing sector grew successfully and provided balance. The overall winner from the economic development and growth was the standard of living and the quality of life.

From the ashes of the barter system, grew a capitalistic economy with adequate wages being the reward for labour, profits the reward for successful enterprise and success for good governance being measured in increased population, increased capital and the overall increase in wealth.

Diversification of agriculture and manufactures was the result of a market economy, although trade maintained that balance between exports and imports and government usually kept in check the desirability of overspending and therefore virtually eliminate deficit spending. Economic cycles were imported like many of the goods and services brought to the colony and speculators although welcomed were regulated by these cycles much in the way imported capital was regulated and protected by the legislation over financial institutions.

Hartwell's reference to 'dependence and synergism' is dependent upon the colonial reliance on the British funding of and support for the colony. This responsibility was short-lived and the colony rebalanced itself to become less reliant and more proactive–each governor had been instructed very precisely to 'save money' wherever and whenever possible. One governor[203] spent less by cutting services and benefits. One governor[204] took civilians off the commissary support lists and then cut the rations to those remaining.

---

203 Governor Bligh

204 Governor Hunter

One governor[205] introduced local taxes to supplement British revenues, and so what eventually became the situation was that the British Treasury funded the transfer and support of their convicts, and paid for most of the civil list. The exceptions here were, at least, that surveying, a reasonably large and significant charge, on the colonial government[206] was paid for from land sales revenues, and convict land clearing was incorporated into the land sales price. Crown land revenues were not used to directly enrich the colony, but were initially used as a supplement to British Treasury payments before concern emerged about the legalities of using commandeered land sale revenue to return to the conquesting countries treasury. At this time the British Treasury and Colonial Office broke with precedent and used the crown land revenues[207] for 'benevolent purposes, such as supporting sponsored immigrants, modernizing aborigines and a little bit (15%) to government for discretionary purposes in the name of the Crown. Local revenues supported the colony from very early in the colonial annals (1800) and thus the concept of dependence was removed even further and self-reliance and responsibility was added to self-support as the catchcry of the colony.

It is worth asking if political stability encouraged economic growth. There was a very flaccid form of political stability in Westminster at this time and government after government was installed protem, in much the same way those NSW governments (post-self-government), after 1856, were often of short-lived duration. This British political quasi-instability impacted mainly on migration and capital transfers to the colony. Within the colony, the governors were on a regular 5-year assignment and there was only limited opportunity to extend an administration in the event a governor was found to be a great success in that post. No extensions were made between 1821 and 1850 so one can assume that there were no outstanding governors, and although this in itself did not contribute to instability, policies invariably changed from one administration to the

205 Governor King

206 From the 'Blue Books', refer Beckett 'William Lithgow'

207 From the 'Blue books' we can calculate that 50% of revenues went to Immigration; 15% to support Aborigines; the Civil List received a further 20% and discretionary expenditure was the remaining 15% (HRNSW)

next. This caused the Legislative Council to be depicted[208] as the forum of a populist body with extraordinary powers to sway and be swayed by popular moods. Often the populist Council came into conflict with the traditionalist governor but essentially the Council was limited to the role of 'advice and consent'[209] rather than leading the way in new movements and this was seen during the 1841-43 Big Depression when Sir George Gipps would not act to curb the run on the banks or to curb speculators from damaging the colonial economy and although the Council spent much time in debating the problem only two minor pieces of legislation came out of the Committee installed to consider the public concerns, both of which the governor refused to sign and so the depression deepened and no corrective action was taken. A weak governor and a limp Council headed the depression into a longer, deeper and more damaging trough than had been necessary.

The growing public service was the rock of stability, even though it was the only source of savings in successive budgets, which governors were bound not to put into deficit. Overall political stability and administrative stability assisted the perception of sound colonial administration and attracted migrants and investors, which in turn supported, encouraged and achieved almost continuous growth between 1788 and 1850

The economy was to a large extent based on trade and there is no doubt that wool was the main export with seal skins whale oil and timber, running at lower values. Consumption goods were mainly imports and in spite of local fresh meat, salted meat continued to be a large import item until the early 1820, Governors persevered to keep a balance between exports and imports, and by optimising exports, they were able to maximise their collection of duties and tariffs on the growing volume of imports. Capital came in with immigrants but also by transfers from land speculators and private investors wanting to benefit from the overall growth in the colony. Opportunities abounded in trading and manufacturing in the colony, and every chance was taken by entrepreneurs and government to introduce new industries, usually with great success. Government rarely acted

---

[208] Wentworth' Historical & Statistical History of NSW'

[209] Epitome of History of NSW P267)

pro-actively but recognised the need for certain locally made goods and commenced or encouraged others to commence the operation.

The Colonial economy grew sufficiently to allow the standard of living of all to rise, of all convicts available for work, to be put to work, and for immigrants to be welcomed, often at a faster rate than was being attracted into North America. Trade and entrepreneurial investment underpinned the growth and in turn attracted growing amounts of capital, at the same time the internal economy was creating its own capital formation. The economy grew successfully and peacefully whilst supporting the British goals and meeting the self-sufficiency and self-supporting ambitions of the British Treasury. It was relevant that the British Government meet all the costs of transporting, housing, feeding, clothing convicts, and indeed they met the majority of these costs. They refused, to the aggravation of the NSW Legislative Council, the costs of the local police force and operating the goals in the colony.

Conclusion

In trying to reach a suitable and appropriate conclusion to this essay, and keeping in mind that a second Appendix to the study is the 'economics of N.G. Butlin–with respect to the colonial economy', I have decided to follow the lead of Professor Butlin and set down a number of 'Theories or Guiding texts' that define the essence of the colonial economy. Butlin formulated 14 such 'theories' but I have limited the number to 8, which are essentially the 6 main periods that occurred between 1788 and 1850. It should be noted that Butlin's theories are included in his 1984 paper 'Contours of the Australian Economy 1788-1860'.

I have also included 2 observations about the pre-1788 Aboriginal economy, which Butlin also refers to in his 'Economics of the Dreamtime'.

Conclusions on the Pattern of Economic Growth in the Colony 1788-1860

i. The Aborigines (pre-British occupation of 1788) were careful custodians of the land who had utilised the land in accordance with tradition and expectations of affinity and as a food source. The aborigines sought to preserve a practice long in existence that did not overdevelop or over use the land or its resources but which produced all the needs of its limited population

ii. If there is any worthwhile validity in comparing farming systems between the pre–and post 1788 practices, then they are comparable to the extent that both systems supported, at various times differently, their population. Native grasses vs. improved pastures, and domesticated livestock vs. native livestock. Both yielded sufficient 'value' from the land to support individual needs; both could co-exist but the 'invaders' wanted unrestricted access to the land; their ways were only to 'clear fell' the country, thus transforming the land from its natural cycle to an unnatural cycle of waste of natural resources, removal of underlying 'natural support' system of replenishment, and of over-utilising the natural burden of the land.

iii. Post-1788, and until 1802, economic growth was limited to subsistence farming, and a settling in system, whereby the more intellectual civil servants and colonists took time to understand the land, its abilities and limitations. This prefacing to development was essential in order to lay the foundation for a longer-term successful future. Then, as now, there were two types of thinking and planning–rush ahead and do whatever it takes to succeed in the short-term, or move cautiously with intent and some knowledge to succeed long-term. The governors mostly were of the latter mindset but were equally aware of the limitations imposed on the colony by irregular supplies of food arriving from the 'home country' and the growing quantities needed, as well as the directions made by the British Colonial Office to be self-sufficient, self-supportive and live within a shrinking budget. The most outstanding example of this 'conflict' was the livestock brought with the first fleet, was left untouched even though the colony was starving. On the other hand, the conflict with the aboriginals resulted in a failure to utilise the native wildlife or the sea-life adequately or appropriately as a transition arrangement and evidence of planned co-existence. This first period was like 'treading water' rather than making progress.

iv. The second period (1802-1821) was a period of consolidation, planning and moving ahead at great speed. Although the last of the naval governors–King and Bligh–were pre-occupied with internal conflict and curbing civil unrest, the period was unrestrained in terms of individuals pursuing self-interest–not in an entrepreneurial way, but as a means of doing 'for ourselves' what the administration should be doing. This was a period of transition when the systems were being developed and being 'bedded in'. It was a period of learning, of exploring, of making 'ends meet' with limited resources, great ingenuity and more than a modicum of luck. The economic growth was reflected in the survival of the people; the ill-treatment of the native peoples; the spread of settlement and the resulting open plains and broad acres which unshackled the limitations on grain production and livestock grazing previously experienced; the transformation of the economy from the 'barter' economy pre-Macquarie to an economy with a monetary system; the transformation of the economy from a mindset of 'penal colony' to that of a colony with a future; the organised and structured building and construction boom. The period came to an end with the 'reflections' of a bureaucrat (John Thomas Bigge), who became a tool of the influential and a pawn of the blinkered few who could not see a future for the colony. The greatest gains during this period came from the unlikeliest of sources–the development of a road system, the intelligent harnessing of convict labour, but the greatest gain of all came from the imposition, collection and utilisation of the colony's discretionary revenues. These revenues collected from a 'tax' or duty imposed on imports, gave the governors access to discretionary expenditures which otherwise would not have been funded. Subtle improvements in the quality of life, which the British Government would not have supported. The Colonial Office in London drew on the policy of people in the colony not having a standard of living higher, whilst in the colony, than they would have enjoyed at 'home' and certainly not the convicts. It was this local revenue, for many years outside the influence of Whitehall, which made the difference to the people in the colony. Macquarie refined the collection of these revenues and people could physically see the change in the colony, and their spirits rose accordingly and there was less unhappiness, more positive thinking and expression and an overall more productive economy with greater growth and positive movement.

v. The third period was short 1821-1827. It was as if the Bigge Report, based on his assessment between 1819 and 1822, but his findings were not published until 1823, placed a yoke around the neck of the collective colony and struggled to restrain the urge to move ahead, whilst going through a radical restructure of the way ahead. A different type of governor was installed and they were made very aware of the 'new' post Bigge approach to developing the colony–more convicts would arrive; expenditure for their support would be minimised, and local revenues would be used to run the colony on a daily basis. Both Brisbane and Darling acted responsibility, advanced the political changes for the local administration with its advisory bodies, and encouraged an open, free and 'creative' colony–entrepreneurs were welcome, but then so were speculators, and that was what brought this period to a close–a depression of 1827.

vi. The fourth period was longer, 1827-1842, with growth of manufactures and the primary industries (led by wool) growing at an equally fast rate. The pastoral /wool industry brought most of the capital, created most of the export trade and showed the greatest capital creation and returns on capital. The manufacturing industries attracted the free settlers and provided an employment base for the growing army of emancipists. Its greatest benefit lay not in its meagre exports, but in its successful import replacement. This period witnessed large population growth, large livestock numbers, large quantities of exports (always matched by continuing import needs) and growing wealth creation. As with the third period, it closed with a major depression, man-made, with imported downturns from Britain, withdrawal of speculators and then investors, a slowing of migrants arriving

vii. The fifth period was 1842-1850. If my assumption is valid that 'periods' were defined not by people, such as the arrival of a new governor, but by events, then there is a natural period break in 1850. The discovery of gold, the rebalancing of export composition from wool and grain to gold, and the dramatic surge in local revenues led to marvellous change in the colonial economy. A migrant inflow, previously unexpected by Governors, was the first step, and the second was the spectacular benefits of the coming of rail.

viii. The sixth period was 1851-1856. This period was defined by political instability leading up to independence and the fight between the British Treasury that could see the burgeoning local revenues, worth protecting and fighting for, and the local Legislative Council, that could sense independence through self-government coupled with the growing local revenues which could be otherwise lost to the colony, if self-government without conditions was not achieved.

Notes on Appendices

Two appendices are attached to this essay, as a means of further exploring and_explaining the concepts of the colonial economy 1788-1850.

The first addendum is a collection of special and meaningful collection of statistics relating to the colonial economy.

The second addendum is a commentary by this writer on the Works on the Colonial Economy by its pre-eminent authority, the late Professor Noel George Butlin.

CHAPTER 12

THE ECONOMIC WRITING OF NOEL GEORGE BUTLIN (1921-1991)

Noel George Butlin (19/12/1921-2/4/1991) was the foremost Australian academic on the Economics of the Colonial period of Australian History.

The purpose of this essay is to compile a comprehensive listing of the writings about the colonial economy between 1788-1850, which will lead to a compilation of his colonial economic history writings and result in a better understanding of the colonial economy by its champion–N.G. Butlin.

The Butlin Books

1. 'Investment in Australian Economic Development 1861-1900' (**1964**–CUP)
2. 'Our Original Aggression' (**1983**)
3. 'Colonial Statistics before 1850' (**1986**-CUP w/–Ginswick & Statham)
4. 'General Return of Convicts in NSW–1837' (**1987)**

Posthumous publications

5. 'Economics and the Dreamtime' (**1993**)
6. 'Forming A Colonial Economy **(1994**)

Articles

I. Private Capital Formation in Australia: estimates 1861-1900 (**1954**)
II. Australian Domestic Product, investment & foreign borrowing 1861-1938' (**1962**)
III. Close encounters: modelling aboriginal depopulation 1788-1850 (**1982**)
IV. Yo Ho Ho and how many bottles of rum (**1982)**
V. Aboriginal Populations in South-east Australia 1788-1850 (**1983)**
VI. Macassans & Aboriginal smallpox: 1789 & 1929 epidemics (**1984**)
VII. Contours of the Australian Economy 1788-1860 (**1984**–WPEH)
VIII. Australian gross domestic product 1788-1860: estimates, sources and methods (**1984**)
IX. What a way to run an empire, fiscally (**1985**)
X. White human capital in Australia 1788-1850 (**1985**)
XI. Colonial Statistics before 1850 (**1986)**
XII. Bicentennial Perspective of Australian Economic Growth (**1986**)
XIII. 'The Cost of Convict Transportation: Britain to Australia 1796-1810'(**1987)**
XIV. 'The palaeo-economic history of Aboriginal Migration (**1988)**
XV. Economics and the Dreamtime: a hypothetical history (**1993)**

THE COLONIAL ECONOMIC WRITINGS OF N.G. BUTLIN

'*Colonial Statistics before 1850*' was the precursor to understanding the colonial economy, and this compilation of Australian statistics (previously largely undeveloped) came in order to complete his major works of 'Economics & the Dreamtime' (1993) and 'Forming a Colonial Economy' (1994). Both works were published posthumously, Butlin having died in 1991.

Butlin acknowledges the assistance provided from '*Foundation of the Australian Monetary System 1788-1851*' by his brother, S.J., completed in 1953, and claims 'it is by far the most important published secondary source, even though it is essentially confined to money and banking. Even then, S.J. did not have access to the detailed British financial records'. Butlin also acknowledges the contribution of T.A. Coghlan in '*Labour & Industry in Australia*' (1918), which work 'exploited rather than portrayed the available statistics'. Other collections of useful statistics used by Butlin in 'Colonial Statistics before 1850' was R.M. Hartwell's manuscript 'The Economic Development of VDL' (1954) and B.R. Fletcher's 'Landed Enterprise & Penal Society' (1976), which deals with NSW agriculture to 1821. He asserts that much of the information in 'The Blue Books' (1822-1856) is unreliable, although they, together with the Governor's Returns are fundamental sources. 'Much of the information in these sources needs to be checked, and often corrected, by reference to other returns and records, whether returns by various individuals in the colonies or records of officials in Britain who amended many of the figures returned to Britain'.

Butlin throws some light on his reluctance to use official sources such as the Commissary Returns. "For example bills drawn on Britain and issued by the Commissariats may seem to be straight forward, on the surface. Regrettably, this is a superficial impression. For example, the mass of bills *seem* to be issued to shippers supplying goods to the colonies, the goods being taken into the Commissariat for public purposes. In reality, it seems highly likely that apparent bilateral transactions conceal a complicated three–or four-way trade, with many of the apparently public imports ending in private hands. It is necessary to warn readers against unduly simplistic interpretations of the statistical record'.

Butlin associated himself in the 'Colonial Statistics before 1850' with Mr. Jules Ginswick 'who is about to publish (in 1986) a massive assembly of statistics of New South Wales'. 'This work has greatly influenced the selection and emphasis of the tabulations included in '*Colonial Statistics before 1850*'.

Butlin does not apologise for concentrating on NSW statistics, firstly because, for a bicentennial year (1988), NSW takes dominant position. However, "this concentration on NSW is not as narrowing as it may sound. The original colony covered the whole of Eastern Australia until 1825, when Tasmania was separated. The original Port Phillip became the Colony of Victoria constitutionally separated in 1851, while the present Queensland remained part of NSW until 1859. Western Australia was founded in 1837 and South Australia formed in 1837. Dr. Statham has contributed statistics for the colonies, other than the eastern coast colonies'.

Butlin refers to other sources of information (sources other than S.J. Butlin's *Foundations* and Coghlan's *Labour & Industry*) as being 'limited, with the exception of some private collections such as the Macarthur Papers'. He does acknowledge that Commissioner Bigge improved the coherence, 'but not necessarily the quality' of early statistics, but that there was an overall improvement after 1822 and the commencement of the Blue Books. He claims the spread of settlement following 1813 interfered with the collection of information to the point that successive Blue Books only recognised this problem by omitting large areas of information, particularly those relating to farming and livestock–they were obviously too difficult to physically collect and too unreliable to be of any value. This was partially corrected when 'a system of population censuses were initiated with the NSW census of 1828'. The censuses became a point of attention for Butlin, and we recall the massive work of Butlin, Cromwell and Suthern–'The General Return of Convicts for 1837' (1987).

It would be hard to take exception to Butlin's conclusions about the 'Blue Books', but for all their transcription errors, their value in terms of a valid and accurate set of financial records of the colony each year must remain unchallenged. It should be pointed out that although they are loosely described as being 'The General Returns of the Colony' they are principally a financial statement of income and expenditures, and a 'balance sheet' of sorts being incorporated by exception into the records (the Blue Books recorded official inventories and government personnel in the military and on the civil list with great accuracy), and then only on a secondary basis do they become a source (albeit unreliable according to Butlin) of livestock in the colony, together with indicative pricing and details of manufactures. The musters followed then by the upgraded census included a definitive count of people, livestock, living conditions and family income.

Butlin et al presents us with 34 tables relating to NSW in his collection of statistics and they are all of interest and valuable in their assembled construction. In addition there are numerous statistics relative to the other colonies, both before and after they became independent of NSW.

It is of interest to report, as an aside note, that Butlin's former colleague at the ANU, Dr. H.M. Boot, does not quote Butlin, at all, in his 8,000 word essay on 'Government in the Colonial Economies' but relies mainly on second level writers such as McMartin, Finn, Barcan, McLachlan, Sinclair, Buxton and Thompson. He does however, afford us a general note of 'my debt to Butlin is the same as that of all economic historians of the Australian economy: immeasurable'.

I will turn, at this point, to the forerunner to the last Butlin work published, being 'Forming the Colonial Economy'. Butlin prepared his first Working Paper on Economic History in 1984 and entitled it '*Contours of the Australian Economy 1788-1860*'. This working paper is a lengthy, well presented documentary of the colonial economy, loaded with supporting statistics but full of doubts and apologies by the author for possible inadequate sources, inadequate statistics and

Butlin first reviews the existing writing on the early colonial economy–'Coghlan has very little on the growth and structure of the colonial economy'; 'there have been some extremely valuable monographs of economic issues, the most notable of which is, S.J. Butlin's *Foundations* and Hartwell on VDL'

Butlin sets his goal for writing the paper in interesting qualitative terms 'to present some broad outlines of the economic history of Australia between 1788 and 1860, based predominantly on '*social accounting*' measures with some references to other information'. Butlin places quite severe limitations on his instant writing 'there is no monetary history (*refer S.J. Butlin Foundations*); a second is the changing distribution of income and wealth (Butlin refers his reader to Butlin & Sinclair 'Australian Domestic Product 1788-1860–Estimates Sources & Methods'); a third is the age, sex and occupational composition of the workforce; a fourth admonition is 'the figures in this paper–because of the high-risk figures for this early period–must be treated as rough approximations only'. Butlin omits these three limitations from the 'broad outlines' of the colonial economy.

Butlin presents us in this long paper (there are 35 closely typed pages, together with various statistical tables) with 14 conclusions or (in some cases) theories and then proceeds to discuss them.

Theory Number 1

Butlin reduces his observations on the growth of the white population in the colony economy work to four conclusions,

'The growth of white Australian population was the product of four main influences

- Convict in-flows,
- Free migrant in-flows,
- Local birth rates and
- Local death rates

Butlin writes:

- o "Convicts were the dominant source of income until the early 1830s
- o The civil composition of the population has massive swings in the proportion of convicts in the total white population
- o These factors indicate a 'free' labour market, but the identification of the tendencies towards an open labour market is much more difficult and uncertain"

Butlin could be challenged on each of these conclusions, as they appear to defy the facts as we know and understand them.

The growth of population mirrored and was encouraging of the growth of the colonial economy. Butlin starts his argument, of white population growing and thus influencing the growth of the colonial economy, by assuming that convicts carried with them the optimum funding by Britain.

Although the British Government funded the cost of transportation and the maintenance (supposedly clothing, food, housing), we know that convict labour furnished the food supplies, convict labour demolished trees for wooden barracks, or made bricks for brick barracks and supplied the labour for the Lumber Yard, the Female Factory (both being part of the Commissary operation) in order to supply clothing and other sundries for the convict population.

Butlin then suggests that free immigrants brought with them large amounts of capital. His later studies (Capital Formation in Australia) confirms that immigrant capital, although important and significant, was much less than private capital transfers from Britain which attracted dividend and profit transfers back to Britain.

Butlin's third and fourth point about the local birth and death rate, contributing to a net population growth, is self-explanatory, but what was his point? The rates in Australia between 1801 and 1834 were not as high as in the Americas, but in the colony, such birth rates had a natural in-built limitation. Literacy and wedlock were both low, and there was a local campaign against children born out of wedlock and those illegitimate children were taken off the streets and gathered into a growing number of orphanages around the towns. The Marsden campaign to this end was well funded by the missionary societies and had popular support amongst the general population. The legitimate births were only what could be expected by a relatively illiterate population, and even if full employment prevailed, and a growing standard of living could be witnessed, there was still the cloud of 'penal settlement' hanging over the populace, and the constant concern about the withdrawal of British funding from other than convict and essential services, all led to a feeling of a temporary settlement, rather than a permanent 'home-land'.

The economic contribution of a permanent free population was taken by Butlin as being, in itself, of significance when it was by default rather than planned, and of little economic consequence rather than of major benefit. It created a challenge rather than a prop!

Butlin ignored in his 'growth of the population in the colonial economy' two elements that provided real benefits. His four main elements should have been:

- Foreign investment
- Convict flows
- Agricultural/pastoral success, and
- Free immigration

Butlin's preoccupation is with domestic GDP, capital formation, and demographics.

These attributes are all important to the colonial economy, but the economy needed firstly to be self-sustaining and this would only come with broader based production within the economy–meaning both agriculture and manufactures needed to be funded and grow. This in turn needed trade and overseas markets (Britain), as well as entrepreneurs and speculators. Risk-takers and punters were an essential and integral part of the growing colonial economy. Demographics and private funding were well down the list of actuals in the colonial economy. The main reason for including free immigrants in my list at position number four was not because of their contribution to the population number, nor of their contribution to a more favourable balance between free and 'convict' in the population, nor because of the private capital they brought with them, but because of the large public outlays expended on them from revenues of crown land sales, and their contribution towards decentralisation, by opening up new lands and outlying settlements.

Butlin admits that "paucity of information on the rates of absconding convicts, and the remission rates of convict sentences, and the rates of emigration prevents any adequate analysis–the summary outcome in terms of the civil condition of the NSW population is indicated from a limited number of musters and censuses". That may be so, but the philosophical absence of such enormous detail should be of little consequence. Surely, the economic history of the colony of NSW does not rise or fall on such meagre statistics, when we have social history 'opinions' from those present at the time and who left us with detailed and reliable information on life and living conditions, and then from official records which explain and justify how the settlers lived, worked, and survived; we also know from the record how the convicts were employed and how they were fed, clothed and housed and most important just how much they cost to support and maintain. If Professor Butlin needs additional information for a database or modelling exercise then surely he can extrapolate sufficient approximations to be still relevant and worthy and not then have to throw his hands in the air because his findings cannot be guaranteed to the umpteenth decimal point. There becomes an optimal point when we know too much, and cannot separate the 'wood from the trees'. Economic history of colonial NSW is the attachment of an economic understanding and interpretation to actual historical events. If Professor Butlin's temerity in postulating theses to the actual events is unnerving, then his successors and students show no such reticence. Abbott and Hartwell regale us in their volumes with theories and interpretations, as do Shaw, Fitzpatrick and even Dr. Boot. What is the mystery about not knowing the convict percentage of the overall population? For one thing, the output of the convicts was never counted in the Blue Books or in Butlin's GDP computations. The convicts were not being carried in any official records as a burden. They bore a cost of being transported (at a rate of approx £13 per head, but little more and this was in fact a transfer cost from the Home office in London to the Secretary of State's Office for the Colonies. The British Treasury recognised that the convicts worked and supported themselves and that is why year after year the contribution per head of convict cost the British Government a lesser and lesser amount. In the end the British people were only paying for their shipping costs and their initial 'set-up' (their maintenance until they were put into productive work)–the British Treasury would not even pay for the law and order component of the general government costs in NSW. They believed the convict maintenance of lawfulness could be controlled locally and within local budgets since the early magnanimous contribution of British funding paid for the gaols and the local taxpayer should now pay for the police establishment and the continuous outlay for maintenance of these services. Butlin's statistics don't reflect the nuances of the politics between the 'mother' country and its subservient daughter, nor do they understand the social history and the non-business history that was evolving on a continuous basis within the colony.

Theory Number 2

Butlin's next main theme is:–'the early white settlements were supplied with much more than convicts who were successfully assigned and became freed labour. The white were, in fact, provided with an enormous subsidy by the British government much of it unwittingly and to British chagrin. Though this subsidy declined relatively to Australian gross product, it remained substantial until the early 1830s".

Can we take exception with this Butlin conclusion? I think, again, he misunderstands the circumstances of the British inclination and policy towards the colonial economy of NSW. The colony became the dumping ground for British prisoners and other misfits into British society. By transporting these people to the colony, which had been established for this specific purpose, and only later structured into a joint penal/free society, the British Treasury saved themselves a substantial sum in the opportunity cost of keeping maintaining and rehabilitating these people within Britain. So here we have a growing army of 'misfits' in need of rehabilitation. They are to feed, clothe and house themselves. This venture probably takes a theoretical steady-state population of some 35,000 convicts, but the British Government has many more than this number to transfer overseas. So how will they be gainfully 'employed'? If for a few years they build government buildings, roads, bridges, wharves, stores and houses, that would be a worthwhile enterprise, but there needs to be a growing population to utilise all this excess labour. And this new population cannot be kept by the government just to use the surplus convicts. So this population needs to become part of the agrarian society, till the land, grow crops and graze livestock. All these activities were probably carefully considered by the Home Office in London and then placed into the equation, at least from about 1830 onwards were the revised social policy of the Government. For how long they would ask can we keep dumping our prison population onto a colony in transition? How long can we ignore dealing with this social scourge ourselves and tackling the underlying cause of the predatory problem, which was poverty?

So the challenges to the British planners was one of transferring prisoners from the British gaols and courts to the colony, supporting free immigration subsidised by government revenues, fiscally supporting a free society in the colony, and all that came back was trade, dividends and raw materials. The social planners and liberals took grievous unease in this emerging pattern. One solution was to 'place' (by assignment) the 'better' convicts and have them supported by the free landed population. But was this a subsidy to the landed populace? How could it be both a direct, and large, saving to the government and a subsidy to the local farmers? In the thinking of the day, clearing the land, planting and then harvesting the grain, transporting produce to the commissariat store, was not so much a subsidy as a plan of immense common sense. What else could be done with them? Holding them in official barracks was not the end of the matter. They required supervision; they required exercise of the mind, the soul and the body. In the tightly controlled economy this was an additional cost burden that no one wanted to pay for–so the assignment system solved many economic and social problems. Subsidy, indeed! To offer another example, a subsidy could only be created if the offer of a convict for the charge of 'feeding, clothing and maintaining' could only be thus described if its economic benefit to the user (or farmer settler, as Butlin implies) is greater than its cost. Coghlan castes a lot of doubt on the general economic value of the convicts. He claims that they were lazy, always looking for the opportunity to be out of sight and out of mind, and that they were only 40% as productive as a normal free farm labourer. We can therefore assess whether or not a typical convict cost or saved his 'keeper'. Annual maintenance cost the keeper (according to Coghlan P64) was £36, viz. £26 for food and lodging, and £10 a year for work after 3 o'clock: according to Bigge (claims Coghlan it was £25. 12s. Coghlan concludes that "both figures are probably correct, the larger estimate for the years prior to Macquarie's arrival, and the lower figure for the closing years of his administration". Coghlan goes on to conclude "taking the value of a free labourer at only twice that of an assigned convict, it would apparently have paid an employer to hire free labour at a wage not exceeding £1 per week, in preference to accepting the services of an assigned convict–according to regulations, the wages of a free labourer was to be no higher than 2/6d per day, or 15s per week. So that, allowing for lost time and other breaks, the earnings of a free immigrant or convict who had become free would have been little, if anything, better than those of a prisoner, if the official views could have been made to prevail". However, the official wage of 2/6d per day would have meant an employee would have had to work all day every day for a bare subsistence. Naturally, many labourers would have had to work for official wages in those early years, but it is clear that the majority of able-bodied labourers would not accept the regulation wage. Labour was in short supply, and Governor King writes in his despatches that 5/–was the average daily wage in the competitive labour market. But this was paid largely in goods, spirits and thus represented a much lower money wage. Towards the close of the Macquarie administration the average seems to have settled (according to Coghlan (P 65) at 4/–per day. This was about 2 ½ times the cost of keeping an assigned servant, but with productivity adjustments taken into account, it was profitable to use free in preference to assigned labour. So just what is Butlin concerned about in his statement that "the early white settlers were supplied with much more than convicts and provided with an enormous subsidy". He offers us no further explanation than this glib, questionable comment. Butlin does tell us that 'the fact that Britain may have gained from these expenditures (on convicts) is irrelevant since no charges were placed against the settlers for the use of this resource". I am not convinced of this conjecture.

Butlin uses the phrase, in the quoted text "early white settlements were supplied with much more than convicts". I think the 'much more' refers to the government-sponsored basis infrastructure of roads and other services which allowed the relocation of new white settlers to outlying areas possible, as well as the provision of government-owned markets, government owned (and loaned) breeding stock. Why does Butlin place a value to settlers on these otherwise government essential services? If he refers to the VDL situation, he would find that Governor Sorrel, as a means of improving agriculture in VDL purchased with government funds, better strains and quality of livestock and loaned them to the small farmers who could not otherwise afford such animals, and at no charge. Why then was 'exploration' and then roads, livestock services, markets etc of such concern to Butlin?

Theory Number 3

The third Butlin theory is "the arriving whites confronted an aboriginal population that was ill-adapted to an outside challenge to their land use . . . Faced with competition, the Aborigines lacked effective technology of warfare to prevent the inroads of whites"

What Butlin is telling us, is that in his opinion, the 'invaders' took advantage of the Aboriginals lack of technology and culture and claimed the land as 'terra nullius' irresponsibly? Can this claim be reasonably justified? I would ask, what nation being invaded in the 1700s was technically equal to Britain, France, Spain or Portugal, and when did that differentiation dissuade an invader from claiming territory it found attractive and desirable? We think of the Africa, the South Seas Islands, the Dutch East Indies and the West Indies and cannot point to one situation where territorial claims were made between equals. Surely what Butlin should be pointing to is the absence in British Colonial Policies of any policy that compensates the invaded natives for their land or any policy on uplifting or upgrading those natives to the level of British astuteness. Neither policy was created any time between 1788 and 1856, when self-government was awarded to the white population and after the original native population was decimated. Tokenism took a first step towards recompensing the natives when the Crown decided to spend a meagre 15% of 'crown' land revenues on improving the plight of the natives but this was short-lived and no record exists of any expenditure, other than Marsden's meagre and failed attempt to educate aboriginal youth in groups of 5 so that 'not too many natives would be educated at the one time. Butlin is correct in his words but one cannot draw a detrimental conclusion without laying the blame for a bad situation at the feet of the invaders.

Theory Number 4

Butlin turns here to the racist aspect of colonialism. Butlin claims, "Australian economic (and social) history should be seen not in racist terms but as a clash between cultures. Between 1800 and 1860 Australian white expansion collided against a black population with ensuing biological and economic conflict. A non-racist perspective reveals a dramatically different picture from the conventional white success story, given that one would now trace an expanding white and contracting black economy.

By itself this statement is not persuasive as a statement of economic history of the colonial economy, but Butlin goes on to state 'the significance of this issue depends on one's understanding of the size and rate of decline of the black population and the relative productivity levels of the two cultures.

Butlin's surmise is that there was not room for the two disparate groups to live in harmony and to coexist together. This premise is highly questionable, and cannot be supported in economic terms. Butlin presupposes that the population decline of the blacks and the inverse incline of the white means economic disparity (in rounded thousands).

Year	Butlin's' Black Popln•	White Popln
1788	1100	1
1815	850	15
1860	375	1145

What exactly is the point Butlin is trying to make? He has already told us that the British takeover of the country in 1788 was because of technological differences between the blacks and the whites, and now he is trying to tell us that it was racism and exploitation of the blacks and a culture difference that led to this economic disparity between the two cultures. For two hundred years, assimilation has so far failed, so why does Butlin think the British economic advances should have kept pace with and matched the economic advances of the natives. If the native culture has different standards to those of the whites and economic advancement, materialism and commercialisation does not appeal to the Aboriginal race, then why not accept a peaceful co-existence, mutual obligation and gradual assimilation. Butlin's understanding of Aboriginals is based on white-man's thinking and standards and harmony or reconciliation cannot be brought about. If we can accept the premise that not every component of the population has to bring economic gain, then the Aborigines who are not inclined to be assimilated and be gainfully employed can contribute in a immeasurable cultural way and be supported and subsidised by the rest of the population, in the same way, disadvantaged whites are carried by the rest of society. Butlin must accept the two concepts of mutual obligation and self-determination. Not every aspect of multi-culturalism can be measured in economic terms, and there are many forms of direct and indirect economic contribution that support better living standards and a better quality life even if they are non-traditional.

Butlin relies on Blainey to further try to quantify economic progress for both black and white society. Butlin quotes Blainey by suggesting that "some (e.g. Blainey) propose that black 'living standards' were as good as or better than whites' early in the 19th century".

But again, just what is Butlin trying to say? What is the point of developing some to establish 'black output expressed in terms of white prices"?

The only value could be that a great many important foods consumed by aborigines e.g. fish, fowl, eggs, major animals and fruit were represented in white consumption. But even assessing these values appears without academic merit because none of these food items were grown or produced by the native population and should therefore not be adding value to the native's economic output.

Theory Number 5

Butlin return to his Aboriginal themes and makes the claim that "the blacks imposed high costs on the extension of white settlement. As their effective resistance in the south was beaten, the way was opened for rapid white settlement and for faster growth in white productivity and in population absorption. Then, unhindered by blacks, whites occupied the liberated natural resources shaped for them over the centuries by prior black use".

Butlin is suggesting that there was an 'opportunity cost' to blacks limiting in some way the spread of white settlement. This was the 'high cost' imposed on the extension of white settlement. But then Butlin implies that 'once unhindered by blacks, the whites were able to make much more productive use of the land previously occupied by blacks. This again appears to be a misconception by Butlin of the black affinity with the land and the 'value' they placed on the land. It was a previous Butlin contention that the black population pre-1788 was limited by the amount of natural and native food the land was able to reproduce. Why was it not within Butlin's comprehension to place an intrinsic value on the black's use of the land, and not see productivity from land as being solely in terms of direct utilisation for grain or pasturing? Was it not possible that the de-foliating of the land had a negative economic value and was wasteful, whereas untouched native grasses, periodically burnt by the Aboriginals added value to the land and encouraged larger numbers of native animals, which in turn supported a larger native population?

Butlin further explains that 'blacks imposed high costs on the whites through destruction of white lives, and white owned livestock and property'. It is almost as if Butlin envisages a white life have substantially more value than a black life and white-owned livestock having a greater value than natural native animals, which were just as much a part of the diet for blacks as cattle and sheep were for the whites.

Butlin offers us his explanation for population growth and sets down the 'compound growth between 1788 and 1899

1788-1814	10.9%
1815-1825	11.6%
1816-1828	2.6%
1829-1840	10.4%
1841-1842	12.5%
1843-1844	4.7%

Is Butlin trying to make us conclude that the already high population growth would have been higher if the Aboriginals were not trying to impede the spread of white settlement and protect their lands?

Theories Numbered 6 & 7

Butlin turns from Aborigines to GDP growth and makes some interesting conclusions

- 'The growth in GDP shows a remarkably steady trend other than in the early 1840s and the steep rise during the early gold period' (of the 1850s)

- 'The conventional triad of gaol, wool and gold as important activities in the white economy' need to be tempered by the acceptance that
    - o 'The role of the public sector dwindled quickly as a direct contributor to white economic activity, particularly after 1820 and became minor after 1835'.

Butlin admits that there are 'conceptual problems in the valuation of public contribution activity, given the problem of measuring convicts' services'. What he is saying is that when government farming was all but terminated in 1805, the public sector was no longer a producer, and after 1810, the Police Fund dealt with public works. "Above all, the Commissariat appears as the medium through which the British Government was induced–often unwittingly–to continue massive support to the settlement and to establish standards of living at a very early stage at a level, most probably, few of the settlers had attained in Britain. Not so much the presence of government but the role and significance of the Commissariat appeared to need drastic revision".

Butlin is making unchallengeable statements:

The steady growth of the colonial economy as reflected in the GDP figures was only to be expected. The economy was in transition. From firstly, an economy devoted almost wholly to government enterprise, it changed to an economy of basic private enterprise that is without the speculators and with minimalist manufacturing, but a growing concentration in the agricultural sector. The economic growth was being limited by the shortage of labour and so the growth was largely due to trade, with imports and exports matched, and new local government revenue being imposed on to imports.

Butlin's reference to a commissary in crisis (in need of 'drastic revision') is not the common held view of the commissary under Macquarie. Macquarie was the second governor to 'reform' the commissary–the first had been Governor King, and the third was Governor Brisbane.–But Macquarie's reforms were mostly in the restructuring of commissary operations so that the expected increase in convict numbers could be coped with. Macquarie saw the needs of the immediate future to be for the commissary to have a structure to feed, clothe and employ these growing numbers of male and female convicts. To cater for the female convicts, Macquarie planned to rebuild, expand and change the structure of the Female Factory in Parramatta. To house the majority of male convicts in Sydney town, he planned on building the Hyde Park Barracks. The growing number of youth convicts required separate treatment and housing from the older men, and the Carter Barracks on brickfield Hill was expanded to cater for housing, training, and educating these youth. Macquarie then created the commissariat 'employment centre' which consisted of the Lumber Yard, the Dockyard, the Brickyard, the Stone Yard and the timber harvesting gangs located in Castle Hills and Pennant Hills area, The timber gangs were located in these areas not only for the better quality timber available there, but its proximity to a river in which the logs could be cut on site and then floated down the river to the commissary store to the dock on High Street north, sand then manhandled to the Lumber Yard on the corner of High Street and Bridge Street. High Street was eventually renamed George Street but remained the main thoroughfare in the colony.

The commissary was staffed by the deputy Commissary-general, usually a military officer, supported in turn by a limited number of storemen, mostly convicts, but without any skilled book-keepers. Macquarie issued instructions that the increased store activities would involve more stock, more transactions, stricter rations and therefore tighter controls. This, he meant to cover, by requesting a skilled commissary accountant be appointed. But Bathurst took until 1823 to agree to such an appointment, although Macquarie's successor formally made the same request of Bathurst, and again Bathurst demurred until the answer came from Sir Ralph Darling, the next Governor of the colony in NSW who wanted to transfer ahead of his arrival in the colony, the deputy-commissary-general (of accounts) in Mauritius, a young man of great experience–William Lithgow. Lithgow arrived in 1823 to handle the accounting side of the commissary and to fill a new commissary role of internal auditor. This was an attempt to rectify the absence of skilled storekeepers (as opposed to storemen)–Lithgow recognised the absence of appropriate purchasing procedures. His drawing attention to some areas of weakness such as purchasing, a forward planning for supplies, and a more appropriate pricing policy, could not be regarded as a commissary in crisis, but was non-the-less a commissary badly need of reform, and so Brisbane finished what Macquarie had commenced. These reforms accommodate the commissary role in improving convict management, improving convict work practices, as well as housing, productivity, and certainly trimmed even further the cost of convict and therefore commissary operations.

So Butlin recognised a commissary in need of reform but he failed to note that the reform was already underway during the period Butlin decided the commissary was in need of this 'drastic revision'.

Butlin notes, "Acquiring access to British resources wholesale, it was the medium whereby British Government subsidies were passed to individual settlers directly and indirectly through the provisioning of assigned servants".

Butlin ends his section on the growth of GDP in the early economy by unfairly criticising Macquarie. Butlin writes "Contrary to the view of his restructuring of the economy towards a gaol system, he does not appear as responsible for stemming the early decline in the public sector's share of gross product nor, despite his alleged propensity for building, does he appear to have absorbed an increased share of the settlement's output as compared with his immediate predecessors. Rather, he might be seen as failing to allow the resumption of the 'decline' in the public share as the growth of local population and activity occurred".

Butlin contrives his gathered evidence on the growth rate of the colonial economy to suggest that an apparent a slowdown of output during the Macquarie administration is due to a lack of interest by Macquarie in developing the economy. Nothing, it would seem, could be further from the truth. Factually the Macquarie administration would have recorded the most aggressive of economic development of any governor in the first 50 years of settlement. It was this admission before the Bigge Commission that caused Bigge to write negatively of Macquarie's wastefulness He heard evidence from a free architect within the colony, Butcher, that Macquarie had spent nearly one million pound on building materials and supplies on public building projects between 1810 and 1820. This figure (the figure actually quoted to Commissioner Bigge was £942,834) does not suggest inactivity or lack of interest in economic development but rather the opposite. It also clearly suggests that the majority of convicts supported by the government were productively employed in the public sector. It also means that the source of local materials–the stone yard, the brickyards, the tile factory and the timber millers, were working very hard and employing quantities of raw materials in order to meet the commissariat production goals which in turn met the governor's output goals. In addition, all of these convicts were housed, fed and clothed by the commissary interests, which meant a great number of other government convicts were gainfully employed in the colony.

Far from being a declining public sector, there was a frenetic amount of economic activity underway from building contractors, to importers, traders, farming and agriculturalists, all filling government contracts for goods and services.

There was no 'alleged' propensity for building–it was an actual frenzy of building, supported factually and fully by the presentation to the Bigge Commission by no less a person that Francis Greenway, who firstly claimed he was the architect for the Macquarie building and construction program and submitted a list of 75 public works he personally had designed, costed and supervised for the governor. He then submitted an account for a further £26,000 on account of architectural fees due to him from work commenced and planned but which never got underway. Greenway was calculating his emolument on the basis of an 'agreed' 8% fee for design and supervision. In settlement of this claim, Greenway accepted a grant of land to which he relocated having failed, after the departure of Macquarie to make any inroads as a private architect.

It must be obvious that the public sector performed well until at least after the Macquarie withdrawal, and the level of building activity, if valued correctly, would account for a significant uplifting of the public sector activity and GDP. In keeping with previous comments made in this study that Butlin did not value 'convict output', the true value of economic activity and public sector economic growth can only be made if the value of convict output is valued and there is a value assigned to the full employment of convicts. I.e. productivity levels were high, output was high, underemployed convicts were unknown in the settlement and therefore secondary crime was down. Each of these activities had a flow on effect throughout the settlement, and further valued 'GDP from the public sector'.

Theory Number 8

Butlin turns from the Macquarie period to the supposedly safer ground of the agricultural economy. From his 70 years of GDP statistics, he concludes "Throughout the entire 70–odd years, there were only seven (scattered) years in which pastoral activity exceeded non-pastoral primary production. The agricultural sector of the economy warrants greater prominence than has been accorded it. Possibly also the views about the engrossment of land by squatters and the importance of wool exports as the driver of growth may need critical inspection".

If Butlin tries to shock us by questioning the 'traditional' view of Macquarie being a colonial builder', then he is trying the same tactic in questioning that wool and pastoralists were not the primary economic drivers between 1800 and 1860. He does bend a little when he makes the concession that the 'colonial economy grew faster due to the pastoral activity during the 'Pastoral Age', but does not tell us what period constitutes the pastoral age.

Once again, Butlin does not flesh out or put into perspective his conclusions. He does admit however, early in his discussion of this theory that 'there must be several qualifications to this general assessment. The pastoral series omits imputed value of livestock increase and the non-pastoral primary series includes farm construction". He misses the obvious point that early large-scale land holdings worked at crop production as well as livestock production (mixed farming) and this overall contribution needs a special 'valuation'. In outlying and new areas, perishability and transportation was a natural limiting factor in cropping activities.

We should accept the statistics of Butlin, Ginswick and Stratham, if for no other reason that they have given a lifetime to assembling, correcting and interpreting these statistics, but there are other facts and circumstances that throw doubt on their conclusions especially with regard to the agricultural sector of the colonial economy not being the dominant driving force in the settlement for other than 7 years between 1788 and 1860.

The circumstances which impacted largely on the success and strength of the agricultural sector would have commenced in 1824 when Lord Bathurst, acting on British Government policy arranged for the first of three large land grants to be issued to the Australian Agricultural Company (the other two which followed some years apart, are the Van Diemen's Land Company in 1826 and the South Australian Company in 1835). The purpose of these land grant companies was to release large areas of agricultural land into the hands of private investors in order to raise livestock and raw materials for British industry, to diversify agricultural development, to extend the areas of settlement and to encourage remote settlements at the same time new lands were being opened up. Bathurst hand in mind the utilisation of huge areas of remote lands, possibly as a means of fending off any foreign 'invasions' of unoccupied lands, or as a means of attracting direct investment into the pastoral industry in the new colony, or of endeavouring to recoup some Treasury costs of opening up the new country by imposing a 'quit' rent on the land grant companies. In all, in just three grants he released nearly two and one-half million acres into the hands of British investors, in exchange for less than a million and a quarter pound of future investment.

But this policy sparked great interest in the pastoral industry in NSW, encouraged new breeding of livestock and commenced a vigorous export industry. When Butlin denigrates the value and output of the pastoral industry he should make adjustments for differential raw material prices in London. Wool prices were much higher for European wool than they were for the colonial wool, which was not only of an inferior quality but was uncleaned and very greasy. So, in terms of production, the land was being utilised in an economic manner but at a lower value than competitive sources of the raw material to the end-buyer. Wool followed the golden days of trade in sealskins and whale oil, but grew without in-built limitations other than a breeding cycle too slow to fill the available grazing lands. It took the next 20 years for Australian wool to dominate the English wool market and reach a 50% foothold in the market (in the early 1850s)

Butlin may be correct in producing and reading his statistics but the perception of the colonial economy between 1788 and 1860 is that the agricultural economy dominated growth in the period.

Theory # 9

Butlin turns now to the essential elements of the colonial economy.

He states, "The complexity of the economy beyond mere food production and pastoralism shows up strongly from a very early stage and throughout. The omission of services from consideration is common to most studies of economic structure and development. The variability of the service shares, points to some intriguing economic and social questions that have not been explored to any substantial extent".

Butlin refers here to 'personal' services, which he points to as being rent. The concept is good, even if limited. We need to consider the overall situation in the colony between 1788 and 1817 (this is Butlin's first turning point, with 'the share of services tending to fall to 1817, rise once more to close to the mid-'thirties, stabilise until the late 'forties, and fall once more to 1860.

To limit the concept to 'rent' is misleading. The situation between 1788 and 1817 is that all convicts were housed in single storey wooden barracks until the Hyde Park (a 3 storey brick building) was opened in early 1818. By 1817 only a few houses other than government owned houses were available, so nothing was available for rent before this time. Any emancipists or tick-of-leavers were generally directed out of the town onto small land grants or onto smallholdings as employees, since there were no jobs in the town. So rent did not come into question until after the development of small houses, which would become available as rental dwellings or as boarding houses for the growing number of itinerant emancipists and the increasing demand for accommodation.

Thus, Butlin's premise is obvious and acceptable. From 1817, the 'rent' equivalent was a growing figure for no other reason than supply and demand. Between 1817 and the first depression of 1827, the economy grew rapidly in both agriculture and the first of the manufacturing industries being established. The depression in that year hurt towns' people and the banks, rather than have detrimental effects on the colony as a whole. The impact was on those small landowners who faced price declines in livestock and grain. The Governor directed the Commissary to reduce the price of grain, into store, even though the store held little by way of reserves. The result was even less grain available to the commissary in the following year, which caused a dramatic increase in the buying price (by the commissary)

The 1812 *Select Committee on Transportation* P.13, records "At the expiration of the time to which the convicts have been sentenced, their freedom is at once obtained, and they are at liberty either to return to this country (i.e. Britain), or to settle in NSW: should the latter be their choice, a grant is made to the unmarried, of 40 acres of land, and to the married, of something more for the wife and each child; tools and livestock are also given to them and for 18 months they are victualled from the Government stores. In this manner, they have an opportunity of establishing themselves in independence, and by proper conduct to regain a respectable place in society." Although Butlin would have been aware of this procedure, at least employed until the mid-1820s, he should have noted it as an influence in the question of personal services. In addition to a 'rent equivalent', mention should have been made of an 'income equivalent' from which the personal exertion of growing food from their own holdings could be deducted. Butlin should also have included the 'value' of emancipists remaining on the stores.

The Committee also reported on the 'assignment' system, which prevailed from the 1790s to the late 1817-1818 period. The Report of the committee states, "The convicts are distributed amongst the settlers, who cloth, support and lodge them; they work either by the task or for the same number of hours as the Government convicts; and when their set labour is finished, they are allowed to work on their own account". These are the points that Butlin should have included in his personal services–value of subsidy; value of unpaid labour; value of grant; value of improvements; or he could have retitled the idea to be 'personal exertion services', and included the value of 'allowances and external support, such as commissary items and land grants or assigned servants, in lieu of just rent".

This was the last pre-1860 theory that Butlin discussed, except he restated his quasi-racist theorem that 'the domestic white Australian market was generally the overwhelming component of total rural sales. The broad similarity of the structure of each white colony's economy makes it more necessary to qualify the significance that is usually accorded to wool output".

What Butlin appears to be stating is that the British wool market was central to the growing colonial economy before 1860! Why he inserted the term 'white' between domestic and Australian suggests a precision in terminology that is pedantic in the extreme and pedagogic. The concept is a strange one for he fails to admit that wool sales to the colony of NSW and VDL were important at all times, even during the days of the gold rush when gold overtook wheat as the prime export cash trading commodity, and for this reason the Australian wool share in Britain declined during the decade of the 1850s, but that did not detract from the fact that primary industry including the extraction industry was of great importance, and both could, and would, have been stronger if additional labour and/or technology had been available in the colony. But the mere hint of riches from the soil was sufficient to bring further speculation to the colonies and attract investors, which kept the economy on the boil until the turn of the century. Butlin asks 'did the gold rush have a negative impact on the wool trade?' In 1840 the market share was only 20%, but by 1850, the share had jumped to 53%. Butlin concludes that during the 1850s the percentage declined to 40%. Does this mean a negative impact within Australia? The figures suggest that it did not! As a percentage of GDP, wool sales accounted for a steady and regular 10.5-15% between 1820 and 1850. The agriculture sector as a whole represented, in each colony, a steady 17.5-20%. The decline from 53% to 40% of the British market can be attributed to other influences and factors.

In spite of Lord Bathurst's attempt to have the colony produce 'fine;' wool, both the AAC and the VDL Company failed in their endeavours. The woollen mills in Britain had improved technologically over the year and in the 1850s could process 'fine' wool at a cheaper rate than continental mills, thus they demanded a higher proportion of fine wool. France had changed its flock composition so that by 1850, it was able to produce fine wool for export. Thus the first of the factors influencing a declining colonial domination was that the market had changed–the market for fine wool products increased, the raw materials were not readily available from the colony, and Britain purchased from a more local source. Before 1850, wool exported from the colonies, arrived in Britain at a lower price than the wool available from continental sources–this impacted on volume of colonial wool. Then when the prices began to equate, quality came into prominence. Colonial wool was too greasy, unwashed and cost more to process, so the price differentiation was importance to cover both quality and extra processing. When this price differentiation began to vanish in the early 1850s, obviously volume suffered, although this volume decline was minimal. The British share of the wool products market both at 'home' and abroad was growing.

A decline of 13% in an expanding market did not have any dramatic effect on volume of wool leaving the colonies, nor on the overall price received. The significance of this conclusion can be seen in the fact that wool exports as a percentage of colonial GDP remained constant during this period in each colony. It also evidenced the importance of wool production and the agricultural industry generally to the colonial economy.

We can support this last Butlin premise that wool production was the most important element of the agricultural economy, and that the share of colonial wool declined, but without detriment, in the British markets. Butlin rightly relies on his colonial statistics to support his various theories, but could have validly concluded, as well, that manufacturing growth was having an important effect as well. Manufactures never enjoyed a dominant share of the export market but offered substantive benefit to the import replacement market, and this in itself was of significance because it relieved, a little, the pressure being placed on exports to generate wealth and growth in the colonial market. The manufacturing sector also provided employment for the immigrant working population and the slow but steady movement from the rural sector to the towns. Butlin makes this point in a different context. Butlin states, "The growth rate of white population and GDP turned down from about the mid-1860s, with a somewhat slower rate of GDP per head

Summary

Butlin's first foray into writing about the colonial economy was in his (Working Papers in Economic History) Paper for the ANU 'Contours of the Australian Economy 1788-1860'. It preceded his more formal volumes of the Economy and the Dreamtime and Forming the Colonial Economy, and followed his assembly of various statistics for the same period.

Structuring the paper in an unusual format, he poses 16 'conclusions' and then discusses each 'conclusion' in support of his contention or claim.

One cannot in all efficacy, discount Butlin's conclusions since his 50 years of concentration prior to his death in 1991 of studying the colonial economy makes him a pre-eminent student of the period, but one can with a little insight into the same topic question his statements as being absolutes and offer an alternative for further study. Butlin does make some statements, 'wild' is not quite the right word, but 'questionable' in its strict definition, and should not be an unacceptable portrayal of some of his more radical claims.

Butlin portrays the Aborigines in the first 30 years of occupation as downtrodden, but then suggests they had an under-performing economy in their own right because they did not 'work' the land, and grazed no livestock in their own right. He probably although thought they did not invent or utilise the 'wheel'. He then concludes that by defending their native lands they slowed the rate of growth of the settlement and therefore interfered economically with the white economy. Aborigines are a passing interest to Butlin who then turns to the growth rate of the white colonial economy. This discrimination if not distinction between the 'black' and 'white' economies is daunting, as any attempt to compare the internal growth rates of each economy is stricken to disaster. There can be no validity in a comparison, for omissions make the results futile and doubtful. He omits to value the output of the convict production in the white economy, and for the first 500 years this should be the focus of any GDP measurement. He fails to accept that 'native' grasses to the Aborigines were as important if not more than the 'improved' pastures for the white settler. He also omits to value the native 'livestock' of the Aborigine, but claims the slaughter of proper livestock by Aborigines was extremely costly.

Butlin creates a dilemma, which he fails to explain or solve.

When he moves onto the post-1800 colonial economy, he first accuses Macquarie of tardiness in economic development and suggests the traditional understanding of the success of the Macquarie building program is but myth. He is far from the truth in this claim and in fact his misconception of the output during the Macquarie administration throws doubt on his more general conclusions and theories.

He finally turns to a statement validated by his own statistics. That in only seven years between 1788 and 1860 did pastoral activity exceeds non-pastoral primary production. This, on the surface, flies in the face of his other general theories that the dominant economic sector came from the pastoral industry and that same sector in fact drove the overall economy.

In all Butlin raises many interesting and contentious thoughts about the colonial economy, but surely offers himself the foundation for his later two works, following a time gap in which he took time to re-think some of his more basic propositions.

Special Theories on the Pattern of Economic Growth in the Colony 1788-1860

ix. The Aborigines (pre-British occupation of 1788) were careful custodians of the land who had utilised the land in accordance with tradition and expectations of affinity and as a food source. The aborigines sought to preserve a practice long in existence that did not overdevelop or over use the land or its resources but which produced all the needs of its limited population

x. If there is any worthwhile validity in comparing farming systems between the pre–and post 1788 practices, then they are comparable to the extent that both systems supported, at various times differently, their population. Native grasses vs. improved pastures, and domesticated livestock vs. native livestock. Both yielded sufficient 'value' from the land to support individual needs; both could co-exist but the 'invaders' wanted unrestricted access to the land; their ways were only to 'clear fell' the country, thus transforming the land from its natural cycle to an unnatural cycle of waste of natural resources, removal of underlying 'natural support' system of replenishment, and of over-utilising the natural burden of the land.

xi. Post-1788, and until 1802, economic growth was limited to subsistence farming, and a settling in system, whereby the more intellectual civil servants and colonists took time to understand the land, its abilities and limitations. This prefacing to development was essential in order to lay the foundation for a longer-term successful future. Then, as now, there were two types of thinking and planning–rush ahead and do whatever it takes to succeed in the short-term, or move cautiously with intent and some knowledge to succeed long-term. The governors mostly were of the latter mindset but were equally aware of the limitations imposed on the colony by irregular supplies of food arriving from the 'home country' and the growing quantities needed, as well as the directions made by the British Colonial Office to be self-sufficient, self-supportive and live within a shrinking budget. The most outstanding example of this 'conflict' was the livestock brought with the first fleet, was left untouched even though the colony was starving. On the other hand, the conflict with the aboriginals resulted in a failure to utilise the native wildlife or the sea-life adequately or appropriately as a transition arrangement and evidence of planned co-existence. This first period was like 'treading water' rather than making progress.

xii. The second period (1802-1821) was a period of consolidation, planning and moving ahead at great speed. Although the last of the naval governors–King and Bligh–were pre-occupied with internal conflict and curbing civil unrest, the period was unrestrained in terms of individuals pursuing self-interest–not in an entrepreneurial way, but as a means of doing 'for ourselves' what the administration should be doing. This was a period of transition when the systems were being developed and being 'bedded in'. It was a period of learning, of exploring, of making 'ends meet' with limited resources, great ingenuity and more than a modicum of luck. The economic growth was reflected in the survival of the people; the ill-treatment of the native peoples;

the spread of settlement and the resulting open plains and broad acres which unshackled the limitations on grain production and livestock grazing previously experienced; the transformation of the economy from the 'barter' economy pre-Macquarie to an economy with a monetary system; the transformation of the economy from a mindset of 'penal colony' to that of a colony with a future; the organised and structured building and construction boom. The period came to an end with the 'reflections' of a bureaucrat (John Thomas Bigge), who became a tool of the influential and a pawn of the blinkered few who could not see a future for the colony. The greatest gains during this period came from the unlikeliest of sources–the development of a road system, the intelligent harnessing of convict labour, but the greatest gain of all came from the imposition, collection and utilisation of the colony's discretionary revenues. These revenues collected from a 'tax' or duty imposed on imports, gave the governors access to discretionary expenditures which otherwise would not have been funded. Subtle improvements in the quality of life, which the British Government would not have supported. The Colonial Office in London drew on the policy of people in the colony not having a standard of living higher, whilst in the colony, than they would have enjoyed at 'home' and certainly not the convicts. It was this local revenue, for many years outside the influence of Whitehall, which made the difference to the people in the colony. Macquarie refined the collection of these revenues and people could physically see the change in the colony, and their spirits rose accordingly and there was less unhappiness, more positive thinking and expression and an overall more productive economy with greater growth and positive movement.

xiii. The third period was short 1821-1827. It was as if the Bigge Report, based on his assessment between 1819 and 1822, but his findings were not published until 1823, placed a yoke around the neck of the collective colony and struggled to restrain the urge to move ahead, whilst going through a radical restructure of the way ahead. A different type of governor was installed and they were made very aware of the 'new' post Bigge approach to developing the colony–more convicts would arrive; expenditure for their support would be minimised, and local revenues would be used to run the colony on a daily basis. Both Brisbane and Darling acted responsibility, advanced the political changes for the local administration with its advisory bodies, and encouraged an open, free and 'creative' colony–entrepreneurs were welcome, but then so were speculators, and that was what brought this period to a close–a depression of 1827.

xiv. The fourth period was longer, 1827-1842, with growth of manufactures and the primary industries (led by wool) growing at an equally fast rate. The pastoral /wool industry brought most of the capital, created most of the export trade and showed the greatest capital creation and returns on capital. The manufacturing industries attracted the free settlers and provided an employment base for the growing army of emancipists. Its greatest benefit lay not in its meagre exports, but in its successful import replacement. This period witnessed large population growth, large livestock numbers, large quantities of exports (always matched by continuing import needs) and growing wealth creation. As with the third period, it closed with a major depression, man-made, with imported downturns from Britain, withdrawal of speculators and then investors, a slowing of migrants arriving

xv. The fifth period was 1842-1850. If my assumption is valid that 'periods' were defined not by people, such as the arrival of a new governor, but by events, then there is a natural period break in 1850. The discovery of gold, the rebalancing of export composition from wool and grain to gold, and the dramatic surge in local revenues led to marvellous change in the colonial economy. A migrant inflow, previously unspeculated upon by Governors, was the first step, and the second was the spectacular benefits of the coming of rail.

xvi. The sixth period was 1851-1856. This period was defined by political instability leading up to independence and the fight between the British Treasury that could see the burgeoning local revenues, worth protecting and fighting for, and the local Legislative Council, that could sense independence through self-government coupled with the growing local revenues which could be otherwise lost to the colony, if self-government without conditions was not achieved.

CHAPTER 13

EXPLAINING THE COLONIAL ECONOMIC DRIVERS 1788-1856

In order to understand the growth of the colonial economy, we must understand the economic drivers that underpinned, sustained and supported the colonial economy. There are at least six, if not seven, such economic drivers. They include the factors of (a) population growth, the (b) economic development within the colony, the (c) funding sources such as British Treasury appropriations and the (d) revenues raised from within the local economy (for example, taxes and duties on imports) and (e) foreign investment (both public and private). The traditional concept of growth within the colonial economy comes from (f) the rise of the pastoral industry. A seventh driver would be the all-important Land Board, which played such an important role within the colonial economy The Land Board played an important role in co-ordinating crown land policy, controlling land sales, squatting licenses and speculators, re-setting boundaries of location, establishing set aside lands for future townships and for church and school estates, carrying out the survey of millions of acres of land transferred by grant and sale, and offering terms sales for crown lands and being responsible for the collection of repayments, rents, license fees, quit-rents and depasturing fees. In addition the land board was vested with road reserves for hundreds of miles of unmade roads but important rights-of-way that would well into the future protect access to remote pastoral and farming properties. The main thrust of published material about the Land Board is in conjunction with crown land sales policy, but the Board had a much larger role and the overall Board policies sand performances are what are to be reviewed here.

Although an important factor it is no more important that our other five motivators of the colonial economy between 1802 and 1856. Why have I selected these two specific dates? 1802 was when Governor King first imposed an illegal, but justified and well-intentioned impost on the local free community to build a local gaol to replace one burnt to the ground through a lightning strike but which the British would not replace. The local residents thought a more solid and durable prison was a worthwhile community investment. At the other end, the year of 1856 signalled the first real representative and responsible government in the colony, and although it was not the end of the colonial era, it was certainly the end of Britain's financial support of sand for the colony and as such the colony was expected to stand on its own two feet.

These six factors will be discussed as mechanisms for 'growing the colonial economy between 1802 and 1856'

One consideration that must not be forgotten is the externally enforced pace of colonial expansion, particularly through the organised rather than the market-induced inflow of both convicts and assisted migrants. What this means is that instead of market forces requiring additional labour and human resources, extra labour and resources were imposed on the colony and there was an obligatory process of putting these people to work, in many cases by creating a public works program and pushing development ahead at an artificial pace rather than at a time and rate suited to the local economy. In much the same way, the 'assignment' system in the 1810-1830 period forced landowners to create clearing and development programs in order to utilise the labour available rather than only develop land as demand required.

1. Population growth including immigration of convicts & free settlers

The reason the colonial society did not change very much in the 1820s is that relatively few immigrants arrived. During 1823, Lord Bathurst,

Colonial Secretary, sent instructions to Governor Brisbane (Macquarie's successor) altering the administration of the colony of NSW in most of the ways Commissioner Bigge had recommended in his reports.[210] One result of the Bigge Reports was that Macquarie was officially recalled to Britain even though he had canvassed his retirement before Bigge's arrival in 1819. Macquarie was distressed by the Bigge Reports and took very personally the recommendations made for change. Although there were many implied criticisms Macquarie considered that the public perception was that he had not acted properly in his role as Governor. Macquarie set to and compared the circumstances of the colony at the time of his arrival in 1810, with the great achievements he had made through 1821. In hindsight, Macquarie had accomplished much, mostly by means of arrogantly pursuing a series of policies without the pre-approval of the Secretary or the Government in London.

The arrival of only a few immigrants was because Bigge and the Colonial Office believed that only men of capital would emigrate. Labourers and the poor of England should not be encouraged and, as these people rarely had money to pay for the long passage to Sydney, few of them arrived.[211] Although the numbers were small, few of them came unassisted. In 1821 320 free immigrants arrived and this increased each year; 903 in 1826; 1005 in 1829, but slipping to 772 in 1830. Mostly they were family groups with some financial security.

In 1828, the first census (as opposed to musters) of white persons in NSW was taken. 20,930 persons were classified as free and 15,668 were classified as convicts. However, of the free persons, many had arrived as convicts or were born of convicts. In fact, 70% of the population in 1828 had convict

---

210 Commissioner J.T. Bigge had been sent by Bathurst to Enquire into the State and Operations of the colony of NSW in 1819; the House of Commons had demanded an inquiry into the colony and had threatened to hold one of its own; Bathurst pre-empted a difficult government situation by appointing Bigge with a very broad and wide-ranging terms of Enquiry. Bigge held two years of investigations in the colony and reported to the Commons in 1823 with the printing of three Reports.

211 Australian History–The occupation of a Continent *Bessant* (Ed)

associations. However, by 1828, one quarter of the NSW population was native born; 3,500 were over 12 years of age

There was another side to this migration of unregulated souls. Shaw writes" The cost of assistance, the unsuitability of many emigrants, their ill-health, and the numbers of children and paupers that were sent–all these gave the colonists a source of grievance".[212] A large part of the problem was that the English wanted emigration–but those they wished to see emigrate were not welcomed in the colony. A growing opinion in the colony was that free migrants could not work with convicts; the convicts by themselves were too few and with growing expense; therefore transportation must stop and immigration be encouraged. However, immigrants of a good quality were not those the English wanted to send; its preference was for the paupers and the disruptive in the society. To stop transportation would be "attended with the most serious consequences unless there is previous means taken to ensure the introduction of a full supply of free labour". [213] In the next five years, the number of free immigrants increased so much that transportation could be stopped with little political backlash. Between 1835 and 1840, the colony was quite prosperous (it was a case of boom and bust–the great depression came in 1841); sales of crown land were large, and consequently the funds available for assisting immigrants were plentiful.[214]

In 1838, land revenue was over £150,000 and assisted migrants numbered 7,400; in 1839, land revenue was £200,000 and assisted migrants 10,000; in 1840 revenue was over £500,000 and assisted migrants 22,500.

---

212 Shaw, A.G.L. *The economic development of Australia* p.44

213 HRA Bourke to Colonial Secretary *Governor's despatches* 1835

214 The British Treasury had agreed to put 50% of land sale proceeds into assisting immigrants with shipping costs; a further 15% into assisting Aborigines' and the balance was for discretionary use by the crown. These percentages changed in 1840 when all sale proceeds were spent on immigration but the land fund still ran out of funds in 1842 and no further assistance was made to immigrants other than by the colonial government borrowing funds in the London market through its own credit.

Between 1832 and 1842, over 50,000 assisted and 15,000 unassisted migrants arrived in NSW; or they might have arrived as convicts, and over 3,000 arrived that way each year. Thus between 1830 and 1840 the population of the whole of Australia increased from 70,000 to 190,000, with 130,000 of those in 1840 being in NSW. Of these 87000 were men and 43000 were women; 30,000 had been born in the colony; 50,000 were free settlers, 20,000 were emancipists and 30,000 were convicts.[215]

2. Foreign Private Investment

We need to make the distinction between foreign public investment, and foreign private investment. The British Treasury appropriated specific funds for infrastructure programs in the colony, such as public buildings, churches, gaols, roads etc.

One reason that local colonial taxes and duties were imposed on the colony was to give the governor the funding source for discretionary expenditures in order to improve his administration. There were many instances of expenditures which could not be covered by the British funds, such as a bounty to recapture runaway convicts, building fences around the cemeteries and whitewashing the walls of public buildings (for instance barracks) in the settlement. The British Treasury would have considered such items of expense as being unnecessary. Road repair and maintenance was intended to be covered from toll receipts but they were never sufficient to make necessary repairs. Governors Hunter and Bligh did little to improve public and community buildings, roads and bridges and by the time Macquarie arrived in the colony in 1810, there was a major backlog of building work and maintenance to be undertaken. Macquarie expanded the local revenue tax base in order to give himself more flexibility in pursuing improved conditions for the settlers and the population at large.

Although Macquarie did not specifically seek new free immigrants for the colony, word of mouth circulated that the colony was in a growth stage and worthy of being considered for either immigration or investment. Usually

215 Shaw *ibid*

one accompanied the other. The first private investment came with the immigrants. Free settlers would either cash up in England or transfer their possessions to the colony, and this small level of private investment was the start of a major item of capital transfers to the colony.

However, private capital formation took many forms; the early settlers, bought or built houses, they built or bought furnishings; they had carriages and often employed water conservation.

As the system of land grants was expanded and farming was encouraged the spread of settlement required a combination of public and private investment.

The government had to provide roads and townships, and the settlers had to provide pastoral investment. This pastoral capital formation consisted of five main types of assets:

Buildings–residence, outbuildings, wool shed or grain storage
Fences–stockyards, posts and rails
Water conservation–dams, tanks, wells
Plant–cultivators, tools
Stocks–food, clothing, household items, materials for animal care and general repairs–livestock

Stephen Roberts offers an interesting insight into the colony of 1835.[216]

"It did not need much prescience to foresee the whole of the country united by settlement–so much had it outgrown the coastal stage of Sydney town. It was a new Australia–a land of free settlement and progressive occupation–that was there, and the old convict days were ending.

Both human and monetary capital were pouring into the various colonies and transforming the nature of their population and problems. Convicts no longer set the tone; even autocratic governors belonged to a day that was passing, and instead, the country was in the grip of a strangely buoyant, and equally optimistic, race of free men".

---

216 Roberts, S.H *The Squatting Age in Australia 1835-1847 (published 1935)*

As part of our private capital formation, we must remember the growth of human capital and the needs for specific labour. Capital requires labour with a specific role. The establishment and expansion of farming meant more than shepherding and ploughing. There was a considerable demand for building skills, for construction and maintenance of equipment such as drays and carts, harness making and repair, tool-making etc. It became important, in order to support and sustain capital growth and economic development to be able to employ labour with multi-skills. This was a new phenomenon for the colony, especially since Britain did not develop these types of broad skills and self-motivation in its criminal class. The Rev. J.D. Lang sought a temporary answer by specifically recruiting 'mechanics' in Scotland as immigrant for the colony.

3. British Public Funding transfers

Public Capital formation is obviously different to private capital formation. I have given an example of rural-based private capital formation elsewhere in this study and will do so again here, in order to demonstrate both types of capital investment.

Private capital formation took many forms; the early settlers, bought or built houses, they built or bought furnishings; they had carriages and often employed water conservation techniques, which included tanks or earthen dams.

As the system of land grants was expanded and farming was encouraged the spread of settlement required a combination of public and private investment.

The government had to provide roads and townships, and the settlers had to provide pastoral investment. This pastoral (rural-based) capital formation usually consisted of five main types of assets:

Buildings–residence, outbuildings, wool shed or grain storage
Fences–stockyards, posts and rails
Water conservation–dams, tanks, wells
Plant–cultivators, tools

Stocks–food, clothing, household items, materials for animal care and general repairs–livestock

Public capital on the other hand was a socio-economic based government asset, and included:

Roads, bridges, crossings, drainage, excavation and embanking, retaining walls

Hospital, storehouses, military barracks, convict barracks, Court-house, police posts, government office buildings

Market house, burial ground, Church, tollhouse, military magazines.

Obviously the list can go on and on.

MAJOR PUBLIC WORKS IN NSW 1817-1821

Roads
Sydney to Botany Bay
Sydney to South Head
Parramatta to Richmond
Liverpool to Bringelly, the Nepean and Appin
Buildings
Sydney
A military hospital; military barracks; convict barracks; carters barracks; Hyde Park
Toll-house; residences for the Supreme Court Judge, the Chaplain and the
Superintendent of Police; an asylum; a fort and powder magazines; stables for
Government House; a market house; a market wharf; a burial ground; St. James
Church
Parramatta
All Saint's church spire; a hospital; a parsonage; military and convict barracks; a
Factory; stables and coach-house at Government House; a reservoir
Windsor
St. Matthew's Church; military barracks; convict barracks
Liverpool
St. Luke's church; a gaol; a wharf; convict barracks

4. Economic Development

K. Dallas in an article on *Transportation and Colonial Income* writes, "The history of economic development in Australia is concerned with the transplanting of British economic life into a unique and novel environment. All colonial societies resemble each other in the problems of transplanting, but only in Australia was there no indigenous communal life vigorous enough to influence the course of future development"[217]

Dallas in the same article declares, "The economic effects of the transportation system are usually misunderstood. The real development of Australia begins with the pastoral industry and the export of wool in the 1820s. Until then, penal settlements were a base for whalers, and made the pastoral possibilities known to English capitalist sheep farmers earlier than they would otherwise have known."[218]

Since this is such a major point on which much disagreement exists, an analysis of its merits is required. No less an authority than N.G. Butlin, J.Ginswick and Pamela Statham disagree, and they record in their introduction to 'The economy before 1850 'the history books are preoccupied with the pastoral expansion in NSW. It is reasonably certain from the musters that a great many complex activities developed and Sydney soon became not merely a port town but a community providing many craft products and services to the expanding settlement".[219]

The next section of this study outlines the remarkable contribution of Governor Macquarie between 1810 and 1821, most of the physical development taking place before the arrival of Commissioner J.T. Bigge in 1819. The table of infrastructure and public building development below confirms that the greatest period of economic development in the colonial economy took place under the Macquarie Administration and did not wait until the spread of settlement and the rise in the pastoral industry (which brought with it so many economic problems) in the late 1820s and 1830s.

---

217 Dallas, Keith *Transportation & Colonial Income* Historical Studies ANZ Vol 3 October 1944-February 1949

218 Dallas *ibid*

219 The Australians: Statistics Chapter 7 'The economy before 1850'

CHAPTER 14

ECONOMIC GROWTH DURING THE MACQUARIE ADMINISTRATION

Governor Macquarie arrived in the colony in December 1809 and commenced his administration on 1st January 1810

In 1812 a select committee of the House of Commons was appointed to enquire into the colony of NSW. The circumstances related mainly to the disposition of former Governor Bligh and the many complaints received in England regarding the hardships caused by the monopoly of the favoured class".[13] A new Charter of Justice was conferred on the colony as a result of the committee report in 1813[14]. The Governor's Court was a 'modification of the previously existing tribunal'[15]. The Supreme Court was to consist of a judge, appointed by the Governor–the first Judge Jeffrey Hart Bent arrived in July 1814 but following a dispute with Governor Macquarie, Bent was recalled by Earl Bathurst and replaced by Mr. Barron Field, an English Barrister who arrived in 1817.

Macquarie oversaw a period of agricultural expansion and a series of explorations in order to open up new grazing areas in the inland

In 1813, the first crossing of the Blue Mountains took place and the Bathurst Plains were discovered. This search for new, more fertile land was made necessary because of the repeated droughts and the unsuitability of the coastal plains for agriculture or pastoral purposes. The three explorers

Wentworth, Blaxland and Lawson "affected a passage across a chain of mountains clothed with dense timber and brushwood, and intersected by a succession of ravines, which presented extraordinary difficulties–not so much from their height as from their precipitous character".[16] Within fifteen months from the discovery, Governor Macquarie ('with characteristic promptitude'[17]) caused a road to be made; sand many new settlers quickly transferred their flocks and herds to the newly discovered country.

In 1817, Captain P.P. King (son of former governor King) sailed from Sydney to survey the east coast to Cape York. In the same year Surveyor-general John Oxley explored the Lachlan River following it for more than 400 miles. During his return he came across an extensive and fine pastoral country, which he named Wellington Plains and he finally reached the Macquarie River. The following year Oxley traced the Macquarie River and reached the Liverpool Plains and discovered the Hastings and Manning Rivers.

In 1818 Hume discovered the pastoral district of the Monaro of which Goulburn is now the centre. In the following year Hume traced the Murrumbidgee River, and the Riverina district.

With these discoveries, the known area of the colony grew by twenty times its former extent, and "the new sources of wealth, of incalculable amount, were thrown open to the industry and enterprise of its inhabitants".[18]

With the new agricultural lands had to come a new agricultural policy and this came in the form of minimum prices for produce purchased by the Commissariat. But the colony was experiencing a new lease of life as was expressed by a correspondent to the *Morning Chronicle*, printed in September 1825. The nom-de-plume of 'Austral-Asiaticus' supposedly belonged to Lt. G.T.W.B. Boyes, who had been appointed during the Macquarie administration to head up the Commissary accounting and audit systems.

The letter was a response to printed criticisms of Macquarie policies, and the incredible deterioration since the resignation of Macquarie and read in part "Under Macquarie's judicious administration, commerce and agriculture flourished, because they received from the Executive Government that fostering protection and encouragement which, in turn, in the infant state of the colony, were indispensable for their growth. The farmer received for his corn, the grazier for his cattle, such a fair equitable price from the Commissariat, for the large purchases made on account of government (namely 10/–per bushel for wheat and seven-pence per pound for beef) as enabled them respectively to support a state of decent mediocrity, suitable to their sphere of life and encouraged increasing industry and perseverance in their pursuits. The merchant was not embarrassed in his commercial speculations by the difficulty of making his remittances, but could, at all times obtain Treasury Bills for that purpose without paying, as at present, a premium of from £15 to £20 per centum for the accommodation. Under the change of system, introduced on the accession of the present governor, an entire and distressing alteration of affairs took place . . ."[19]

However successful Macquarie was with his encouragement of exploration and his agricultural policy, the most remarkable feature of Governor Macquarie's administration was the number of public buildings erected, the total reaching 250. His roads policy almost must also be noted for the benefits it produced.

Commissioner Bigge had been directed by Earl Bathurst to "examine all the laws, regulations and usages of the territory and its dependencies, and into every other matter or thing in any way connected to the administration of the civil government, the state of the judicial, civil, and ecclesiastical establishments, revenue, trade and resources".[20]

Macquarie did little to defend his administration other than writing an extremely long letter to Bathurst which commenced" I found the colony barely emerging from infantile imbecility and suffering from various privations and disabilities; the country was impenetrable beyond 40 miles from Sydney; agriculture was in a languishing state; commerce in its early dawn; revenue unknown; threatened with famine; distracted by faction; the public buildings in a state of dilapidation and mouldering to decay; the population in general depressed by poverty; no public credit nor private confidence; the morals of the great mass of the population in the lowest state of debasement and the religious worship almost totally neglected–Such was the state of the colony when I took charge in 1810. When I left the colony it had reaped incalculable advantage from my extensive and important discoveries. In all directions, including the supposed insurmountable barrier called the Blue Mountains to the westward of which are situated the fertile plains of Bathurst; and in all respects enjoying a state of private comfort and public prosperity"[21]

Colonial revenues and expenditures

Local Colonial Revenues 1810-1820

The summary financial statements[22] show that Macquarie used a significant proportion of local revenues for road making and maintenance and public building construction and their maintenance. Although there was a 'tacit' agreement between Bathurst and Macquarie that the British government would fund military and the main church buildings, the colonial revenue would be used for infrastructure and most 'public' use buildings

The point being made here is that although the British Treasury was burdened with nearly £100,000 of colonial expenditure per annum[23], the local community, by having to pay higher prices for its imports was carrying about 50% of the British expenditures which include much that rightly should have been paid by the home government. In addition to British ownership of the public buildings, colonial government departments and divisions were paying 'rent' for the use of those buildings. The local commissary was paying £200 per annum rent for the use of the 'bonded' store–a building that cost only three times that when it was built in 1818 by convict labour and local materials. A loan by the Colonial Fund to the Commissary account of £19,000 is never shown as being repaid, so the British government was being directly subsidised by the people of Sydney Town.

It was left to Brisbane (Macquarie's successor) to recommend construction only through the tender process. It had been Macquarie's submission to Bathurst that the tender process would be expensive to the colony and add unnecessary costs to buildings. As Lithgow was to later recommend that no building under an outlay of £200 should need any British approval, thus obviating the time-consuming preparation of plans, estimates and waiting 18 months for project approval. (HRA 1:11:386)

The Report of Major Ovens and William Lithgow[24] in reform of convict work organisation offers a principled insight into the obligation of convicts to work for the government and the various trade's roles entered into by convicts. A sub-enclosure to the report lays out the expenditures on maintaining convicts, being £12.8s 2d on rations per annum, plus an amount of £7.8s3d for 'indulgences' to convicts, offset by 'contra' of the value of 'production' or output per convict. Ovens concludes that convicts 'pay their way' provided they are made to work and be productive. Thus if each convict were only paid 3/–per day, the cost would be £46.16s 0d per annum. Against this is the cost of £20 for their maintenance, justifying the loss of 50% productivity that Oven's envisages by convicts not committed to their work.

A wide range of Macquarie era statistics is available to demonstrate economic growth during the period 1810-1821

Macquarie encouraged exploration in a practical way, by using government funds and government stores to support a practical program of exploration. By 1815, cattle were being moved across the Nepean, Bathurst was a settlement, grain and vegetables were being grown on the Bathurst Plains, Blaxland, Lawson and Wentworth were enjoying the governor's plaudits while each were receiving a thousand acres of land, but only Lawson chose to have his land across the ranges. The road to Bathurst of 191 miles in length was completed and travellers were using it daily, together with bushrangers, and aboriginals. The Lachlan River and the Liverpool Plains region were being opened up and Oxley was exploring north to Morton Bay. Even Bathurst was amazed when he heard of the discovery of the Macquarie River–he did not expect 'after the fruitless attempt by Captain Flinders to discover any considerable river, to expect that such a river as the Macquarie would be found in the interior of the continent flowing so far westward'. Bathurst ordered further exploration along the stream to verify if 'a few hundred miles beyond the penetration of the continent, the Lachlan and Macquarie Rivers ran into the western sea'.

Macquarie took to heart the need for town planning, improved roads and a better image for the still young colony. New roads, even before the major 191-mile road over the Mountains to Bathurst, were being built by soldier labour to South Head and the colony's first turnpike to Green Hills on the Hawkesbury had reached Parramatta. The two bridges in Sydney had been widened at the cost of much good liquor currency. Everywhere were to be seen the evidence of the Macquarie ability to contribute to the 'ornament and regularity of the town of Sydney, as well as to the convenience and safety of the inhabitants thereof'[220]; these monuments included the new stone wharf at Sydney Cove, the improved wastes of Brickfield Hill, the completion of Macquarie Place and the houses of Sydney not to be built unless approved by the governor; they were not to encroach on the street, less they be forced to move back into line. Each house was to be numbered at the cost of 6d to the owner. Neat frontal palings of 4 feet high must guard all dwellings; wood must not be cut in the public parks, and shirts were no longer to be washed in the Tank Stream.

Macquarie needed to convince the majority of settlers in both the towns and the rural areas of the need for 'ornamental' improvement in the colony. These were the poor, uneducated people, many emancipists and ticket of leave people, married or de facto with children to protect and look after. Already under previous administrations, differences of opinions between

---

220 The Australians: Statistics Chapter 7 'The economy before 1850'

Year	Beckett's figures	Ginswick figures
1810	6489	3272
1811	11359	10939
1812	11347	13494
1813	23109	14621
1814	8378	13325
1815	16544	17994
1816	18076	17782
1817	23709	24706
1818	28996	31006
1819	38684	40844
1820	40389	42968
1821	45338	44507
Total	**272418**	**275460**

HRA 1:7:427 Macquarie to Bathurst

these people and the propertied segment had developed, and the local newspapers even with their small circulation were quite influential and persuasive not only of government but have public opinion as well.

Summary Revenue of the Police Fund 1810-1821[221]

James Thomson writes,[222] "The imposition of customs duties and other taxes in support of the public revenue was left entirely to the discretion of the governor of the colony. Tariff and duty rates set by Brisbane remained in force until new rates (slightly increased) were proclaimed by Governor Darling on 16th October 1828.

In the tears between 1824 and 1840(16 years), the customs revenue had increased at the rate of 578%. In 1824, the population of the colony was

---

221 The Police Fund first commenced in 1802, under the name the Gaol Fund. Governor King intended to replace the original Sydney Town Gaol constructed of woods but which burnt in 1801 with a new gaol, built with British Government funds; the British Treasury declined to approve the funding so the governor sought voluntary community funding to finance the building but this appeal fell short so he used Treasury funding with the understanding it would be replaced by local revenues. He imposed a duty on spirits and liquor coming into the colony, until Macquarie decided in 1810 to use this source as discretionary revenue to supplement the funding for his building program. The revenue growth within the colony was embarrassing to Macquarie's predecessors and King decided to introduce an Orphan Fund and share the revenue, initially 3:1 but then changed the role of each fund and shared the revenue 7/8ths to 1/8th. The Police fund paid for road repairs, fencing, and wood for heating public buildings, building repairs and often civil salaries, when other funds were not available. The quarterly results for both funds were published in the *Sydney Gazette,* after 'auditing by the Lt-governor. Darcy Wentworth was treasurer of the Police Fund and Samuel Marsden was Treasurer of the Orphan Fund, whose monies were used for building the Female Orphanage in Parramatta and sponsoring schools and teachers in the colony.

222 *Financial Statements by the Treasurers of NSW 1855-1881* with explanatory notes by James Thomson p.490

32,702 and customs revenue was 17s 7d per head. In 1840, population was 129,463 and duty was at £1.10.11/2d per head. By 1875, writes Thomson, with population at 606,652, customs revenue per head was still at only £1.12.11/2d per head.

CUSTOMS REVENUES RECEIVED IN NSW 1824-1841

Year	Amount–£	Year	Amount–£
1824	28763	1833	108466
1825	48437	1834	124501
1826	47733	1835	140424
1827	49472	1836	153682
1828	65116	1837	163286
1829	74731	1838	145330
1830	78657	1839	158232
1831	87803	1840	195080
1832	93864	1841	223845
		1842	215253
		1843	164929

CHAPTER 15

THE GROWTH OF THE PASTORAL INDUSTRY

An important step in growing the pastoral industry was taken by Governor Darling in 1827, when he began issuing grazing licenses to pastoralists. After a brief experiment, the terms were fixed in 1828; the Land Board charged an annual rent of 2/6 per hundred acres, with liability to quit on one month's notice.

Shaw claims "from this small beginning grew the squatting movement and the great pastoral expansion and thus the policy of the early colonial governors that the colony would be a country of farmers was definitely abandoned.

Events before the squatting policy helped the governor make his decision.

The Blue Mountains had been crossed in 1813; Macquarie had opened the settlement in Bathurst and built a road over the mountains linking Sydney, Parramatta and Bathurst; In 1825 the Australian Agricultural Company was given a grant of land by way of a Royal Charter, and in exchange for one million pound of capital, received one million acres and a large number of convicts. The initial selection took much of the rural acres around Port Stephens area on the east coast of NSW, but it was not long before the company exchanged this land for more fertile lands but a similar quantity on the Liverpool Plains, away from the coastal plains, although the company kept 2,000 acres of coal bearing land in the Newcastle area.

Governor Darling, probably unwittingly took British Government transportation policy full circle when, in 1827 he received a message from Lord Bathurst, with a reminder of the background to the transportation program implemented.

In the early days of the colony, there were lots of convicts, free labour, but little work for them and many costs associated with their maintenance. The governors had demanded settlers with capital to employ the labour and develop the land. It was then proposed to limit land grants in proportion to the means (the capital) of the settlers. The colony received settlers, some with capital but many without. Those without had been kept largely off the land in the selection process. When the governor shall be satisfied of the character and respectability of the applicant, and the amount of capital he can command, and intends to immediately apply for agricultural purposes, has been duly ascertained, he will receive the necessary authority to select a grant of land proportionate in extent to the means e possesses".[223]

The system of grants laid down by Brisbane was that every grantee was bound to receive and maintain 1 convict for every 100 acres of land or every 40 acres of cultivated land. Because of this policy, there was a great demand for convicts and 'so much competition exists amongst the settlers to obtain convict labour that it is no longer necessary to hold out any premium to ensure convicts were assigned and taken off the hands of the colonial government'.[224]

So settlers had been demanded to use the convict labour, land was granted with the use of convicts but in 1827, the colony had run out of convicts to assign and there was no apparent need for more settlers, being enticed by a land grant. Thus, there was to be a return to the policy of immigrant workers who would be the poor and the social outcastes of Britain, who

---

223 HRA 1:14:376 Darling to Under-Secretary Hay on 'terms upon which land is granted to settlers in NSW

224 HRA 1:13:221

usually had no capital to bring with them. The new policy declared the *Sydney Gazette* was to be; Land is reserved for capitalists but the capital thee settlement needed was 'capital in labour' to feed the need for more labour that accompanied the transfer of capital assets.

THE LAND BOARD

As an economic driver of the colonial economy, the Land Board played an important role in co-ordinating crown land policy, controlling land sales, squatting licenses and speculators, re-setting boundaries of location, establishing set aside lands for future townships and for church and school estates, carrying out the survey of millions of acres of land transferred by grant and sale, and offering terms sales for crown lands and being responsible for the collection of repayments, rents, license fees, quit-rents and depasturing fees. In addition the land board was vested with road reserves for hundreds of miles of unmade roads but important rights-of-way that would well into the future protect access to remote pastoral and farming properties. The main thrust of published material about the Land Board is in conjunction with crown land sales policy, but the Board had a much larger role and the overall Board policies and performances are what are to be reviewed here.

The main economic drivers supported by the Land board, would include generating land sales and manipulating the use of the land sales revenues for direct economic gain through a successful migration program; the opening up of new counties parishes and townships, led directly to the successful pastoral industry revolution in the colony; and the surveying and funding of public roads developed the communication and transportation infrastructure to support and sustain rural growth;

Background

Coghlan[225] records that "the first regulations dealing with crown land sales were published in 1823 but it took some time before a plan could be

[225] Coghlan, T.A. *Labour & Industry in Australia 1917* Vol 1 p.232

developed that would achieve a fair price for land suitable for encouraging settlement and not interfering with the assignment of convicts. This regulation notified the settlers "it was intended that persons who wished to purchase land would be permitted to do so, after receiving the governor's assent to their written application, but no individual was allowed to purchase more than 4,000 acres, nor any family more than 5,000 acres. The usual price was 5s per acre, but land in the Sydney Region (County of Cumberland), the price was fixed by Lord Bathurst at 7/6 to 10/–per acre.

In 1824, the Colonial Office, viewing the need for a complete change in the law, indicated that Commissioners would be appointed to divide the colony into counties, and parishes, and make a valuation of all the land in the territory with the view to fixing an average price at which all disposable land would be sold. Matters moved quickly from this point.

Commissioners were appointed in January 1826, and in September 1826, the (now called) Land Commissioners placed values on available lands in certain districts. These lands were then put up for sale and it was open to anyone to apply by sealed tender for those lands with the minimum (government) price to be recognised by buyers. This tender system did not last long, and did not provide many land sales, and so in September 1828, public auctions were introduced. All sales were to be published for two months beforehand but no one was admitted that did not have the Governor's permission to bid.

Neither system was successful and very little land was sold in this way. In NSW, only 13,672 acres were sold between 1823 and 1831. The second problem was that 'payment was evaded for much of the land that was purchased', due to administrative failures.[226]

The regulations drawn up for the sale of crown land were not only aimed at setting a fair price for the sale of the land, and the qualifications of the buyer, but also of promoting the cultivation of the soil. Until 1831, none of these objectives was attained. The regulations provided that 'grants should be only given to persons who possessed capital available for the cultivation

226 Coghlan *ibid* p.233

of the land granted, equivalent to half its value. Enquiry was made of each applicant, and reviewed by a board of officials (the Land Board). However, what constituted capital and how should it be valued? Material, plant and stock, as well as money, would constitute capital for the purposes of the grant but placing a value on it was found to be difficult by the Board. Resumption after seven years was imposed, if certain development had not taken place in the interim.

Edward Gibbon Wakefield appeared on the scene and proposed a whole series of changes to the system including displays of surveyed land maps, a 10% deposit and some guarantees of future development with penalties for failure to deliver.

One explanation for the low number of acres sold in the colony is that the large number of land grants had diminished the demand for land purchases–the demand for land had been fairly well satisfied by the grants already made. A second explanation is that the colonial government was unprepared for the demands of mapping and surveying that was required for the sales program. A third explanation is the reluctance of the buying public to accept the system of sale by auction for cash as a final settlement of the government crown land sales program.

In 1832 and 1833, the land disposed of was quite small in acres sold, but from 1834, a significant movement (sales picked up rapidly) occurred, which was to deliver great difficulties to the colony and its government.

LAND SALES IN NSW 1832-1840[227] (IN ACRES)

Year	Grants	Sales	**Year**	Grants	Sales
1832	15	20860	**1837**	200298	370376
1833	70117	29025	**1838**	179929	316160
1834	84408	91399	**1839**	310250	272619
1835	160137	271947	**1840**	225742	189787
1836	47633	389546	**1841**	101726	203884

[227] Ginswick *Manuscript* (as quoted by N.G. Butlin in *Forming a Colonial Economy)*

These tables show that whilst land sales were raising revenue for the Crown, the governor was issuing large grants without a capital charge, but with the land carrying an annual quit-rent.

Town lands were of a very different nature. Until 1829, the usual dealing with town lots was by lease, although Macquarie had made a few grants of town lands in fee simple. The usual lease rates were 1d and 2d per rod in country townships.[228]

When quit rents were abolished in 1831, the town lots were priced for sale at between £2 and £20 per acre, with most parts of Sydney being priced at £50 per acre. Coghlan reports that prime sites in George Street, Sydney sold at £18,150 per acre (Cnr. George & Bridge Street in 1834) and £27,928 per acre (Cnr. George & King Street in 1835)

The Government took another significant step in October 1829, when it proclaimed 'the limits of location'–the government was setting outside boundaries for the colony–a person may go outside these limits but not purchase lands or grazing rights thereto, to the exclusion of anyone else. It would not be until 1836 that the squatter's rights would be recognised on land outside the limits of location of the nineteen counties–in 1836, the first licenses were issued 'to depasture the vacant crown lands beyond the limits of location'.

The future Land Board was confronted with a huge backlog of surveying and mapping works–From 1788 to 1823 the amount of land grants in the colony was 520,077 acres; from 1823 to 1831 the area of land granted and sold was 3,557,321 acres; but in this last figure is included the grant to the Australian Agricultural Company in 1825 of 1,048,960 acres and various lands reserved by Governor Brisbane for church and school purposes, amounting to 454,050 acres; from 1831 to 1838 sales amounted to 1,450,508 acres, so that in total the Crown had parted with 5,981,956 acres all within the boundaries of location. The original mapping of the nineteen counties included 24,669,000 acres much of which was mountainous and unusable.

---

228 Coghlan *ibid* p.241

Development of farmland, under Brisbane and Darling, in NSW was slow. When Macquarie departed from the colony, in 1822, he was proud to advise Bathurst that 32,000 acres were cleared and cultivated. However, 12 years later, even though a further 3,500,000 acres had passed into private hands, the amount of cultivated acres was still showing at only 60,000[229].

The *Votes & Proceedings* of the NSW Legislative Council for 1833, records that in July the Governor (Richard Bourke) presented a Bill to regulate the affairs of the Church & Schools Land Corporation. The Bill passed all stages and transferred ownership of all lands previously belonging to the corporation to the Crown, through an agent with specific, but limited, powers to deal with these lands.[230]

No final resolution to the legality of either this transfer (or the original transfer to the corporation) was made until The *Imperial Land Sales Act of 1842* (5 & 6 Vic, c.36-1842) was passed, and in which statute was "reserved to the Crown the power of disposing of all waste lands for any purpose 'of public safety, convenience, health and enjoyment'.[231] Two other local acts assisted in clarifying the Crown Lands debacle–The Crown Lands Alienation Act and The Crown Lands Occupation Act, both passed in 1861, and which permitted anyone, of any age or sex to select between 40 and 320 acres of Crown land anywhere in the colony for £1 per acre, whilst the auction system (with a reserve of £1 per acre) was re-instituted; a terms payment system was authorised, with a deposit of 25% in cash and the balance within 3 years. Nominally, the selector had to live on his land but no policing was undertaken of this requirement. These acts became known as the Robertson Acts after John Robertson, the NSW Minister for Lands.[232]

S.J. Butlin is the only economic historian (other than T.A. Coghlan) that has a word to say about the Land Board activities, but he only records

229 Epitome of Official History of NSW (1887) p.235

230 Epitome of Official History of NSW (1887) p.56

231 Epitome *ibid* p.358

232 Epitome *ibid* p.358

a plan to broaden the economic role of the Board in 1841, which the Governor disallowed.[233]

"It was a member of the NSW Legislative Council[234], who in constructing a plan to extricate NSW from the major slump of 1841-43, recommended that the Land Board be empowered to buy up mortgages in exchange for deferred Land Board notes or certificates, bearing 7% interest. The council passed a Bill incorporating the Holt plan in spite of Sir George Gipps having threatened to withhold Royal assent".[235]

Although this would have been an important step in strengthening the role of the Land Board and of limiting the damaging economic impact of the depression of 1841, Governor, Sir George Gipps refused to support the Bill and it lapsed, and what could have become an important mechanism for alleviating pastoral failures was lost. Obviously Butlin refers to this Holt plan as a means of evidencing the negative role Gipps played in not acting positively to minimise the effect of the depression.

How and Why the Land Board was formed

The first step in the formation of the Land Board was the appointment of Land commissioners in 1823 by Governor Brisbane.[236] The first 1825 despatch from Bathurst to Brisbane was date 1st January 1825 and detailed the problems surrounding the granting and settling of crown wastelands[237]. Bathurst directed that "a general division of the whole territory of NSW be made into Counties, hundreds and Parishes". Bathurst also made the point that this arrangement would be created by an Imperial statute and that the NSW Legislative Council "will not be required to enact any law for the purpose". This reference by Bathurst would have been an unwelcome revelation by the Legislative Council, which had only been formed two years previously and was very protective of its rights and responsibilities.

233 Butlin, S.J. *Foundations of the Australian Monetary System* p.331

234 Thomas Holt

235 HRA 1:23:231 Gipps to Stanley; *Sydney Herald* 6th December 1843

236 HRA 1:11:925-30 Bathurst to Brisbane

237 Bathurst terms them 'waste Lands of the Crown' HRA 1:11:434

It's appointed members had hoped, together with Brisbane, that there would have been more local debate and public discussion on such an important issue–the land issue affected the future of local government, the future direction of the limits of location, and the regulated spread of settlement for the pastoral industry.[238]

Bathurst in the fifth paragraph of his despatch directed that to meet and implement these policy decisions, a Commission should be established and a survey made of the whole colony. [239] Bathurst directed that each county be 40 square miles, so that each county could conveniently be re-ordered into hundreds (a 100 square miles) and parishes (25 square miles). This despatch consists of 30 HRA typed pages and so would have been 200 + of handwritten pages, also included a proposal to establish a corporation for holding church and school lands (to be called estates, suggests the despatch in para.18); also a direction that all lands be valued (the instructions for valuing were that an average be struck for each parish, taking into consideration the topography of the lands and the fertility of the soils-para.15); a statement that all future sales will be settled only using 'ready money' (Para. 16) and instructions for the reservation of lands for public purposes (para.17).

Bathurst set the maximum amount of land for any one purchase at 9,000 acres, and reserved the right to collect a 'quit-rent' at the rate of £5 per cent upon the average value. Such payment could be lump summed at 20 times the annual amount, thus pre-paying 20 years of such rents. As an offset, each convict that was fully maintained (at no expense to the government) would be allowed 32/–per annum.

---

238 In the third Bigge report on Agriculture and Trade, the recommendation was "that the country intended to be settled be laid out and surveyed, and subdivided into farms in suitable sizes for land grants and that each district be no more than 36 square miles. (1823 Report p.49)

239 By 1825, 5 counties had already been established in the colony (Cumberland, Westmoreland, Camden, and Argyle). Bathurst was proposing a further 14 counties as stage 1 and then the rest of the territory as settlement spread from Sydney. (Note 103 p930 HRA 1:11)

Bathurst stresses that the success of the overall plan depended on the survey and valuation being completed as a priority move and within the survey to set aside public lands and future townships. Bathurst attached to the despatch a draft charter of incorporation of the Church and School estates, and a summary of Rules for Emigrants going to New South Wales. It was later challenged in the Supreme Court of NSW as to whether Crown Lands could legally be transferred to a separate corporation and that is why the ratifying legislation was passed in 1842.[240]

The three commissioners appointed in June 1825 were John Oxley, William Cordeaux and J.T. Campbell[241]. Brisbane also advised Bathurst in the despatch that Oxley had declined to accept the £500 per annum emolument offered.[242] Following the appointment of the three Land Commissioners, Bathurst refined his proposal and directed the formation and structure of a Board of Commissioners to be known as the Land Board.

In his despatch dated July 1825, Bathurst recommended to Darling (Brisbane's successor) that in the "exercise of the powers granted to you by your commission and Instructions, for the sale and granting of Waste Lands of the Crown within your government, it will be found convenient

240 This situation is not unlike the taxes and duties imposed on imports to the colony from 1802, and which were shown to be illegal and it took until 1819 for a ratifying statute to be passed by the House of Commons

241 John Oxley was the Surveyor-General and an explorer of note; Cordeaux was a military officer who had accompanied Oxley on some explorations; and accompanied Commissioner J.T. Bigge and Oxley on an inspection trip to Bathurst in 1819. Cordeaux also operated the commissariat store in Liverpool; John Thomas Campbell had been official secretary to Macquarie, helped found the Bank of NSW, and Brisbane recommended he be appointed to the NSW Legislative Council and Darling appointed him Collector of Customs to replace John Piper

242 HRA 1:11:680 (note 199, p.948 confirms the named commissioners) Oxley was not being as generous as may be first thought. He was in receipt of a civil salary as surveyor-general. He also received a percentage of the survey fees which usually amounted to £1,500 per annum extra for Oxley, so declining a £500 honorarium, was quite self-serving and protecting his positions.

to establish a Land Board.[243] for . . . "reviewing applications for grants and from whom you can receive reports on the claims of the different applicants". You are authorised to constitute a Board of this nature to consist of not more than three persons, who must permanently reside in Sydney. Gentlemen engaged in public office, should be given preference. They can be granted remuneration for these services not exceeding £100 per annum. You will lay down guidelines for them, for the despatch of their business. The establishment of the Board should not be made unless it improves Public benefit. As soon as the division of the territory into counties is completed, you will name a commissioner of the peace in each county and they will act as a magistrate".[244]

Darling advised Bathurst on 5th May 1826 that he had formed the Land Board and made suitable appointments.[245]

"The members of the Land board are Colonel Stewart, the Lieutenant-Governor; William Lithgow, Colonial Auditor-General; J.T. Campbell, formerly Secretary to Governor Macquarie"

Darling claimed that it was an opportune moment to establish the board, at a time when new arrangements were being made for the "disposing and granting of land. Stewart is a competent man of business and Lithgow is invaluable from his perfect knowledge of business and information on all points connected with official details".

Darling added, "I should state to your Lordship that the total disorganisation of the departments and indeed every branch of government, when I assumed the administration, encouraged me to form an advisory board–the Board of General Purposes–which gives me advice and recommendations on any particular points which may require investigation".[246] It appeared to be important to Darling that he establishes his Land Board along sound principles lest he be thought of as being a lax administrator.

---

243 HRA 1: 12:21 Bathurst to Darling

244 HRA 1:12:21 Bathurst to Darling

245 HRA 1: 12:266 Darling to Bathurst

246 HRA 1: 12:266 Darling to Bathurst

Another important despatch by Darling to Bathurst dated March 1826, takes 80 pages in the HRA, so it was probably several hundred handwritten pages.[247]

The main contents were government orders relating to 'gratuities' for convicts employed by government[248]; a Report by the Board of General Purposes[249]; a Report by the Land Board and minutes of the Executive Council.

The Land Board reported to the newly arrived Governor Darling on 26th January 1826, providing a background briefing by the Surveyor-General's office that informed the Governor that between 1788 and 1810, successive governors had extended grants to individuals (mainly to convict settlers and averaging less than 100 acres each) amounting to 117,500 acres; and over 12,000 acres had been set aside for use by Churches and schools in Sydney and Parramatta (including the Female Orphan School in Parramatta); that Governor Macquarie, between 1810 and 1821 had granted lands in excess of 400,000 acres, much of which was selected at large (i.e. uncontrolled) and remained unsurveyed at the time of his departure).

John Oxley, as Surveyor-General, had directed the survey of the colony and "divided the territory into Counties, Townships and sections of a square mile, reserving in each township, four square miles or 2,560 acres in the most suitable situations for future villages etc. However, the reservation of land for Church and school estates had not been ordered nor completed at that time. Governor Brisbane, the report confirmed, had

---

247 HRA 1:12:363-444

248 "Gratuities" were to be paid to convicts employed as Overseers, storekeepers, clerks or in any other capacity, at the rate of 1s6d per day or £22/16/3 per annum, plus an allowance for clothing and rations, with each gratuity conditioned upon the good conduct and responsibility of the convict.

249 Darling had established the Board of General Purposes, at no cost to the government, or with any remuneration to the participants in order to advise him on solutions to specific situations. He had surrounded himself with eight advisers, knowledgeable and experienced in a variety of areas, and organised them into various sub-committees to consider a specific problem and report back to Darling with a solution.

made appropriations of over 1,068,000 acres, of which 200,000 acres were to be Crown reserves and 334,000 acres contracted to be sold to individual settlers, with the balance of land being by grants. Oxley revealed that his was a difficult task of surveying properties that were scattered over "an extent of country of nearly 250 miles in length by 140 miles in width".[250]

The Land Board noted in its second report to Darling that the quit rent had been increased from £5 per centum to 15s. Per 100 acres, with the prospect that this increase would stall the sale of crown lands. The report also noted for Darling's information that there were four types of land grants:

i. Lands granted by Macquarie but not yet approved under seal–meaning that they could still be disallowed
ii. Lands granted on condition of permanently maintaining a certain number of convicts
iii. Lands on which a quit rent of 15/–per hundred acres is imposed; and
iv. Purchased lands

Upwards of 1,800,000 acres of land had been appropriated in NSW under any one of the above methods, and these were located in one or more of eight counties and over 80 parishes covering 35,000 square miles–for which the boundaries (of these counties and parishes) were still undefined in 1826.

The reservation in each parish for future roads initially caused concern, as they could not be vested in other than the crown, because the existing statute did not allow those reserves to be vested in any other authority. It was later decided to vest them temporarily in the Land Board, until active roads were developed within these reserves.

The land board proposed to Darling that by following the instructions issued by Bathurst and former governor Brisbane, the probable average price of the 2,000,000 acres of mixed description lands suitable for settlers would be only 3/–per acre. Obviously, this figure had been influenced by

---

[250] Oxley to Darling 1826 HRA 1:12:380

the new increased quit rent of 15s per 100 acres, in order to maintain the quit-rent to value ratio at about a 5% level. However the Board noted that 'if, as directed, the average of the whole parish was to be taken as a value, then the price could not exceed 1s 6d per acre.

This land board report demonstrates that the Secretary of State's office in London had little understanding of the practicalities of life in the colony of NSW and was intent on making policy in an absurd vacuum, including such acts as selecting people for government appointment in London, and setting land prices and regulations in isolation without regard for local conditions or demands. This was further reflected in the disappointing volume of Colonial land sales, where only a cash settlement was allowed at the time of sale and there was insufficient means in the colony to make such settlement. The Board concluded that only the opulent man could make such payment arrangements and this would cause the most valuable property to be purchased by speculators and land jobbers. "These unprofitable occupants (absentee landlords) would be enabled to maintain a decided advantage over the free immigrant settler, who receives his land with interest terms, and then has to pay for the improvements". Such land for free immigrant settlers will be what land did not sell on the open market (so the Land Board advised Darling), so it may not be fertile land and there may not be any means for expansion since most of the sold land is held by speculators and non-residents who will ask any price for their holding.

This second report also drew attention to the enormous task of surveying all crown lands and the shortage of people to carry out the work. This was to be a continuing problem for the Land Board for many years, especially the mechanics of verifying that land sale conditions were being met. For instance, Colonial Secretary (Frederick Goulburn) had issued instructions in November 1823 placing conditions on grants by Governor Brisbane that of each 30 acres granted at least 10 acres would have to be cultivated or buildings, fences or other improvements made (to a value of £50), within five years, or the grant would lapse and revert to the Lands Board. The Lands Department, the commissioners or the Board never verified these conditions, before new regulations were issued in 1827.

The Board recommended to the Governor in late 1826 that town lots in Parramatta, be offered on a leasehold basis rather than remain unsold and undeveloped. At least, stated the Board, the government would be receiving rent as revenue. The Board was quite critical of a government notice informing settlers that they are offered "an additional grant of 100 acres of land for every convict maintained by the settler free of expense of the Crown for one complete year". The Board pointed out that this arrangement was unauthorised and that the original Secretary of State proposal was to be a 'credit' of 32s to be allowed to settlers for every convict employed. The computations show that for each 100 acres at 3/–per acre or £15, and then offering an additional 100 acres of land is equal to almost 10 times what the original allowance would be. The Board also recommended the cancellation of all tickets of occupation (i.e. squatting licenses)

Later in 1826, and in another briefing paper to the new governor, Ralph Darling, the Board stated that the survey work was still very much incomplete from both the days of Macquarie and Brisbane grants; the Board could not set a land price for unappropriated lands and could not establish suitable set aside areas for Church and school establishments. 'Since', they wrote, 'the Board could not carry out the required actions of the Secretary of State, but they appear to be very urgent, we have deemed it necessary to ask your Excellency to decide on a solution with the least possible delay". William Lithgow, J.T. Campbell and William Stewart signed this report for the Land board.[251]

The Land Board in Operation

This section highlights the participation in the Land Board of William Lithgow, the Colonial Auditor-General who had also been appointed a Commissioner of the Land Board. Such appointment was probably a potential conflict of interest situation since Lithgow was a large pastoral landowner, who obtained grazing licenses on large tracts just outside the limits of location, before any survey work had been completed and on

[251] HRA 1:12:413 Land Board Report attached to despatch from Darling to Bathurst, July 1826

the back of exploration by Oxley (a fellow commissioner) and Hamilton Hume (a close friend).

The land board had been created in response to the decision to slow the staggering rate of land grants, and commence the sale of crown lands. It was designed to be an overseeing and monitoring body, with the authority, to enforce the collection of fees and quit-rents associated with grants of crown land.

William Lithgow had been appointed a member of the Board in 1826 by Governor Darling with his expectations that the very large job of surveying crown lands, both granted and sold, would soon become current and continue to meet on-going demands for surveys of new townships, and the large pastoral lands that needed to have boundaries surveyed for identification purposes.

Lithgow as a member of the Land Board officially wrote to Governor Darling on 11th March 1826 concerning the delay in surveying land granted during the past 5 years. The letter recites: "The surveyor-General (John Oxley) states in his report 'that the principal portion of 400,000 acres, granted by the late Governor Macquarie remained unsurveyed at the time of his departure, and that out of 1,068,000 acres appropriated by Governor Sir Thomas Brisbane by grant or sale, or as Crown reserves, the boundary lines of at least half remain unascertained". The letter urged Darling into action to recruit more qualified surveyors from England. The letter also responded to Darling's instructions ordering the division of the country into counties, hundreds and parishes. The Land Board explained that the policy could be implemented only if further manpower was provided.

We can see Lithgow's concerns in a further letter from the Land Board to Darling dated 29th March 1826. The submission recommends that the Surveyor-General's Office was far too busy with boundary identification to be collecting quit rents. Instead, Lithgow and other members of the Board (including J.T. Campbell and William Stewart) recommended that the position of Collector of Land Revenue be located within the office of the Colonial Treasurer.

The Land board was required to handle many disputes, and the report of one such dispute was handed to the Governor on 25th December 1826 along with a stinging rebuke on a flawed policy:

"The board recommends that the governor does not grant further lands to applicants who *do not even intimate any intention ever to become resident in the colony,* which will reduce the great abuse in the future distribution of crown land in the colony" [252] Lithgow also recommended that locals residents not be allowed to act as 'agents' for absentee landlords, especially those who used their influence in England to gain an unfair advantage.

The Land Board remained in existence until the Robertson Acts installed a Board with broader powers in 1858.

The House of Commons passed The Sale of Waste Land Act of 1828, and this statute raised the minimum reserve price of crown land to one pound per acre, except that large acreage of land in remote areas could be sold at a lower price, and it established a formula for the use of the land revenue; fifty percent was to be spent on immigration, the rest was to be expended by the Governor in accordance with British Government directives from time to time[253]. The Governor was to continue to have power to issue depasturing licences and to make regulations for the use and occupancy of unsold lands, but the existence of the Sale of Waste Lands Act placed an important restriction on the colony by implying a continuing prohibition against the Legislative Council legislating on these matters. The first directive on how the Governor was to spend a portion of the fund, enjoined the Governor to spend a proportion on Aboriginal protection and another on the roads; he was left free to hand any surplus over to the Council for appropriation; but it was made clear that the whole of the second fifty percent was to be considered as an emergency reserve for Britain, if the Council proved difficult". McMinn sheds some further light on the Crown Lands mystery but there still remains the question of whether, year after year, these funds were fully used or just included as a contribution to general revenue. It would appear that somewhere there is a firm directive from the British Treasury that the revenues from Crown Lands sale was to be used to 'offset'

---

252 Government Despatches–*Land Board*)

253 Epitome of Official History of NSW

some of the British costs of maintaining the Colony. The 'Blue Book' is evidence that as general revenues, these land funds were already being used to pay for the costs of feeding, clothing, and housing convicts, and we know they were specifically used to pay for 'sponsored immigrants', aboriginal 'protection', and new roads. The costs of the military establishment were charged against general revenues so in the quite large 'pot', nearly all Colonial expenditures were subsidised or offset by revenues from the Sale of Crown Land. Britain it seems, offered to pay only for the shipping and supplies costs of getting their prisoners to the Colony. After 1828, we know that convict production–both agricultural and mineral–went a long way to paying their expenses, so perhaps the British Treasury did in fact get off very lightly indeed, especially for the benefits it derived.

Two financial statements (being summaries of the Blue Books) for 1827 and 1828 place further doubt on the application of funds derived from crown land sales.[254]

PUBLIC DEPARTMENT AND ESTABLISHMENT COSTS [255]

Establishment	£ for 1827	£ For 1828
Governor's office	4825	5000
Col. Secretary's Office	6125	6000
Legislative Council	800	800
Collector of Customs	5530	5670
Coll'r of Internal Revenue	670	800
Surveyor-General	4550	6000
Land Board	2700	2800
Colonial Treasurer	1570	1600
Colonial Auditor	1300	1400
Other	21000	20000
Supreme Court	11200	12000
Police and Gaols	14500	15000
Civil Engineer	2435	2000
Church & Schools	4000	4100
Total	**82095**	**81400**

[254] HRA 1: 13:541 and 689

[255] Costs which form a charge on the Colonial Revenue of NSW to meet annual expense of several public departments and establishments

The HRA does not offer a detailed breakdown of government expenses by establishment for 1828, but rather offers 29 categories of estimated costs, which would today be similar to a budget appropriation. These estimates have been used for comparison purposes.

ABSTRACT OF COLONIAL REVENUES

Revenue Item	1827	1828
Duties on Spirits	41429	
Ad valorem Duty	9000	
Wharfage & Light House duty	5000	
Sale of Newcastle coals	1254	
License fees	4530	
Tolls & ferries	3450	
Fines collected	771	
Government fees	2900	
Sale of gov livestock	3236	
Total Revenues	74470	
1/8th portion to C & S estate	-5595	-5800
Colonial Revenue	68874.11.9	73509.13.8

The question of Crown Land's revenues remains. It is apparent from the 'Blue Book' notations that this revenue was initially 'reserved' for specific allocation by the Crown and remained in the Colony as an offset against British Government fiscal obligations (e.g. Civil List salaries) until self-government in 1855. A relevant quotation from the 1887 Financial Statements of the Colonial Treasurer of New South Wales follows:

"Prior to the passing of the Constitution Act, the Territorial Revenues of the Colony belonged to the Crown, but upon that coming into operation in 1855, they were placed at the disposal of the local Parliament, and together with the taxes, imposts, rates and duties were formed into one fund, under the title of the Consolidated Revenue Fund. In lieu of the Crown Revenues thus given up to the Colony, an annual Civil List of 64,300 pound was made payable to Her Majesty out of the Consolidated Revenues of the Colony." What this means is that the British Treasury allowed the offset of all direct British payments made on account of the Colony against revenues raised by the sale, rent or lease of Crown lands, until 1838 when the decision was made to allocate a 50% portion of Crown Land Revenues towards subsidising immigration to the colony, and a further 15% towards the support of 'natives' in the colony, and the balance was to be made discretionary, although Britain chose to use most of the excess for administrative (e.g. civil salaries) purposes.

The Blue Books for 1828 include a *Statement of Outstanding Debts,* due to the Governor. The relevance of this statement is that whilst revenue from land sales started as general revenue it was re-allocated to the Land Fund, but the debts to the government from mostly land sales sources are showing to be part of the Consolidated Revenue Funds. These mixed signals require clarification.

STATEMENT OF OUTSTANDING DEBTS PAYABLE TO THE GOVERNMENT

Type of Debt	Amount of Debt
Promissory Note on land sale	42760[256]
Promissory Note for sale of livestock	10543
Promissory Note for sale of other Gov. Property	1782
Rent of lands in arrears	396
Quit Rents in arrears	5765
Tolls & Ferry Lettings	1919
Market Dues	125
Auction Duties	1025
Coals Sold	52
Fees & Fines from Courts	685
Rent on Gov. Buildings	175
Loans with interest	498
Service of Gov stallions	918
Due to Lumber Yard	30
Cattle sold from Gov herds	14
Cows on Loan	2495
TOTAL	69189

256 Governor Darling had supported the 1827 recommendation by John Oxley that terms sales should be allowed with a nominal interest charged on outstanding amounts. The initial interest rate was set at 5%pa.

The Land Board became a department of state in 1835 and changed its name to the Lands Department. The Lands Department and the Public Works Department were merged in 1856. I have referred earlier to the new activity of 'jobbing' in land. This 'land banking' by individuals or speculating by buying key sites was abhorrent to Governor Darling, and he proposed[257] that original purchasers of land be not allowed to resell for a period of 7(seven) years from the date of purchase lest any sale be declared illegal. Darling also considered that the impost of quit-rents was an alternative to ordinary taxes and sufficient quit-rents should be collected to meet the ordinary needs of Government.

The Land Board struggled with the question of preparing an average value of land in each parish. Their concerns, as expressed to Darling,[258] was 'should the different quality of land within a parish reflect in the average price. The Board kept quoting the earlier direction from Bathurst, which was impractical and had caused all the delays and confusion (refer Page 5 this study). A second concern was that the quit-rents to be collected were an ongoing charge against the land and would, in effect, drive down the sale price of the land by the equivalent of the capitalised quit-rents[259].

THE LAND FUND

Coghlan writes about the Land Fund[260]

"When in 1831 it was decided to abolish the system of free land grants, and to dispose of the public estate by auction in lieu of private tender, it was also decided that the proceeds of land sales should be paid into what was called the Land Fund, from which were to be paid the charges incidental to the introduction of immigrants; and it was from the inability of the Land Fund to meet these charges that the public debt of NSW first had its rise. From 1831 to 1834 the Land Fund was sufficient, but in 1841 the engagements for immigration purposes were so heavy that it

---

257 HRA 1: 14:294 Darling to Huskisson August 1828

258 HRA 1: 14:294 Land Board to Darling August 1828

259 HRA 1:14:298 *Commissioner of Survey to governor Darling*

260 Coghlan in 'Wealth & Progress of NSW' (P837)

became necessary to supplement the fund in some way and it was decided to borrow against the security of the Land Revenue. On 28th December 1841 a debenture loan of 49,000 pound was offered in the colony through the Sydney Gazette, the first loan raised in any colony.

The Military chest and The Land Fund

The military chest, as an account style for the colonial treasury was identified in the financial statements contained in the 'Blue Books', and we can readily identify the revenues credited to that account as well as the expenditures charged against the military chest.

However the Land Fund is without mention in the 'Blue Books' at least through the end of 1838, and the origin of this nomenclature must be accepted as 'untraceable' without proper basic evidence. We know only of its existence in firstly, the Australians: Historical Statistics P112, and then its mention in the works of economic historian, S.J. Butlin.

That assumption must be as follows:

A. If the military chest is accepted as a predecessor to the 'Land Fund' then its purpose must have been essentially the same. The military chest took its revenue from the proceeds of sale of crown lands, sale of stores sent from England, sale of produce from the Convict Establishments and sale of crown livestock. In other words, only material items possessed by the crown; and that is most probably why the notations on the Blue Books changed from 'Receipts in Aid of Revenue' to 'Revenue of the Crown'. This important change occurred in the 1834 financial statements.

B. Obviously the Land Fund was so designated either officially or by Australian Economic Historians to be the account into which official 'crown' revenue is deposited and from which crown reserved expenditures are drawn. The crown reserved its use of portion of the funds for conveying selected immigrants into the country, and for (15%) aboriginal welfare. We will return to the official sanctioning of these funds later.

C. S.J. Butlin in his masterwork "makes several passing references to the 'Land Fund' without fully identifying its source or use.[261]

S.J. Butlin writes that "in February 1838, William Rucker, a Melbourne storekeeper, announced the opening of a Derwent Bank agency, to 'receive deposits and discount bills and orders for account and under the responsibility of the Derwent Bank Company in Hobart. He fixed the discount rate at 20%, letting it be known that Hobart rates would apply when a court was established in which debts might be recovered. Attempts were made, with what success it is not clear, to secure the accounts of the Customs Officer and of the Land Fund for the agency. But the agency met with considerable difficulty."

In 1846 there was a squabble between Stuart Donaldson, NSW Treasurer, Murray MHR and Dr. Bland MLC as to where certain colonial debentures were to be funded. Donaldson wanted the subscription to come from the public; George Murray thought the Trust and Loan Bank should do the funding, but "Dr Bland wanted the loans to come from the Land Fund"

"Because of its late settlement and mining boom, land purchase in South Australia was heavy in the late 'forties and the local accumulations in the Land Fund were more than the local commissariat required. The practice developed, with English blessing, that any surplus in the Fund was paid to the commissariat which shipped the specie to other colonial commissariats in need, especially that in New Zealand, the amount being credited to the colony's account with the Land and Emigration Commissioners in London"[262]

Grey, in South Australia, decided to use, contrary to official directions from London, to use any bank he chose for Government business, and he used the Bank of South Australia. Being contrary to official direction, this action permitted a penalty. The Land Fund, which was a transient deposit remitted to England for immigration payments, was divided between the

[261] Butlin, S.J. Foundations of the Australian Monetary System 1788-1851

[262] Butlin *ibid* p.490

Australasia and the South Australia, but all other government business was given to the Australasia."[263]

"In 1851, the SA Treasury decided to require banks to hold cash at least equal to the government deposit, and to insist on this for the Land Fund."

Some of these references throw doubt on the strict governmental use of the Land Fund.[264]

"It was Lord John Russell's opinion in 1840 that the general revenue ought to provide for the general expenditure, leaving the Land Fund, apart from 15 percent to be used for expenditure on Aborigines, free for immigration purposes as originally intended"[265]

Coghlan in his extensive work helps place some of these matters in relation to sale of crown land & immigration into perspective.[266]

"It was upon emigration from England at the cost of the land revenue that the colonial authorities finally placed their confidence. They offered in 1822 to set aside 10,000 pound from the Land Fund for emigration purposes; of this sum they desired that about two-thirds should be devoted to promoting the emigration of unmarried women, as the proportion of men in the colony was excessive, and that about one-third should be used in loans for the emigration of mechanics. The colonial office objected vigorously but the British Treasury agreed to the proposal with the proviso that no further sum should be expended upon immigration until the money received from the sale of land had reached 10,000 pound."[267]

"It had been Edward Gibbon Wakefield's philosophy that the idea of land disposition in the colonies was adopted . . . . If the land was sold, the proceeds of the sale might aptly be applied to transferring labour from

---

263 Butlin *ibid* p.539

264 Butlin *ibid* p,540

265 'Historical Records of Victoria-Volume 7–Public Finance p.35

266 Coghlan, T.A. "Labour & Industry in Australia "-Vol 1, p.220

267 Historical Records of Victoria-Volume 7–Public Finance p.35

Britain to the colony without which labour the land would be of very little value. In 1831 the English Government resolved to alter the land system of Australia with the view of throwing open the country more freely to settlement, and thereby increasing immigration."[268]

In the first four months of 1832, 103 mechanics reached the colony but were disappointed to find pay rates considerably less than those promised in England. The female emigrants all found ready employment, chiefly as domestic servants.[269]

"Considering its resources, the colony went into the immigration business in a big way. The estimated expenditure of 1838 was 120,000 pound of which 80,000 were spent in chartering 26 ships, and 40,000 expended on bounty immigrants."[270]

"With the overall success of the program it was decided that the whole of the rapidly increasing land revenue of New South Wales should be devoted to immigration and in 1837. 3093 immigrants arrived of whom 2688 were sponsored and 405 arrived under the bounty regulation of the colonial government."[271]

Land Fund 1833-1850[272]

Year	Revenue £'000			Expenditure £'000[5]		
	Land	Other	Total	Immigr.	Other	Total
1833[6]	26.1	0.1	26.2	9.0	17.2	26.2
1834	48.2	42.9	60.8	7.9	52.9	60.8
1835	88.9	121.3	131.9	10.7	121.2	131.9
1836	131.4	121.1	263.3	11.8	251.5	263.3

268 Historical Records of Victoria-Volume 7–Public Finance p.218

269 Historical Records of Victoria-Volume 7–Public Finance p.222

270 Historical Records of Victoria-Volume 7–Public Finance p.226

271 Historical Records of Victoria-Volume 7–Public Finance p.227

272 This table extracted from Historical Statistics can only be verified by reference back to the Blue Book Financial statements for those years, provided we make a generous assumption.

1837	123.6	202.6	254.9	44.4	210.5.	254.9
1838	120.2	185.8	353.8	108.0	245.8	353.8
1839	160.8	148.8	321.8	158.3	163.5	321.8
1840	325.3	283.6	480.0	148.0	332.0	480.0
1841	105.8	21.4	386.5	331.6	54.9	386.5
1842	44.1	51.7	117.2	112.0	19.7	131.7
1843	29.3	49.3	56.5	11.6	44.9	56.5
1844	16.9	126.0	127.5	69.0	58.5	127.5
1845	38.0	131.0	127.9	20.0	107.9	127.9
1846	38.8	153.5	146.5	1.2	145.3	146.5
1847	51.7	109.7	212.3	1.0	232.6	233.6
1848	51.7	109.7	212.3	113.8	98.5	212.3
1849	109.0	237.4	296.0	138.5	157.5	296.0
1850	158.5	104.8	373.1	166.2	206.9	373.1

A Practical Dilemma

One can imagine the first 'carving up' of the colony into Counties, Parishes and townships, that the surveyor's task was not an easy one.

For a start the surveyor was looking for 'natural' barriers or identifiable separators, to distinguish counties. A mountain rage, a river or a coastline would make an easily identifiable and recordable boundary. Sometimes a main road might suffice, but mostly they wanted something more than a tree line or a fence post and fence line, which could be dismantled or moved to be a boundary. So establishing boundaries for each division was an important first step.

By 1834, Major Thomas Mitchell (who had arrived in 1827 to become deputy surveyor-General, but upon the death, shortly thereafter, of John Oxley, was to become the Surveyor-General) had prepared a map based on a triangulation approach[273] covering the nineteen counties then existing around Sydney. This map was published in three sheets in 1834 at the

273 Theodolites and circumferentors were used for angle measurement, baselines were measured on the shores of Botany bay and Lake George near Canberra, and the survey was connected to the astronomic observatory then at Parramatta

scale of 8.6 miles to 1 inch and entitled *Map of the Colony of NSW*. It is sometimes called *The Map of the Nineteen Counties*. This stood as the largest, though not the first topographic map to be produced in Australia in the nineteenth century.

However the pressures of land settlement did not permit any further topographic mapping of the country for a further 60 years. It was recognised that the need for topographic intelligence was a necessary adjunct to land management.[274]

The dilemma facing these early 'town planners' was how to create a road network serving the remote townships. The major roads linking inland towns to Sydney town were mostly toll roads, so there was a funding mechanism to create and repair these major links. Secondary roads were of importance only to the local land owners, and the government took the decision to create 'reserves' for future secondary roads and to wait for local landowners (usually those adjoining the reserve) to create a cart track, rather than spending any public monies on this huge network of parish and county (secondary) roads.

John Oxley addressed this dilemma in a memorandum to Governor Darling dated 20th September 1827.[275]

"A clause was inserted in the planning for (land) grants (and the grants themselves) reserving to the Crown the right of making roads etc through the lands of the respective proprietors, but does not seem to be understood, probably in consequence of the nature and description of the settled country not being sufficiently known.

The road reserve is a right to take such land as may be necessary for a public or parochial road through lands granted[276], without paying for the lands

---

274 Lines, John D. *Australia on Paper–The story of Australian Mapping*

275 HRA 1:14:303 *Surveyor-General Oxley to Governor Darling.*

276 The problem had arisen that landowners claimed control over these reserves and often refused to give up the land for planned roads. The dilemma became that the government legality of the reserve and who the reserve land was vested in became the subject of a legal challenge.

taken. A solution would be to cause lines of these roads to be so marked so that they may, most advantageously for the district, communicate with the public or turnpike roads, leading to the towns and settled parts of the country is all that is required of the government, for with the exception of a few slight bridges over hollows and wet places, nature has affected the rest, by affording in most cases a clear and excellent road. The trees stand wide apart and do not impede or slow the passage of carts and travellers. Remote roads are chiefly used by stock and light travelling carts, and it would be useless to specifically plan a road alignment at this time until more use is undertaken.

The cost of construction of the public main roads is at present constructed by the convicts and defrayed by the Crown. There remains the question of cost associated with roads leading to farms not bordering on the great public roads, or those on which the principal towns and villages are situated. These roads, by, by way of distinction, may be termed Cross or Parish Roads. They require little or no formation, as the upper crust of the natural soil will remain passable for years without having the least labour bestowed upon them. There is not much cart traffic on such roads, but a toll may be levied sufficient to defray a portion of the expense of making them.

Oxley also spelled out for the Governor the problem of construction of roads through improved lands.

This was a problem not easily resolved until road reserves were dedicated to a statutory authority, the literacy rate improved so land owners could read and understand their contracts, surveys were brought up-to-date and properly showed road reserves, and

A system of deed recording was invoked for the colony.

Endnotes

i Quoted from the Terms of Reference of the House of Commons Select Committee

ii The Charter created two Courts–the Governor's Court and the Supreme Court

[iii] The Epitome of Official History of NSW–page 30

[iv] Extract from the Official Account of the Trip to Governor Macquarie

[v] The Epitome of Official History of NSW-page 29

[vi] The Epitome of Official History of NSW–Page 31

[vii] The Diaries and Letters of G.T.W.B. Boyes Volume 1 1820-1832

[viii] Bathurst to Bigges–Letter of appointment and terms of reference, 1819

[ix] Macquarie to Bathurst HRA 1:20:653

[x] Summary prepared by this author from quarterly reports of Police & Orphan Fund revenues and expenditures printed in the *Sydney Gazettes*

[xi] Taken from Ginswick MS as reported by N.G. Butlin in 'The Economy before 1850'

[xii] 'William Lithgow–Biography' by G.W. Beckett

[xiii] Quoted from the Terms of Reference of the House of Commons Select Committee

[xiv] The Charter created two Courts–the Governor's Court and the Supreme Court

[xv] The Epitome of Official History of NSW–page 30

[xvi] Extract from the Official Account of the Trip to Governor Macquarie

[xvii] The Epitome of Official History of NSW-page 29

[xviii] The Epitome of Official History of NSW–Page 31

[ix] The Diaries and Letters of G.T.W.B. Boyes Volume 1 1820-1832

[xx] Bathurst to Bigges–Letter of appointment and terms of reference, 1819

[xxi] Macquarie to Bathurst HRA 1:20:653

[xxii] Summary prepared by this author from quarterly reports of Police & Orphan Fund revenues and expenditures printed in the *Sydney Gazettes*

[xxiii] Taken from Ginswick MS as reported by N.G. Butlin in 'The Economy before 1850'

CHAPTER 16

THE WESTMINSTER INFLUENCE ON THE COLONY

The Legal Assumptions behind the Colony

It was the Act of 1784, a statute intituled "An Act for the effectual transportation of felons and other offenders, and to authorise the removal of prisoners in certain cases, and for other purposes therein mentioned", and that empowered King George III, with the advice of the Privy Council, to appoint places to which felons might be transferred. By an order in council dated 6th December 1786, the 'territory of NSW, situated on the east part of New Holland", was appointed a place for receiving the persons within the meaning of the Act.

By letters patent and commission dated 2nd April 1787, Captain Arthur Phillip was appointed Governor and Vice-Admiral of the territory. The letters patent defined the boundaries of his authority, and empowered him to make orders for the good government of the settlement. Through ordinances and regulations, he created offences and crimes previously 'unknown to the law, and made modifications the application of the laws of England in matters relating to police, tolls, and convict labour. His legislative powers were 'assumed to be founded on and justified by the prerogatives of the Crown'. Commissioner Bigge raised, in his 1833 report to the House of Commons the first question as to whether the Crown had authority to delegate such a power to the Governor.

The Judicial authority for the governance of the colony derived from both statute (27 Geo III, c.2) and from prerogative, similarly assumed to exist. This statute created a criminal court similar to a court of Admiralty, and was composed of the judge-advocate and six military officers; by letters patent, dated 2nd April 1787, the Crown created a court of civil jurisdiction having power to deal in a summary way with personal actions and probate and administration proceedings, according to the laws of England. The civil court was presided over by the Judge advocate and two appointees (settlers) of the governor. This arrangement continued until February 1814 when a Supreme Court was promulgated. Responsible government was slow in arriving in the colony and in fact, the Act of 1823, extended only representative government to the colony. The governor remained his own prime minister and the heads of departments worked, at the pleasure of the Crown. This half-measure remained intact until the NSW Legislative Council stepped up its demand for responsible government and the enabling Act 13 & 14 Vic, c59 provided the powers requested

Key Westminster Legislation Affecting the Colony of NSW

Apart from the legislation passed by the House of Commons enabling the land of New South Wales to be used as a penal settlement, the first important pieces of legislation referred to the transportation of prisoners of the Crown to the proposed colony of NSW and the legislation directed to the former North American colonies which included the declaration that Britain will not tax the colonies. The foundation of the proposed penal settlement came in 1787, just before the First Fleet sailed. The legislation commissioning the colony to be operated by a governor and establishing his powers, remuneration and length of appointment also came in 1787 in time for Governor Phillip to assume appointment when he stepped on land at Botany Bay.

The British Statutes disallowed taxation in the colonies including any imposts not approved by the Crown. However, Governor King in 1802, decided to raise a 'levy' to rebuild the town gaol after it had burnt in 1801, and the Secretary of State declined to build it at public expense. Successive Governors continued the levy and expanded the base of effective 'taxation' in the colony until the formation of the Supreme Court of NSW and the appointment of Chief Justice Jeffery Bent in 1815. Bent refused to pay the Macquarie imposed 'toll' to travel on the new Main Roads, and although he was recalled by Bathurst, his successor, Barron Fields, advised Macquarie that, in his legal opinion, all locally imposed taxes were illegal, and the governors could be held responsible to the public for repaying taxes illegally collected. Macquarie hastily advised Bathurst copying him with the Field's opinion and Bathurst took legislation to the Parliament, which protected the governor from any consequences of the imposition of illegal duties. The first legislative review of the colony was commissioned by Bathurst, and declared 'it has become expedient to cause an enquiry to be made into the present state of the settlements in our territory of NSW and its dependencies, and of the laws, regulations and usages, civil, military and ecclesiastical, prevailing therein". The commission and instructions to Bigge are important because they 'determined very largely the form of the three Bigge Reports, printed by order of the House of Commons in late1822'

Petitions were used during Macquarie's term (in 1817) to influence Bathurst, firstly against the excesses and vindictiveness of J.H. Bent. A second petition was presented by assistant Commissary Brougham to Macquarie on March 23,1819 and demanded change to the form of government and 'a removal of the disabilities under which (they thought) they lived'. Many other petitions and requests were made, requests of an economic rather than a legislative interest. They were concerned with agriculture and the pastoral industry, fisheries, shipping, unemployment, excessive taxation and the distillation of spirits. One request that did deal with a statutory restriction was about the Act that limited ships to a maximum of 350 tons, which could be engaged in trade with the colony without permission of the East India Company. However a previous piece of legislation had opened to southern oceans to unrestricted whaling, sealing and fishing. The East India Company fell out of favour for patrolling the southern hemisphere and an amending piece of legislation opened trade of any size to the colony. The House of Commons may well have been influenced by the people's partition of the previous year. Two other pieces of legislation impacting on both the East India Company and the colony were firstly the 1816 Act that reserved all major trade to the East India Company and the earlier Act that incorporated the Charter of Justice and included regulations for the East India Company. In between these two Acts, legislation setting forth the public offices of the colony was passed

Background to establishing the colony of NSW

In this study we are revisiting the traditionalist theory that the only reason for the colony of New South Wales was as a penal settlement. It was carefully planned and discussed at all levels based on the simple submission by Sir Joseph Banks in evidence before the House of Commons Select Committee on Penitentiaries in 1774.

The traditionalist argument is, in its most simplistic structure:

Upon Cook's news that he had taken possession of a great country (New South Wales), England did not immediately decide to colonise it. She already had a huge empire, and wanted no more for the present, for colonies were expensive to govern, and they oftentimes caused wars. With the American Colonies in mind, it seemed that colonies brought no profit while they were struggling and expensive, and that when they became prosperous they rebelled.

Even though Cook and Bank's journals were doctored by Hawkesworth before publishing to make NSW sound better than it was, the choice of a new colony would have been (in the opinion of F. Hawke) New Zealand or the Friendly Islands before Botany Bay was selected.

However the need was different now with the revolt by the Americas and the accumulation of over 1,000 prisoners each year in Britain. They were being kept in prison and in hulks tethered together in mid-stream, and soon became over-full. It was Banks that suggested Botany Bay as a new penal colony, which is surprising when we remember what Banks said about NSW. He now seemed to think it was just the right place. It was far away and no danger of prisoners escaping. Thus the colony was simply to be used as a jail for prisoners and a repository for the poor of England! Russel Ward in *Australia* puts it simply "In 1788 the Australian nation was founded by and for Great Britain's surplus of convicted criminals, a fact which used to give many respectable Australians pain and which threatened a few with schizophrenia."

But this is over-simplistic, for Ward implies that Britain was blinded by all other considerations than the placement of prisoners somewhere other than in Britain. As any economic Historian would know, if nothing else the economic considerations of adding another colony to the British Empire was just extra expense. But there was something else! Foreign policy issues, trade and industry issues, ridding the homeland of the poor and unemployed, following the Industrial revolution were all considered and the penal colony idea was the icing on the cake, and not the sole determinant.

Why does the traditional view need reviewing?

The record needs setting straight for future generations and at least for the next 50 years!

The answer to the question 'what are the reasons for the settlement' once seemed obvious. In the 1780s England was facing an urgent problem–jails were overflowing, crime was increasing; the solution was transportation–but to where? Botany Bay was selected!

This is the traditional copybook answer repeated for the past half-century!

In 1888, a British historian, Gonner, suggested a larger story–Botany Bay was settled for economic reasons, to compensate Britain for the loss of her American Colonies. This theory found no support in Australia until R.M. Dallas (a Tasmanian historian) discussed it in 1952. Dallas asked–Why would a nation of merchants go so far and pay so much money, if it were merely to dump convicts? It was Dallas that even set Geoffrey Blainey to rethinking the rational explanation.

Lord Sydney, as Secretary of State, had stated the problem and the government's position in 1780: The traditionalists bought this explanation without much question or even concern.

"The several gaols and places for the confinement of felons in this Kingdom, being in so crowded a state that the greatest danger is to be apprehended not only from their escape, but from infectious distempers which may hourly be expected to break out among them".

However these were the reasons for the policy of 'transportation' and not for settling the colony!

Some Background to Events leading to the Government 1786 decision

In the 18th Century, England was in the throes of domestic upheaval. She was going through the Industrial Revolution. The country was being transformed from a rural-based economy to an industrial one. Farms were closing. Factories were opening. People were relocating from the country to the city. The results were overcrowding, primitive sewerage, disease and an increase in crime, mostly due to higher levels of poverty. On top of that there was no police force, only a collection of corrupt wardens. The English penal code was to be made even more severe than it already was! Gaol was to be no more of a rehabilitation or preventative strike then, than it is now. The gaols were overflowing and short-term (7 years or less) convicted persons were placed on 'hulks' tied together in mid-stream of the Thames

Men were escaping from the hulks in growing numbers and there was a real fear that the situation would get out of hand. Crime, cost and prisoners were increasing–finance, accommodation and patience with the problem were not.

Building more prisons (made permissible by the Penitentiary Houses Act of 1779) was one solution, where convicts could be employed in hard labour. The scheme foundered because of wrangles over location and cost. By 1784, the authorities moved again to transportation and a 1784 Act to resume transportation was passed but without a specified location. Parliamentary Committees investigated Africa, but the unhealthiness of the climate, the infertile soil and a fear of hostile natives combined to rule out the region. A disastrous experiment at Cape Coast Castle resulted in a 45% death rate amongst convicts in a single year.

Even in 1785 and 1786, sites in Canada and the West Indies were under consideration, but by 1779 Joseph Banks had proposed Botany Bay just before Matra wrote his report to the Admiralty in 1883. Matra emphasised the great commercial advantages of Botany Bay, based on his having been a midshipman under Cook during his 7-day stay on the East Coast of new Holland. The colony could serve as a base for trade with China (tea), with Nootka Sound (furs) and the Moluccas (spices) and for the cultivation of flax.

Sir John Young, another adviser to the Peel government, submitted a plan in 1785 for a settlement suitable for convicts and commercial gain. The Beauchamp Committee of the House of Commons rejected both schemes. The cost of transportation was the main objection. The evidence suggested a passage cost of about 30 pound, which was 6 times the cost of passage to America. Although Botany Bay was rejected in 1785 as too expensive, just one year later, on 18th August 1786, it was chosen as the site. Botany Bay was selected as the last resort, almost in desperate circumstances. Circumstances pressuring the decision included the debts of the Prince of Wales, negotiations for a treaty with France, and growing agitation against the 'slave trade'. The convict problem appeared small, in comparison, but deserved and got a rapid solution. The government's aim was mercantilist–colonies or settlements were only useful if they benefited the mother country. England was a trading nation with imperial ambitions. Botany Bay was selected for the general advantages it offered as well as being a place suitable for transportation.

These general advantages included:

- Botany Bay was useful as a naval base and a refitting port in the South Seas.
- England's interest in the Pacific had increased, especially after the loss of the American colonies.
- Rivalry with the French in the East became a foundation for a base.

- The colony of NSW had important commercial attractions; flax and timber, essential for naval supplies could be grown there. Convicts were not dumped at Botany Bay; they were sent as the first settlers for a naval base and refitting port.
- That is why the early emphasis on rehabilitation. From that base, the vital trade routes could be tapped-tea from China, fur from North America, and the whaling industry and South American loot carried on Spanish ships.

After 1785, when the French and Dutch alliance was renewed, the French revived their-own East India Company into the Pacific. In 1786 the British annexed Penong and Botany Bay was settled as a useful base for trade. The official documents do give us the profit motive, which the English needed to undertake the venture. These official documents included

- Cook's report of Norfolk Island having superior quality of the 'spruce pines and flax'; and the 'greatest consequence to us as a naval power'-Matra.
- Phillip was instructed to cultivate flax, which Phillip did within one month of arriving at Botany Bay. The flax and pine timber were as important in 1788 as steel and oil are today.

However, the traditionalists still argue that Botany Bay was settled *at a certain point in time* because the government needed to solve its convict problem. The revisionists argue–why that place and not another? The pressure groups won the day in 1786–

- The politicians saw the disgraceful and frightening state of the hulks;
- The 'opposition' in parliament needled the government for its failure to find a solution;
- Powerful economic groups (of merchants) were well represented in the discussions for protecting trade against competition from national rivals.

The government made a sudden, but not hasty, decision in the face of all this pressure.

Revising the Interpretation

A revisionist theory draws a very different analysis whereby there were numerous basic determinants (other than the penal colony) of the formation of the colony and that it became only a means to an end to send convicts from the overflowing British prisons to the early colony.

For a start, the fact was that no British government in the past had been directly responsible for initiating the permanent settlement of any territory. The American colonial enterprises, dating back to the early seventeenth century, had been the work of individuals seeking a better life, or of companies acting with the general support of the government or under Royal charter, but none had been directly fostered by the government. With no private or commercial interests likely to set up a pioneering enterprise in the newly chartered territories, emigration from the British Isles to various American colonies went on free from any thought of the more distant places as alternatives. 'Not only remoteness but the very nature of the lands observed by members of Cook's expedition inhibited serious interest', writes Younger in *Australia and the Australians* 'whilst New Zealand's ferocious tribesmen inspired fear, and Sir Joseph Banks wrote of New South Wales that "a soil so barren and at the same time entirely void of the helps derived from cultivation could not be supposed to yield much towards the support of man" '.

The British government supported privatisation of colonisation, but the settlement of such remote and unproductive places did not appeal to any private group, and the British government saw no reason for action. A readiness to take possession (as Cook had done in the name of King George III) did not imply a readiness to follow such action with occupation; nor did the mere declaration of possession in itself confer any substantial right or obligation on the British government.

These basic determinants of whether or not to settle the area of *New Holland* included:

- Foreign Policy considerations
- Military (in particular, naval) considerations
- Scientific & technical considerations

- The tyranny of the distance
- Economic (in particular, trade) considerations

Only after quantifying the strategic criteria within these five categories did the rationale of the colony being developed at government expense but being made to pay its own way, as rapidly as possible, did the formation of a penal settlement come about as a means to underpin the economics of the future colony.

Foreign Policy Considerations

Commodore John Byron sailed from Plymouth in 1764 with orders, that in order to avoid arousing Spanish jealousies and retaliation were kept secret. After passing through the Straits of Magellan he sailed on the familiar north-westerly course over the Pacific, making few discoveries; he sighted only outlying islands of minor groups, and after visiting Tinian he went on to Batavia and returned home, completing the circumnavigation in the record time of twenty-two months. On his return to England in 1766 his ship, the frigate *Dolphin*, was placed under Captain Samuel Wallis who, with Captain Philip Carteret in the *Swallow*, set off on another circumnavigation. The two ships were separated soon after passing through the Straits of Magellan. Wallis reached Tahiti (Naming it King George Island), the Society Islands, and the Wallis Archipelago, sailing home by way of Batavia. Carteret discovered Pitcairn Island and sailed through St George's Channel, so proving that New Ireland and New Britain were separated.

For much of the eighteenth century there was a distinct possibility that naval warfare (between France and Britain) would be extended into the Pacific. Both the French and English were doing their share of voyaging in these waters, sometimes no more than a few months, or a few leagues, apart. England's victory in the Seven Years war, acknowledged at the Treaty of Paris in 1763, resulted in England's supremacy over the French in India, and the loss of France's North American colonies to England. (France, however, retained some possessions in India and the best of her sugar-islands.) In the long run the English victory also decided the future of the Pacific.

The real reasons for Britain establishing the Colony of New South Wales

- Cook's news that he had taken possession of a 'great country' did not prompt Britain to colonise it immediately. The British government supported privatisation of colonisation, but the settlement of such a remote and unproductive place did not appeal to any private group, and the government saw no reason for action.
- Botany Bay was seen as having been settled for economic reasons–to compensate Britain for the loss of her American colonies (Gonner 1888)
- Marta's report emphasised the great commercial advantages of Botany Bay. The colony could serve as a trade base for China (tea), Nootka Sound (furs) and Moluccas (spices).
- The Naval demand for flax and hemp made a new supply base a political and economic as well as a defence necessity.
- The naval demand for continuous supplies of timber masts also provided great pressure on establishing a supply base
- Britain was a trading nation with imperial ambitions. Botany Bay was selected for the primary advantages it offered, as well as the secondary advantages of a transportation destination.

These advantages included:

- Botany Bay was useful as a naval base and a refitting port in the South Seas.
- England's interest in the Pacific had increased, especially after the loss of the American colonies.
- Rivalry with the French in the East suggested Botany Bay should become a foundation for a defence base.
- The colony of NSW had important commercial attractions; flax, hemp and timber, essential for naval supplies could be grown there.
- Convicts were not dumped at Botany Bay; they were sent as the first settlers for a naval base and refitting port.

- That is why the early emphasis on rehabilitation. From that base, the vital trade routes could be tapped-tea from China, fur from North America, and the whaling industry and South American loot carried on Spanish ships.
- Circumstances pressuring the decision included the debts of the Prince of Wales, negotiations with France for a peace treaty and growing domestic 'opposition' to the slave trade.

It would seem that the four main and primary reasons for establishing the colony were:

- Foreign policy,
- Trade and economic policy,
- Scientific and technical opportunities, and
- Supplying the military (mainly the naval stores)

These included

- <u>Foreign</u>

    - o Naval warfare between France and Britain could extend into the Pacific and a naval base was required to gain the advantage
    - o Britain had been fighting Spain as well as France: so, New South Wales would be an admirable centre from which to attack the Dutch and Spanish Islands in the Malay Archipelago.
    - o The Treaty of Paris in 1763 between Britain and France resulted in:

- British supremacy in India
- Britain taking over France's North American colonies
- Campbell urged the settling of New Guinea since the 'Spaniards would leave no means unattempted to dispossess the British from that area.
- Potential for future conflict

    - o Between Spain and Britain
    - o Between Britain and France, in the Pacific

Scientific & Technical Matters encouraged further Exploration

- Britain had charted much of the Pacific area, but the great South Land remained unconfigured
- Community pressure was growing to complete the discoveries of unknown parts of the globe
- New availability of instruments, mathematics and astrology made it possible to take exact celestial measurements, and chart a ship's position with accuracy.
- These inventions opened the way for new geographical discoveries
- Dampier returned from the Indian Ocean area in 1701 with thoughts of lands still untouched. Other than the wartime expedition of George Anson, it was not until 1764 that the British sent a ship into the Pacific area.
- Exploration and discovery advanced the 'honour of Britain as a maritime power' (Lord Sydney)

Geographical Considerations

- An alternative and faster route between England and China was available by assuming that a halfway house existed at Botany Bay. Access was via the Cape of Good Hope, around Tasmania, up the east coast of New South Wales, calling at Botany Bay and the weaving a course through the Islands to the east of New Guinea and so north-west to China. England had a rich trade with India and China but it was also a vulnerable trade–it was the envy of powerful European nations, who commanded the sea approaches to India and China.

Economic & Trade Considerations

- The South Sea Company and undiscovered lands in the Pacific all created an aura of untold riches for Britain, waiting to be discovered, and Britain should be there first. Expectations of great wealth were conjured up, although the scandal of the South Sea Bubble cause disillusionment

- It was believed that the Pacific would create opportunities for new enterprises for those with foresight and courage to act.

<u>Other secondary considerations for establishing the Colony Transportation</u>

- The favourable opportunity cost of housing, guarding, accommodating, feeding prisoners as compared to doing the same thing in Britain.
- In the 18th century Britain was in the midst of economic upheaval following the industrial revolution. Transition from a rural to an industrial economy caused a population shift from country to town, resulting in unemployment, overcrowding, disease and crime.
- As Russell Ward states: 'in 1788, the Australian nation was founded by and for Britain's surplus of convicted criminals.
- Men escaping from hulks in growing numbers created a fear the situation would get out of hand. Crime, costs and prisoners were growing–finance, accommodation and patience with the problem were not.
- The pressure for a decision also came because
- The British politicians saw the disgraceful and frightening state of the hulks;
- The 'opposition' in parliament needled the government for its failure to find a solution;
- Powerful economic groups (of merchants) were well represented in the discussions for protecting trade against competition from national rivals.

    - The convict transportation proposal was in essence a form of compulsory, assisted migration. It provided the basis of populating this strategic colony quickly and inexpensively as well as overcoming the challenges of immediate free migration.
    - The colony could eventually be structured so as to attract men of capital and speculators–it could offer free land and free labour

I came across a quotation recently that is quite suitable for finishing this section. It is unusual, as you will see, when I reveal the source at the end of the quotation.

> *We have progressed a long way from the days when angry colonial parliaments and executives could and did quarrel about 'dictatorship from Downing Street'. Even today one may find traces of the notion that Dominions are places whose useful but unspectacular functions is to grow food and produce raw materials for the inhabitants of the United Kingdom, who will, in turn, supply them with manufactured products.*

If you thought this was a colonial opinion, you would be incorrect. It is the opinion of former Australian Prime Minister (1949-1966) Robert Gordon Menzies as recorded in 'Afternoon Light' (1967).

Benefits of the Colony to Britain

The original estimate of direct gains by the British authorities from the original and continuing investment in the Colony of New South Wales was based on 5 (five) identifiable and quantifiable events

1. The opportunity cost of housing, feeding and guarding the convicts in the Colony compared with the cost of doing the same thing in Britain.

The original estimates, in this category, were based on an estimated differential of ten pound per head-an arbitrary assessment of the differential cost.

However recent and more reliable information has come to hand which gives further validity to a number of 20 pound per head per annum, compared with the original 10 pound per head per annum.

A letter to Under Secretary Nepean dated 23rd August 1783, from James Maria Matra of Shropshire and London assists us in this regard.

It was Matra who first analysed the opportunity of using the new Colony as a Penal Colony; only his estimates were incorrect and ill founded. He had advised the Government that it would cost less than 3,000 pound to establish the Colony initially, plus transportation cost at 15 pound per head and annual maintenance of 20 pound per head.

In fact the transportation was contracted for the second fleet at 13 pound 5 shillings per head and annual maintenance was offset by Colonial revenues from 1802.

However, Matra made a significant statement in his letter to Nepean, when he pointed out that the prisoners housed, fed and guarded on the rotting hulks on the Thames River were being contracted for in the annual amount of 26.15.10 per head per annum. He also writes that 'the charge to the publick fore these convicts has been increasing for the last 7 or 8 years' (Historical Records of NSW-Vol 1 Part 2 Page 7)

Adopting this cost as a base for comparison purposes, it means that the benefit to Britain of the Colony increased from 140,000,000 pound to 180,000,000 pound. This benefit assesses the Ground 1 benefit at 84,000,000 pound.

2. Benefit to Britain on Ground Two (2) is put at 70, 000,000 pound which places the value of a convicts labour at 35 pound per annum. Matra had assessed the value of labour of the Hulk prisoners at 35. 85 pound.
3. The valuation of convict labour in the new Colony should reflect the convicts not only used on building sites, but also on road, bridge and wharf construction. This would add (based on 35 pound per annum) a further 21,000,000-pound.
4. The Molesworth Committee (A House of Commons Committee investigating transportation) concluded that the surplus food production by the convicts would feed the Military people and this, over a period of 10 years, would save 7,000,000 pound for the British Treasury.
5. The benefits of fringe benefit grants of land to the Military etc can be estimated (based on One pound per acre) at over 5,000,000 before 1810.

6. We learn from Governor King's Report to Earl Camden (which due to a change of office holder, should have been addressed to Viscount Castlereagh as Colonial Secretary) dated 15th March 1806 that the Convicts engaged in widely diverse work. The Report itself (Enclosure #2) is entitled "Public Labour of Convicts maintained by the Crown at Sydney, Parramatta, Hawkesbury, Toongabbie and Castle Hill, for the year 1805

Cultivation-Gathering, husking and shelling maize from 200 acres sowed last year-Breaking up ground and planting 1230 acres of wheat, 100 acre of Barley, 250 acres of Maize, 14 acres of Flax, and 3 acres of potatoes-Hoeing the above maize and threshing wheat.

Stock-Taking care of Government stock as herdsmen, watchmen etc

Buildings-

- At Sydney: Building and constructing of stone, a citadel, a stone house, a brick dwelling for the Judge Advocate, a commodious brick house for the main guard, a brick printing office
- At Parramatta: Alterations at the Brewery, a brick house as clergyman's residence
- At Hawkesbury: completing a public school
- A Gaol House with offices, at the expense of the Colony
- Boat and Ship Builders: refitting vessels and building row boats
- Wheel and Millwrights: making and repairing carts

Manufacturing: sawing, preparing and manufacturing hemp, flax and wool, bricks and tiles

Road Gangs: repairing roads, and building new roads

Other Gangs: loading and unloading boats"

(Historical Records of NSW-Vol 6 P43)

Thus the total benefits from these six (6) items of direct gain to the British comes to well over 174 million pound, and this is compared to Professor N. G. Butlin's proposal that the British 'invested' 5.6 million.

Scientific & technical consideration

During the years of struggle, increasing attention was given to scientific inquiry and geographical speculation, both in England and France. Now that practically all the remainder of the world was charted, the Great South Land–Terra Australis or Terra Incognita–had become a matter of immediate concern. Books about voyages in the Pacific and southern seas, proposing further exploration or the founding of settlements, and speculating about unknown parts, contributed to the growing interest.

It was also an era of scientific exploration, undertaken against a background of great expansion in scientific thought. Significant advance in the theoretical sciences of mathematics and astronomy had been made in the 17th century; now these new principles were being applied to navigation. The invention of the sextant in England in 1730 and the subsequent development of the chronometer, made it possible to take exact celestial measurements, and so to chart a ship's position with accuracy. These inventions, with modifications in ship-design resulting in greatly strengthened vessels, opened the way for new geographical discoveries.

Economic & trade considerations

With the founding in 1711 of the South Sea Company, one of London's joint-stock ventures to seize public imagination, the distant Pacific became a region for more than literary fantasy. The South Sea Company was to trade with Spanish America and concessions were gained for it for that purpose, but its great appeal to the speculator lay in its hoped-for trade with the rich lands thought to await discovery in the Pacific. Expectations of dazzling wealth were conjured up, although operations never became profitable. The fraudulent booming of the company's shares was followed by a collapse of the so-called South Sea Bubble in 1720, causing disillusionment as well as great scandal. The collapse brought to a sudden and calamitous end, all speculative interest in nebulous plans for trade in the Pacific. Nevertheless, the English period of discovery had begun.

Distance personified

Between 1744 and 1748, a handsome new edition was published in London of the *Complete Collection of Voyages and Travels* (which had originally appeared in 1705 edited by John Harris) urging further discoveries. As well as narratives of navigators, the book contained prefaces and notations by John Campbell, who sought to draw attention to opportunities for new enterprise believed to exist for enterprising Englishmen. Pointing to the value of commerce, Campbell explained the narratives of travel in the South Sea in terms of the new challenge that awaited those with foresight and courage to act:

'It is most evident from Tasman's voyages that New Guinea, Carpentaria (i.e. Cape York Peninsula), New Holland, Van Diemen's Land and the country discovered by Quiros make all one continent, from which New Zealand seems to be separated by a strait, and perhaps is part of another continent'.

Campbell went on to suggest that there were great prospects for Britain if settlements (or, as he termed them, plantations) were established there. Convinced of the immense value of the southern continent, which he termed Terra Australis, he was opposed to a monopoly being granted to the East India Company to trade there. He made a strong plea that the South Sea Company should have rights there 'as a point of high importance,' and wrote that if Britain wished to make the greatest gain 'it may, indeed be requisite to remove ill judged prohibitions, and to break down illegal exclusions'.

He urged that New Guinea should be settled at once, 'and with competent force, since without doubt the Spaniards would leave no means unattempted to dispossess them.' In the space of a very few years, he believed settlement of New Guinea (and a trade in slaves from there) would prove of great consequence to the South Sea Company. He also recommended the formation of a settlement on the southern coast of Terra Australis. This, he believed, would lead the way to the opening of a new trade route 'which must carry a great quantity of our goods and manufactures.' Such a settlement would also be attended by other advantages. 'There is in all probability,' Campbell wrote, 'another Southern continent which is still to be discovered.'

'Perhaps it was the aura of unreality associated with the southern lands as much as the British preoccupation with European wars, that held back further exploration for so long' writes Marjorie Barnard in *A History of Australia*. Dampier had returned to London in 1701, hinting at prospects in lands still untouched. Yet, apart from the wartime expedition of Captain George Anson in 1739, it was not until 1764 that the British government sent another ship into the Pacific area.

Investigating the New World

These voyages were all undertaken by Britain to advance 'the honour of this nation as a maritime power–and the trade and navigation thereof' (Lord Sydney). The English ships each followed a course through the Straits of Magellan and then struck northwest, finally reaching the coast of New Guinea. Close behind them were the French, who had the same objectives and who directed their efforts to the same area. Captain Louis Antoine de Bougainville reached the Society Islands and Tahiti a year after Wallis, and continued westward, making some new discoveries in the Samoa group. His next landfall was an archipelago that he decided–correctly–was Quiros's long lost and long-sought Australia del Espiritu Santo. Here, he told himself, was the opportunity to solve the old riddle of the Southern Continent.

'So Bougainville sailed away from the Great Barrier Reef. He still believed he had been close to land, but consoled himself with the reflection that it could easily have been 'a cluster of islands' not the east coast of New Holland. His subsequent course took him through the hazardous waters of the Louisiade Archipelago, through the Solomons and New Britain, and north of New Ireland to the Moluccas and eventually to Europe' (Younger).

An English geographer, Alexander Dalrymple, had written a book, in 1769, in which he explained how easy it would be move into what he imagined to be the great, rich, populous continent of the south–a land 'sufficient to maintain the power, dominion, and sovereignty of Britain by employing all its manufacturers and ships.' Dalrymple, who had spent many years in the employ of the East India Company, had returned to London in 1765 and set about a study of material available on the South Seas. He secured a copy of a memorial printed in 1640–discovered by the English expedition that captured Manila in 1762–and from this long-hidden document he deduced the existence of a strait to the south of New Guinea. In a little book, *Discoveries in the South Pacific to 1764*, which was written in 1767 but not published until 1769, Dalrymple included a map in which the strait was marked, as well as the routes of Tasman and Torres. In this booklet he recapitulated all the discoveries that had been made in the South Pacific, including Juan Fernandez Islands off the coast of the Chile, the discoveries of Quiros and Tasman, and those of Le Naire to the north of New Guinea. He drew the conclusion that all these widely separated fragments were probably parts of the same great continent–a continent possibly extending over a hundred degrees of longitude in latitude 40°S, so that it was larger than the whole of Asia from Turkey to the extremity of China!

Cook had no idea of the importance of his discovery of and claims over the East coast of New South Wales. He and his superiors were much more interested in the Great South Land, whose whereabouts were such a puzzle. His second and third voyages were spent in searching between NZ and South America, and between Alaska and north-eastern Asia, but did nothing more in 'our' part of the world. Haskell records that 'England then joined the loyalists in fighting 'our' cousins, the Americans; in the end 'we' were defeated but it set men thinking of the new land in the southern seas. James Matra, a midshipman on the *Endeavour,* drew up a scheme by which loyalists should be set down in NSW to found a colony there, with labourers brought from China and the South Sea Islands to do all the hard work for them. The great difficulty was that the French were also interested in exploring the South Seas, and if Matra's suggestion had been formed as Matra proposed, a strong French fleet would come down upon it and seize the country. Matra asked the Government for help on the grounds that if the scheme were carried out under the direct orders of the Government, there would be no fear of a French attack'. (*Australia and the Australians*–Haskell)

The recent war in the Americas served another argument in favour of Matra's suggestion:

- England had been fighting Spain as well as France; so, if England had to fight them again, NSW would be an admirable centre from which to attack the Dutch and Spanish Islands in the Malay Archipelago. But the argument that prevailed in the end was much more persuasive than that. It was that NSW would be a most suitable place to which to send prisoners.

Impact of the Colonial Isolation During the 1800s

The question of isolation was of positive benefit to the British authorities because the concept of creating a 'dumping ground for human garbage' was synonymous with finding a 'penal wasteland that was out of sight and out of mind'.

However the disadvantages to the Colonial authorities were numerous

a. There was the tyranny of distance-the huge risks, of frightening transportation by sailing ship to a land hitherto unknown, uncharted and unexplored, promising huge risks and great loss of life.
b. Food preservation during the voyage and in the Colony was a challenge with no refrigeration or ice. The only preservatives being salt and pickling.
c. Communications between Sydney and London made exchange of correspondence, obtaining decisions and permission tiresomely long. It often occurred that the Colonial Governor wrote to a Colonial Secretary, who during the twelve months of round trip, had been replaced with another person.
d. Laws and justice, in the Colony, were to be based on British law, but in reality, local laws became a mix of common sense and personal philosophies e.g. Lt Governor Collins, as Advocate-General in the

Colony desperately needed law books to practice, but they were never sent. Bligh, as Governor, ruled virtually as a despot and tyrannical dictator, knowing that a sea trip of seven months was between him and any admonishment or complaints being heard.

Summary

As Marjorie Barnard points out:

"It is difficult to conceive of a plan that is based on a colony of social misfits on a coast that all reports had described as barren, waterless and dangerous. James Matra put a more credible plan forward in 1783. He had at least seen the east coast of the continent and Joseph Banks supported his scheme. Matra wrote

The climate and soil are so happily adapted to produce every various and valuable production of Europe that with good management and a few settlers, in twenty or thirty years they might cause a revolution in the whole system of European commerce and secure to England a monopoly of some part of it, and a very large share in the whole."

These schemes, however credible the source would have fallen on stony ground but for an uncomfortable by-product of the American War of Independence. In the days of the Old Dominion, England had got rid of her felons very easily and inexpensively by shipping them off to the plantations of Virginia. At first the government paid contractors 5 pound a head to carry them across the Atlantic. Later it became a better bargain. The contractors made their profit at the American end. The services of a skilled man for the term of his punishment were sold for between 15 and 20 pound. Women brought from 8 to 10 pound each. This showed a good profit although deaths were usually heavy. The convicts were slaves in all but name. Once handed over the government took no more notice of them.

Our revisionist theory is much more complex than the simplistic traditional opinion.

It would seem that

- foreign policy,
- Trade and economic policy,
- Scientific and technical opportunities, and
- Supplying the military (mainly the naval stores)

were the fundamental considerations in determining to occupy the colony, following which the answer to the question–how are we going to pay for any settlement, especially since this excursion will be government sponsored–was answered with the suggestion that the prisons are overflowing in Britain; it is costing the government upwards of 32 pound per convict per year; why don't we transport the overflow of convicts and the poor and unemployed people to the new colony as fodder for its economic development and divert some, if not all of the funds used to support them in Britain to the support of these people in a new colony; it will only be the original shipment that will be degenerates; their successors will be free peoples able to look after themselves both financially and economically, and Britain will not only have rid itself of these drains on the economy of Britain but have created the basis for future trade with the mother country and its colonies.

LEGISLATING FOR THE COLONY

Westminster legislation that affected the colony of NSW 1750-1850

A full listing of Westminster Legislation is to be found at the end of this Chapter and includes approximately 120 statutes that directly related to the Colonies in Australia. Forty-three of the most important pieces of Legislation have been summarily described in the forthcoming section of this study with appropriate footnote references for further study.

1. 4 Geo I c. 2 (1717)

The intention of this early statute was to authorise transportation of prisoners by contractors. This legislation "legitimised trade in convicts, with convicts being slaves in all but name. Once they were handed over to the contractor the Government took no further interest in them, save devoutly to hope that they would never return. In the 17th century, as a matter of indulgence and to meet a scarcity of labour, prisoners might be pardoned on condition that they worked for five years in some of the King's plantations. At the end of that time they would be granted land, again on a condition, this time that they did not return to England without the King's licence. This more humane form of banishment was still on the statute book in 1718 when this other Act of Parliament (4 Geo I, c.2) entitled 'An Act for the further preventing robbery, burglary and other felonies, and for the more effectual transportation of felons and unlawful exporters of wool etc" superseded it. The effect is in the complete handing over of the convict to the ship-owner who undertook to take him out of the country. The land grant was quietly forgotten, the embargo on return was left to take care of itself as it was sufficiently difficult of achievement to prevent it from being an issue".

2. 4 Geo I c. 11 (1717)

This Act only authorised transportation to the colonies and plantations of North America, and as the independence of the American colonies had been recognised, further legislation was necessary. Accordingly in 1784, the 'Transportation Act' was passed (refer # 9 below)

3. 3 Geo III c. 96 (1763)
4. 16 Geo III c. 43 (1776)
5. 24 Geo III c. 56 (1774)

In 1784, the Imperial Parliament passed this statute, intituled "An Act for the effectual transportation of felons and other offenders, and to authorize the removal of prisoners in certain cases, and for other purposes therein mentioned". This law empowered the King, with the advice of the Privy Council, to appoint places to which felons might be transferred. By an order in Council, dated 6th December 1786, His Majesty's territory of New Holland was appointed a place for the reception of persons within the meaning of the Act.

By letters patent and commission dated 2nd April 1787, Captain Arthur Phillip was appointed Governor and Vice-Admiral of the territory. The commission also defined the territory as 'From the north cape or northern extremity of the coast called Cape York, in latitude 10° 37' south, to the south cape or the southern extremity of the coast in latitude 43° 39' south, and inland to the westward as far as 135° east longitude, reckoning from the meridian of Greenwich; including all islands adjacent in the Pacific Ocean within the aforesaid latitudes"

6. 18 Geo III c. 12 (1778)

Quick & Garran call this statute the 'famous Declaratory Act in which the British Parliament, profiting by the lessons of the American Rebellion, renounced its intention to again tax the colonies. It removed all doubts as to the powers of colonial legislatures to alter or repeal the general mass of English Law, such as the law of primogeniture, inheritance etc not made operative, by statute, throughout the Empire'

The Acts 18 Geo III, c.12 and 28 and 29 Vic.c.63 are the charters of Colonial Independence. By the first it is promised that the British Parliament will not impose any duty, tax or assessment whatsoever, payable in any part of His Majesty's colonies, provinces, and plantations in North America or the West Indies. The latter Act is known as the Colonial Laws Validity Act, 1865, and provides that no colonial law shall be deemed to be void or inoperative on the ground of repugnancy to the law of England, unless it is repugnant to the provisions of an Imperial Act especially applicable to the colony in which such colonial law was passed.

7. 27 Geo III c. 2 (1787)

The judicial authority necessary for the government of the new settlement was derived partly from statute and partly from prerogative, similarly assumed to exist. This Act intituled "An Act to enable His Majesty to establish a court of Criminal Jurisdiction on the eastern coast of New South Wales and the parts adjacent thereto", authorized the Crown by letters patent to erect a criminal court for the trial and punishment of treasons, felonies, and misdemeanours. This court, similar in constitution to a court of admiralty in its criminal jurisdiction, was composed of a Judge Advocate and six naval or military officers to be selected by the governor. There was this ample statutory authority for the administration of criminal law suitable for a penal colony, but none suitable for a free community.

8. 34 Geo III.c. 74 (1779)

This 1779 Act was passed and was designed to supersede the older form of punishment, and gave expression to the hope that even hardened criminals might be reclaimed. The Act provided for the continuance of transportation, to places other than North America, but it also authorised the erection of penitentiary houses, and in the preamble, the expression was made that many of the offenders who were sentenced to transportation, might be deterred from the "commission of further crimes and brought back to industrious habits. The punishment suggested in the Act was "solitary imprisonment, accompanied by well regulated labour and religious instruction"

9. 20 Geo III c. 47 (1780)
10. 24 Geo III. c 12 (1783)

The preamble of this act of 1783 explains the difficulties of the situation, admitting that it would be some time before those difficulties could disappear. As a temporary expedient, Parliament authorised the appointment of overseers, to whom criminals sentenced to transportation might be transferred. The overseers were to permit the convicts to work under proper supervision, but the convicts were to receive only half of the profits of their labour; the other half was to be retained by the overseers, who were, in return, to feed and clothe the prisoners. This approach apparently did not contain the satisfactory solution, for in the following year, a successor act (24 Geo III c.56-refer below) gave the King (in-council) power 'to declare the places in or out of his dominions to which such offenders should be conveyed'. The act of 1783 was repealed except in so far as it affected convicts who had already been dealt with under its provisions.

11 24 Geo.III. c.56 (1784) "Transportation Act"

In 1784, the Imperial Parliament passed this statute intituled "An Act for the effectual transportation of felons and other offenders, and to authorise the removal in certain cases, and for other purposes therein mentioned". This law empowered the King, with the advice of the Privy Council, to appoint places to which felons might be transferred. By an Order in Council dated 6th December 1786, the "Territory of New South Wales situation on the east part of New Holland" was appointed a place for the reception of persons within the meaning of the Act

12. 27 Geo. III.c 2 (1787) "Establishing a Court of Criminal Jurisdiction"

In 1787 this Act intituled "An Act to enable His Majesty to establish a Court of Criminal Jurisdiction on the eastern coast of New South Wales" authorised the Crown, by letters patent, to erect a criminal court for the trial and punishment of treasons, felonies and misdemeanours. This court, which was similar in its constitution to a court of Admiralty in its criminal jurisdiction, was composed of a Judge Advocate and six naval officers to be selected by the Governor. This legislation was suitable for a penal settlement but not sufficient for a free community. By letters patent dated 2nd April 1787, the Crown also created a court of civil jurisdiction having power to deal in a summary way with personal actions and probate and administrative proceedings 'according to the laws of England'.

13. 27 Geo III c.13 (1787)

In 1787, this statute brought the various revenues of the Crown in Britain into a 'Consolidated Revenue' Fund into which flows every stream of the public revenue and from whence issues the supply of funds for every public service. In the colony of NSW, the land revenues were for many years kept distinct from the general revenues; but with the granting of responsible government, a Consolidated Revenue Fund was created. This feature of financial administration, universal in all the self-governing parts of the empire was included in both the NSW (1856) and the Australian Constitutions (1901).

14. 27 Geo III c. 36 (1787)
15. 27 Geo III c. 49 (1787)
16. 27 Geo III c. 38 (1787)

Copyright in prints and engravings were originally secured in 1735 under 8 Geo II, c.1. This second statute secured copyrights in designs for manufacturers. This second statute was subsequently amended by the Act 5 & 6 Vic, c.100, (1842) and 21 & 22 Vic, c.70 (1858). By the Act of 1842 all articles of manufacture and substances on which designs are executed, are divided into thirteen classes; for some of which the copyright of the design was fixed at three years, for others nine months and for others twelve months. By the Act 5 & 6 Will. IV, c.65 the right of printing and publishing lectures belongs to the lecturer, subject to compliance with certain conditions. The subsequent Patent Designs and Trade Marks Act of 1836 (46 & 47 Vic, c.57) consolidated all prior statutes relating to designs. The consolidated act defines the term design as any design applicable to any article of manufacture, or to any substance, artificial or natural, or partly thereof, whether the design is applicable for the pattern, or for the shape or configuration, or by whatever means it is applicable, whether of printing, painting, embroidering, weaving, sewing, modelling, mechanical or chemical, separate or combined, not being a design for a sculpture.

17. 30 Geo III. c.47 (1790)

This statute gave colonial governors authority to issue pardons and to assert that the disabilities and incapacities consequent upon attainder were not removed by such a pardon, unless the name of the recipient were later included in a pardon issued under the Great Seal. Up to that time, the nature and the effect of the Governor's pardons, or remissions of sentences, had been considered as effective in restoring all privileges, of whatsoever kind, that had been lost by conviction. Suddenly the emancipists were told that, owing to the state in which their pardons had been allowed to lie, they might be prevented by judicial form from recovering their rights, that is, whenever their opponents might choose to take advantage of the defect.

Commissioner Bigge wrote of this situation and the legislation in his report on law and order in the colony:

He reported "a power is there (in Act 30 Geo III, c. 47) given to the King or his representatives to remit absolutely or conditionally the whole or any part or terms of the sentences of felons, and that such instruments of remissions should have the like force and effect as if His Majesty had signified his royal intention of mercy under the sign-manual. A pardon, under the sign-manual had been stated by a great legal authority to imply only a preparation for pardon, and if that construction be applied to the situation of convicts whose sentences are remitted by the Governor of NSW, it would seem that the interval that must necessarily elapse between the period in which it is bestowed by them must form an intermediate state of civil existence that is certainly not consistent with a state of freedom".

Bigge concluded on this point "therefore, the words of this statute are only directory and point out the manner in which the effect is to be given to the acts of remission of the governors of NSW; and although there may have been an intention of reserving an exercise of the royal discretion upon them, yet there could have been none of suspending the benefits intended to be conferred upon convicts who received the governor's pardon and continued to reside in the colony".

18. 31 Geo III. c.31 (1791)

This statute conveyed voting rights to people in the Province of Canada, and was quoted by W.C. Wentworth in his deliberations to have a property franchise incorporated into any constitution for NSW. He had expressed in his *Australian* newspaper his willingness to accept the various franchise disqualifications which this statute applied, excepting only that provision which declared that no-one should vote who had 'been attainted for treason or felony in any court of law within any of His Majesty's dominions (sect 23)

19. 34 Geo III c. 84 (1794)

The House of Commons established 'penitentiary houses' under this statute, as an alternative to the Hulks, and transportation to NSW. The debate in the Commons in 1810 led to the formation of a select committee, as it was 'shameful' that the penal settlement had gone on for twenty-four years without enquiry into its success or failure

Many in the House, led by Sir Samuel Romilly, thought the penal settlement was only a social experiment and that transportation was inappropriate–'something should be done to provide for the reformation of convicted criminals. There was a consensus that transportation had been 'inefficacious' on account of the administrative system, which had been adopted there. The Government wanted to avoid a full enquiry and set up a first committee to report upon the expediency of erecting penitentiary houses, but Romilly wanted to expand the scope of the enquiry and this popular move led to the appointment of the select committee on 12th February 1812 to inquire into 'the state of New South Wales'.

20. 35 Geo III. c.92 (1795)

This statute restricted ships of less than 350 tons from the traffic between NSW and the United Kingdom. A companion statute (53 Geo III, c.155–refer # 22 below) forbade ships of less than 350 tons to sail between the Cape of Good Hope and Cape Horn without permission from the East India Company. Reference was also made to the duty of 6/8d, which was charged on every hundredweight of wool imported into England, and to the duty, which was imposed on tanning bark. These taxes, it was argued, checked the development of natural industries in NSW, so the settlers in NSW claimed, and they sought the repeal of the provisions, which regulated the size of ships and also for the removal of the objectionable duties.

21. 39 Geo III c. 51 (1799)
22. 39 Geo III c. 67 (1800)

This statute created the union of Great Britain and Ireland. By this British Act and an accompanying Irish Act (40 Geo III c.38) the two Kingdoms became united into one Kingdom under the name of the *United Kingdom of Great Britain and Ireland.* The two parliaments became merged in one Imperial Parliament of the United Kingdom.

23. 46 Geo III c.141 (1806)

The free settlers in the colony petitioned Governor Macquarie to waive the restrictions on the colony imposed from this statute, which forbade ships of less than 350 tons from the traffic between the United Kingdom and NSW.

24. 53 Geo III c. 155 (1813)

At least one of the petitions to Governor Macquarie from free settlers in the colony concerned the statutory restriction contained in this legislation, which forbade ships of less than 350 tons to sail between the Cape of Good Hope and Cape Horn, without permission from the East India Company. (Refer also # 18 above)

25. 54 Geo III c. 61 (1814)
26. 55 Geo III c. 146 (1815)
27. 56 Geo III c. 27 (1816)
28. 59 Geo III c. 114 (1819)

This was a special piece of legislation, passed to protect the governors of the colony from vexatious prosecution (and the consequences of the imposition of illegal duties, raised to Macquarie by the second chief justice, Baron Field), and to continue existing duties, and to authorise the imposition of further duties still.

29. 59 Geo III.c.122 (1819)

This statute, which was previewed in the Bigge instructions by Bathurst opened the trade between Britain and the colony to ships of every size and released the various products of the colony from payment of duties when the goods were imported into Britain.

30. 59 Geo III c. 52 (1819)
31. 1 Geo.IV.c.62 (1820)

This was a 'continuing' piece of legislation, for the Act 59 Geo III c. 114 (1819). The primary act of 1819, which had the effect of an Act of Indemnity, only ran until January 1st 1821 but its provisions were continued firstly by this legislation of 1820, and then again in 1821 (1 & 2 Geo IV, c.8) and in 1822 (3 Geo IV, c.96). They were then made perpetual by an Act of 1823 (4 Geo IV, c.96)

32. 1 & 2 Geo IV c. 8 (1821)

This was one of three statutes (the other two were 59 Geo III, c.114; 3 Geo IV, c.96) by which the governors of NSW were given limited powers to impose local taxation in the shape of customs duties on spirits, tobacco, and other goods imported into the colony.

33. 3 Geo IV c. 3 (1822)
34. 4 Geo IV. c. 96 (1822)

Three successive Acts, (refer 59 Geo III, c.114; 3 Geo IV, c.96; 1 & 2 Geo IV c. 8) empowered (and then renewed twice) the Governor of New South Wales to impose local taxation in the shape of customs duties on spirits, tobacco, and other goods imported into the country. The first Act, in addition, being introduced in 1819 was used to ratify the acts of Governors from 1800, when Governor King first imposed a duty on spirits. Successive Governors from King (Hunter and Macquarie) were made immune, and protected against any challenge to the revenues raised in the colony between 1800 and 1819. Since this and its successor Act had 'sunset' clauses, the legislation had to be renewed in 1821 and again in 1822. Through this last Act (c. 96) Van Diemen's Land (VDL) was separated from NSW as a dependency. S.24 authorised VDL to be proclaimed an independent colony.

35. 4 Geo IV. c. 96 (1823) "For the Better Administration of Justice"

This Act of 1823 was designed to give Sir Thomas Brisbane immediate but temporary access to 'local self-government'. It was intituled "An Act to provide until the first day of July 1827, and until the end of the next session of Parliament, for the better administration of justice in New South Wales, and for the more effectual government thereof. The old military courts of 1787 were abolished, and a Supreme Court and Court of Appeal, on the English model, were authorised to be erected. The Crown was empowered to create, by warrant, a Council consisting of from five to seven persons charged with certain legislative powers of a limited character. They were to be appointed during the pleasure of the Crown. They could advise but not overrule the governor in matters of legislation, and all laws and ordinances passed with their approval were required to be laid before the British

Parliament. On 17th May 1824, a charter of justice was promulgated, and Francis Forbes was appointed the first Chief Justice"

36. 6 Geo IV. C.50 (1825)

The Chief Justice of the Supreme Court in NSW sent a letter to Darling, in which he expressed the opinion that under the provisions of this legislation, expirees, as well as those that received pardons, were eligible to serve on juries. However, when Darling submitted the correspondence to Secretary of State Viscount Goderich, Darling was informed the opinion was unimportant, as a new Act would 'put an end to trials by jury in the Quarter sessions (HRA 1:14; 394). ACV Melbourne points out that "it is evident, from this reply that the British government did not approve of the way in which the intention of the Act of 1823 (see above, 4 Geo IV, c. 96) had been evaded.

37. 8 Geo IV c. 2 (1827)

This Act was had been designed to provide for the licensing and general regulations of newspapers in the colony, and, with the exception of clauses which, had been rejected by the Chief Justice (Forbes), in was enacted

38. 8 Geo IV. c. 3 (1827)

This second piece of legislation, a companion piece to the one above, contained provisions, which sought to impose a stamp duty on newspapers. The NSW Legislative Council accepted it, but its publication aroused a storm of protest. There had been 'informalities' in the procedure, and because Chief Justice Forbes claimed not to have been given the necessary certificate by the Crown on the statute, and because he therefore expressed the opinions that the measures were repugnant to the laws of England, Governor Darling was compelled to withdraw the Act by public notice (HRA 1:13:291)

39. 9 Geo IV c. 83 (1828)

Difficulties had been created in NSW through the granting of supervisory powers over legislation to the Chief Justice. One concern was the offering of 'technical' objections by the court, but it was accepted that changes were necessary to the Act of 1823 while still providing for the legality of acts of the Legislative Council. One suggestion made was for the enactment of a provision applying all the laws and statutes of the realm to NSW, and giving to the Governor and the Council the power to dispose of doubtful cases by declaratory acts.

40. 5 & 6 Vic. C76 (1842) NSW Representative Legislature

This Act intituled "An Act for the Government of NSW and VDL"; created Legislative Council for NSW, but it did not do so for VDL. The whole of the provisions of this statute, with several minor exceptions, were confined to NSW. The Act also empowered Her Majesty, by letters patent, to separate 'from NSW any part of the territory of that colony lying to the northward of 26° south latitude, and to erect such territory into a separate colony or colonies'. By section 7 of this Act, it was provided that the legislature already existing in VDL under the Act of 1828, might now establish within the colony a Legislative Council, to consist of not more than 24 members of whom 1/3rd should be nominated by the Crown, and the remainder elected by the inhabitants of the colony.

42. 13 & 14 Vic. C.59 (1850) Australian Colonies Act (NSW, Vic, SA & VDL

This legislation amended the above statute in regards to qualifications of electors and of elective members of the proposed Legislative Council of Victoria was to be the same as those of the electors and elective members of the upper house in NSW. This legislation extended power for each colonial governor to draft a Constitution (s.32) 'for the establishment of a parliament' It was proposed that the new parliaments should consist of a Legislative Council and a House of Assembly to replace the existing Councils. For VDL the House of Assembly could consist of 30 members elected by popular franchise and 15 members in the Legislative Council, also elected by qualified voters. Bills for appropriating any part of the revenue, or imposing any tax, rate, duty or impost, were required to originate in the assembly. This bi-cameral legislature thus created could exercise only "the powers and functions of the Legislative Council for which the same may be substituted".

43. 29 & 30 Vic. C74 (1866) (Q & G p40, 59)

This 'declaratory Act was intended to remove any doubts that customs Bills were to be reserved for the Queen's assent. Two new powers were also conferred on the Governor and Legislative Council by this Act, which they did not possess previously. The Governor, in Council, was authorised to impose and levy duties of customs on the importation of goods, wares and merchandise imported into the colony from any part of the world, subject to the limitation that no differential duties could be imposed. Power was also given to the Governor, in Council, to alter the qualifications of electors.

Summary of all Westminster Legislation concerning the Colonies in Australia to 1856

i. Responsible Government

Powers of the Governors[xxiv]
Charter of Justice (1814)[xxiv]

4 Geo IV, c.96 (1823) Act for the administration of Justice in NSW & VDL
Independence of VDL (1825)
9 Geo IV, c.83 (1828) Act for the Administration of Justice in NSW
10 Geo IV, c.22 (1830) Act for the government of WA
4 & 5 Will IV, c.95 (1834) Act creating the colony of SA
1 & 2 Vic, c.60 (1838) Act amending SA constitution
5 & 6 Vic, c76 (1842) Act for the government of NSW & VDL
13 &14 Vic, c.59 (1850) Australian Colonies Government Act

ii Transportation

i. 4 Geo I, c.11 Act for preventing robbery, burglary and other felonry, and for transportation of Felons–(1717)
ii. 16 Geo III, c.43-The Hulks Act-(1776)
iii. 24 Geo III, c.56–Renewal of Transportation–(1784)
iv. 4 & 5 Will. IV, c.95 Forbidding convicts into South Australia (1734)
v. Right of Governor to assign convicts

    1. 4 Geo I, c.11
    2. 24 Geo III, c.56
    3. 5 Geo IV, c.84

vi. Right of Governors to grant pardons

    1. 30 Geo III, c.47 (1790)
    2. 4 Geo IV, c.96

vii. Rights of Emancipist convicts to Land Grants

    1. HRA 1:11:579
    2. HRA III: 5:675

viii. References on the Transportation Program:

    i. *Select Committee on Transportation of 1812*
    ii. *Select Committee on State of Gaols of 1819*
    iii. *Select Committee on Secondary Punishment of 1831-32*
    iv. *Select Committee on Transportation of 1837-8*
    v. *Committee on Convict Discipline & Transportation of 1853*
    vi. J.T. Bigge: *State of NSW–Report No. 1 to House of Commons–1822*
    vii. Macquarie Policy on Emancipists

iii Criminal Code

Blackstone provides a suitable introduction to this section when he writes "It is a melancholy truth, that among the variety of actions which men are daily liable to commit, no less than 160 have been declared by Act of Parliament to be felonies without benefit of clergy, or in other words to be worthy of instant death. So dreadful a list, instead of diminishing, increases the number of offenders. The injured, through compassion, will often forbear to prosecute: juries will sometimes forget their oaths and either acquit the guilty or mitigate the nature of the offence; and judges, will respite one half of the convicts and recommend them to royal mercy. Among so many chances of escaping, the needy and hardened offender overlooks the multitude that suffers; he boldly engages in some desperate attempt to relieve his wants or supply his vices; and if the hand of justice overtakes him, he deems himself peculiarly unfortunate, in falling at last to those laws, which long impunity had taught him to contemn".

27 Geo III, c.2 (1787) Act creating the criminal Court in NSW

iv. Government Infrastructure

Legislative Power of the Governors

v. Civil Code

The list of civil code_statutes must include the three charter companies formed in the British Parliament and which created the Land Grant companies in NSW, VDL and SA.

Van Diemen's Land Company (1824) 6 Geo IV, c.39
Australian Agricultural Company (1824) 5 Geo IV, c.86
South Australian Company (1834) 4 & 5 Will. IV, c.95

FEDERATION & COMMONWEALTH-STATE RELATIONS-A RETROSPECTIVE

a. What provisions did the Commonwealth Constitution make for the States?

S.106 *The Constitution of each State shall, subject to this Constitution, continue as at the establishment of the Commonwealth, or as at the admission or establishment of the State, as the case may be, until altered in accordance with the Constitution of the State.*

S. 107 *Every power of the Parliament of a Colony, which becomes a State, shall continue as at the establishment of the Commonwealth.*

S. 108 Every law in force in a Colony when it becomes a state shall continue in force in the state, until the Federal Parliament makes provision.

S. 109 when a law of a state is inconsistent with a law of the Commonwealth, the latter shall prevail and the former shall, to the extent of the inconsistency, be invalid.

The Sovereignty of the State includes the old powers previously granted by the Imperial Parliament (in 1856) and the new powers freshly granted-these constitute the quasi-sovereignty of the Commonwealth. Quick & Garran (Annotated Constitution of the Commonwealth) suggest (P929) that "in the process of distribution nearly all the new powers and a proportion of the old powers were vested in the Federal Government, the guiding principle being that those powers which could best be exercised by a Parliament representing a united people, should be transferred from the States to the Federal Government. This distribution left the States in full possession and enjoyment of their original institutions and their previously acquired powers, minus only this deduction and transfer. Thus the States retain their Constitutions, their Parliaments, their executive and judicial organisations, subject only to the loss of those powers which by the Federal Constitution are withdrawn from the scope and operation of the State Constitutions and brought within the sphere of the Federal Constitution."

Sir Henry Parkes, in 1891, set out the basis of the transference of powers and the resultant relationship (Papers of the National Convention-1891-P24), ". . . the four most important conditions on which we must proceed.

(1st) That the powers and privileges and territorial rights of the several existing colonies shall remain intact, except in respect to such surrenders as may be agreed upon as necessary and incidental to the establishment of the Federal Government

(2nd) To the highest degree possible, we should satisfy the mind of the Colonies that we have no intention of crippling their powers, invading their rights, diminishing their authority.

(3rd) It is therefore proposed to satisfy each colony that neither their territorial rights nor their powers of legislation for the well-being of their own country will be interfered with in any way that can impair the security of those rights."

The framers of the 1901 Commonwealth Constitution ensured that each state retained the right to hold direct and immediate communications with the Imperial Government in all matters relating to States' business. The point was made at the 1891 Convention by a number of delegates that 'Australia cannot afford to speak with seven voices instead of with one voice-only on matters appertaining to themselves' Deakin, Parkes, Braddon and Kingston all opposed the intention of maintaining direct states contact with England, but the original motion was carried 16 to 6.

In relation to the S.107 provision regarding the 'power of the Parliament of a Colony', Quick & Garran (P933) suggests that ". . . as Federal legislation becomes more active and extensive the powers contemplated by the Constitution will be gradually withdrawn from the States Parliaments and absorbed by the Federal Parliament. The powers to be withdrawn may be classified 'exclusive' and 'concurrent'. Exclusive powers are those absolutely withdrawn from the State Parliaments and placed solely within the jurisdiction of the Federal Parliament. Concurrent powers are those, which may be exercised by the State Parliament simultaneously with the Federal Parliament, subject to the condition that, in the event of conflict, the Federal law prevails.

A third classification is foreshadowed-that of residuary powers. These being the residuary authority left to the Parliament of each State, after the exclusive and concurrent grants to the Federal Parliament, which embrace a large mass of constitutional, territorial, municipal and social powers, including control over

* Agriculture
* Banking
* State borrowing
* Bounties on minerals and metals
* Charities
* State constitution
* Corporations
* State courts
* Various state departments, such as
* Education
* Factories
* Fisheries
* Forests
* Health . . . ."

B Limitations of State powers

S. *114 A state shall not raise or maintain any naval or military force, or impose any tax on property of any kind belonging to the state, nor shall the Commonwealth impose any tax on property belonging to the state.*

S. *115 A state shall not coin money nor make any coin legal tender in payment of debts*

S. *117 A subject of the Queen shall not be subjected to any discrimination by any other state*

S. *118 Full faith and credit shall be given to the laws, the public accounts and records and the judicial proceedings of every state.*

The framers of the final draft removed the splendid reference in the 1891 draft of S.53 and disturbed the rather erudite balance between the states and the Commonwealth. The 1891 draft commenced 'The States Assembly (the Senate) shall have equal power with the House of Representatives'. However the framers of the final 1901 version simply referred to 'The Senate shall . . . .'

c. "The States"

Quick & Garran (P927) see the establishment of the states' rights in this way:

"In accordance with the agreement of the people of the Australian colonies to unite in one Federal Commonwealth under the Crown, the British Parliament, in which resides the supreme and absolute sovereignty of the Empire, has established the Commonwealth and ratified and legalised the Constitution previously approved by the people.

The Commonwealth is the united political society thus established; it consists of the people and the pre-existing colonies, converted into states.

By the Federal Constitution the State Constitutions were confirmed and continued in existence, subject to the grants of power made by the Constitution to the Federal organs of Government. In addition to these assignments of power between the two sets of governing agencies, the Constitution contains a section enabling the people of the united community, in the exercise of their quasi-sovereign power, to amend the supreme instrument of government itself.

States powers and State institutions, Federal powers all spring directly from the same supreme source-British sovereignty.

It may be added that the governing powers reserved to the states are not inferior in origin to the governing powers vested in the Federal Government. The States do not derive their governing powers and institutions from the Federal Government, in the way that municipalities derive their powers from the Parliament of their country. The state governments were not established by the Federal Government, nor are they in any way dependent upon the Federal Government, except by the special provisions of S.119. The states existed as colonies prior to the passing of the Federal Constitution, and possessed their own charters of Government, in the shape of the Constitutions granted to them by the Imperial Parliament."

> **S.119 The** *Commonwealth shall protects every state against invasion . . . .*

S.106 *The constitution of each state shall continue as at the establishment of the Commonwealth or until altered in accordance with the Constitution of that state*

d. Federal-State Financial Relations.

Gareth Evans contributed to a work on 'Australia's Constitution' and their chapter on Federal-State Financial Relations makes numerous points on the subject.

(P104) "Not surprisingly, financial questions dominated pre-federation discussions. Governments are preoccupied with money, and this was no less true in the 19th century than it is today. At that time the major source of revenue for the states was customs and excise duty: the framers of the constitution anticipated that revenue from customs and excise would be more than sufficient for the new commonwealth, and that there would be plenty left over for the states-Sir Samuel Griffith speculated that the annual cost of federation would be less than the price of a dog licence per head of population of Australia.

The constitutional provisions concerning financial matters reflected this view. They gave the commonwealth exclusive powers over customs and excise duties, but otherwise allowed all governments-both state and commonwealth-general taxing powers; they further required the commonwealth to pay surplus revenue to the states.

A combination of political and judicial developments, together with some constitutional amendments, has given the commonwealth an overriding financial supremacy in three critical areas-the raising of revenue, the distribution of revenue and public borrowing.

Sections 105 and 105A of the constitution empower the commonwealth to take over the public debts of the states or to make agreements with the states concerning those debts and the states have been dependent upon the commonwealth at various times to bail them out when budgetary problems have increased.

The general view at the time of federation was that the commonwealth would need little revenue to carry out its functions. This assumption was reflected in the text of the constitution. The commonwealth was given exclusive power to levy customs and excise duties; it was thought that this would generate revenue way in excess of the Commonwealth's actual needs and elaborate provision was made to govern the distribution of 'surplus revenue'. The commonwealth was also given general taxing power, of the kind retained by the states but very few thought that this would ever have much practical significance.

Customs & Excise duties. The commonwealth's exclusive power to levy these duties is found in S. 90. Customs duties presently (1983) amount to about 5% of commonwealth tax revenue. Excise duties at around 15% and sales taxes at around 7%.

The high court's ever more expansive interpretation of the meaning of 'excise duty' has meant that-since the power here is exclusive to the commonwealth-the states have been steadily squeezed out of taxing fields that are available in every other federation; in particular sales taxes, turnover tax and receipts duties.

Other taxing powers S. 51(2) gives the commonwealth its general taxing power. Subject only to the proviso that it cannot be used to discriminate between states. By as early as 1918-19 commonwealth income taxes almost equalled revenue from duties and exceeded the income taxes raised by the states. Income tax has continued to be the commonwealth's major source of revenue although it has broadened its interest into company tax (13% of revenues)

It was s.51 (2) combined with the s.96 power to make conditional grants, which enabled the commonwealth to introduce the uniform tax scheme in 1942. A vital element of the scheme was that a portion of income-tax revenue would be distributed to a state only if it had not levied any income tax itself. In effect, financial assistance was to be granted to a state only on condition that it abstained from exercising a power it had previously exercised every year until 1942. The states challenged its validity twice in the high court, in 1942 and 1957, and although the high court ruled invalid the priority given to the commonwealth tax (over any state collections), the remaining elements of the scheme provided in practice a sufficient basis for the commonwealth to retain its supremacy in the income-tax field.

Indirect Taxes. The exclusive power of the commonwealth to raise customs and excise duties has had a marked effect on the ability of the states to raise indirect taxes. There is a somewhat anomalous exception concerning business franchise licensing schemes, arising from decisions of the high court in the *Dennis Hotels Case* of 1966 and the Tasmanian *Tobacco Case* in 1974. In these cases the court held that state licensing fees based on sales volume were valid, and has since been extended to cover tobacco, liquor and petroleum products, and is estimated at about 10% of states revenues.

Formal Commonwealth State Meetings & Bargaining Bases

a. Premiers' Conferences-involves policy-making functions
b. Loan Council-created following the Financial Agreement in 1927 to coordinate borrowing, debt management and grant activity-backed by the new S.105A of 1928
c. Grants Commission-distributes money to the states, in terms of the financial burden imposed upon state residents etc available in each states-brings equality to all Australians

General Revenue Assistance

The Federal-State Financial Agreements led to a variety of revenue sharing arrangements between 1901 and 2000 and this period has been classified into 6 distinct periods:

1. The surplus revenue period 1901-1910
2. The per capita grant period 1910-1927
3. The financial agreement period 1927-1942
4. The uniform tax reimbursement period 1942-1959
5. The Uniform Taxation Financial Assistance period 1959-1999
6. The GST 'growth tax' period 2000-

Options for Reform

The most obvious problem in Federal-State financial relations remains the continuing imbalance between powers and financial resources. The constitution divides powers between the commonwealth and the states, but there is no corresponding allocation of financial responsibility.

An immediate consequence of the extent of the States' dependence on the Commonwealth is that they have difficulty designing their own budgets and setting their own priorities.

In addition to all this, complaints are made by the three biggest states that they receive too low a proportion of Federal Revenue grants. The Commonwealth Grants Commission Reports of 1981 and 1982 indicated that if tax sharing were based on fiscal equalisation principles, substantial extra sums would go to NSW, Victoria and Queensland.

NSW and Victoria make above-average revenue efforts, while other states can impose relatively low rates of taxation and charges

It would appear that the effect of transferring the revenue raised from the GST to the states will go some way to meeting their needs and past objections that they were not participating in a growth tax. The GST is a growth tax and will offer the states a growing share of indirect taxes. The unknown is how the smaller states will share in extra revenue needed. Will the grant's commission remain in effect and create a base for redistribution of revenue from the larger states to the smaller states? If so, from what source will that revenue be derived? From the GST or from the commonwealth coffers? On a loan basis or grant basis?

e. Destruction of the States

David Solomon sets out in his work-'*The Political High Court*' some of the cases that have contributed to the downfall or decline of the strengths between the Commonwealth and the States. He calls his chapter 'The Destruction of the States' (P62)

"The High Court has delivered so many blows against the states that it is difficult to decide which might have been the ultimate mortal blow to their independence. The history of Commonwealth-state relations is replete with decisions by the court, which helped make them the inferior partners in the Australian federation.

Probably the most important concerned financial matters-in particular taxes and who could levy them. Others involved the extent of the legislative powers of the Commonwealth in section 51 of the Constitution, and the way the court has applied section 109, which provides that where the commonwealth and the state make laws that are inconsistent, the commonwealth shall 'prevail' and the state laws are 'invalid'.

The inevitable decline of the states was predicted only a year or so after the commonwealth came into being. Federal attorney general Alfred Deakin predicted that 'the independence of our states is doomed.' The constitution (he said) had left the states 'legally free, but financially bound to the chariot wheels of the central government. Our constitution may remain unaltered but a vital change will have taken place in the relations between the states and the commonwealth. The commonwealth will have acquired a control over the states, while every extension of political power will be made by its means and go to increase its relative superiority.'

The first legislative and legal steps to establish that dominance occurred when Deakin was Prime Minister in 1908. The constitution makers had given the commonwealth and the states a series of directions about the way their financial affairs were to be organised in the early years of federation. The states were to be paid all revenues from customs duties (less expenses of collection) until such time as the commonwealth imposed uniform customs duties (S. 89) those uniform duties came into effect on 8th October 1901. For the first five years after federation and until otherwise provided by the parliament, the commonwealth had to pay its unexpended balances of revenue to the states (S. 93). And for the ten years after federation, the Commonwealth had to pay 75% of its net revenue from customs and excise to the states, plus any of the remaining quarter of that revenue that was surplus after commonwealth expenditures.

To clarify this position, the parliament enacted the Surplus Revenue Act in 1908 and in October of 1908 the High Court held the Act to be valid despite the preponderance of support in favour of reserve powers. Faced with the need to begin financing a new navy and an old-age pension scheme, the government decided to begin setting aside money to meet future commitments. This action impacted the surplus to be returned to the states and the court decided it appropriate that set-asides were a proper expense.

Chief Justice Sir Samuel Griffith (a delegate from Queensland to the Federation Debates) wrote that '*if a sum of money is lawfully appropriated out of Consolidated Revenue for a specific purpose, that sum cannot be regarded as forming part of a surplus until the expenditure of it is no longer lawful or no longer thought necessary by the government.*'

During World War I the relative importance of the states was further diminished, and the commonwealth entered the income tax field as well as introducing a wide range of other taxes, primarily to finance expenditure on the war. The High Court agreed that the defence of the commonwealth was paramount and that the financial needs of the commonwealth took precedence over those of the states.

The case (Victoria Vs The Commonwealth (1926) 39 CLR 399 involved a challenge by Victoria and South Australia (supported by NSW) against the validity off grants made by the commonwealth to the states for road construction purposes. It was not until the 1920s that the High Court of Australia provided the next shackle to bind the states to the chariot wheels of the Commonwealth.

The decision that 'The Federal Aid Roads Act' was valid was one of the most crucial in the history of Commonwealth-State relations. It meant that the Commonwealth could use its power to make grants to the states under S. 96 for any purpose, not just a purpose within those heads of power given to the Commonwealth parliament.

The commonwealth decided in 1940 following the Moran Case [*W. R. Moran v. Deputy Commissioner of Taxation (1939) 61CLR 735m and (1940) 63 CLR 338]*

That it was time for Australia to have a uniform taxation system (for income tax) when the High Court approved of the arrangement. What the commonwealth did initially was to use its war powers to get a monopoly of income tax powers, and to use its grants power under S.96 to persuade the States to accept the commonwealth's supremacy.

Federalism involves the division of powers between a central government and provincial interests. In the United States and in Australia this was done by allocating specific powers to the national legislature and leaving what remained to the States? In Canada the provinces were given specific enumerated powers and the national parliament had whatever was left.

One of the functions of the high court is to ensure that the provisions of the constitution are not ignored. It is not a function of the court to preserve any sort of balance between the powers and influence of the commonwealth and the states, perhaps not even to ensure that the states are not discriminated against by the commonwealth (except in extreme circumstances).

f. Potential problems amongst and between the states and Commonwealth

LaNauze in his work 'The Making of the Australian Constitution' (P154) suggests two areas of potential disagreement between the future states, neither of which were directly addressed in the final Constitution. The problems of the rivers and attracting interstate trade are both matters, which have plagued the states since federation and even today.

"In principle, the 'problem of the rivers' was an ancient and familiar one, since river-waters were essential to man's life and activities, and nature cared nothing for his territorial boundaries. By custom or law even hostile states in the old world had been able to come to agreements about their use; and though, as always, nature did some very peculiar things in Australia, at least lawyers in the Federation Convention were aware that riparian law had a long lineage.

By contrast the problem of 'differential' or 'preferential' railway rates was recent, selfish, and entirely man made. In Queensland's absence the argument concerned only New South Wales and Victoria. The rich pastoral district of the Riverina lay in southern NSW, north from Melbourne, the nearest great port, and southwest from Sydney, the railways had crept towards it during the last generation. With its inward and outward commerce as the prize to be gained, the two railway-systems had long been concerned in a war of freight rates, which gave large concessions for the hauls to and from the Riverina, each aiming to penalise traffic on the rival system. Up to some undefined point the practice could be justified by a familiar economic principle, but it could hardly be pretended that the actual rates simply reflected the economies of long hauls: they were devised avowedly, to gain trade whether or not they were profitable to the railways themselves. Since the States owned all railways the test of profitable operation was not conclusive. They had been built to 'develop the country'; the community as a whole ultimately met operating losses. The gains to merchant and shipping firms and to the ports of Melbourne and Sydney from the handling of the Riverina trade were indisputable; and since the railways were there, even for railway finances, more freight was generally better than less."

Divisions between the states in fiscal policies and laws were always going to be a point of contention in later years-differential indirect taxation would affect various states and their ability to keep or attract population and industry, time and time again.

Quick & Garran in a personal observation put the case for independent policies in this way, without recognising the impact of their thoughts (P817): "The federal tariff will be framed to meet the wants of the Australian people; and if, when the desirable level of customs and excise taxation has been reached, any states requiring more revenue for provincial purposes, which it is thought fit to raise by direct taxation, then provincial direct taxation and not federal direct taxation is the obvious resource"

A Conclusion

The usage of 1889 figures to construct a constitutional model for 1901 caused a misreading of the real situation in the country-particularly the economic situation. The effect was that only two states were recognised, as being was disadvantaged instead of the four that were truly disadvantaged under the new Federation.

The four conventions became a constitutional debate with blinkers because of the limited parameters-limited, in fact, by the lack of current facts on the economic situation. The delegates were given the 1889 figures instead of the 1899 figures, which showed a very different story. Only New South Wales by recognising the advantages of free trade, in reality, pre-empted the Constitutional provisional to assign all customs revenues raised by the Colonies to the new Commonwealth. NSW had reduced its customs duties as a percentage of total revenues and could therefore rely on its other revenue raising practices to keep its head above water in matching post-Federation expenditures with revenues available.

One can raise the doubt that delegates from the four smallest states (in terms of revenue) were 'snowed' by the two larger states into not considering all aspects of the current economic climate and implications of the post federation period on the economies of each State. That the smartest minds belonged to Deakin, Reid, Dibbs, Garran and Quick (all from the two largest states is not in doubt) but the Griffith (Qld), Play ford (SA) and Forrest (WA) delegates were overridden numerous times in their efforts to defend their states. Economically the smallest four states had most to lose and were ill prepared for their convention struggles.

What should have been the goals of the delegates to the conventions?

* Unification
* Coordination
* Commonality of efforts
* Goals for the future
* A model for a commonwealth government of 6 unequal states
* Rationalisation of government with states, regions and local governments all vying for purpose

* Centralisation of government
* Equity and equality between all peoples of the country

If these were some of the goals, did the new constitution meet them?

The answer is 'no' to all but the centralisation question and with a stretch it can be accepted that we have greater centralisation of government today as a result of the constitution than was anticipated in 1901.

Certain essential clauses are missing from the constitution of 1901 that in Hindsight would have made the economic well being of the country more Equitable.

* The access to grants, loan funds could have been included for all states and

Recognition of need met with less political bureaucracy

* A simplification to Rationalising government
* Better definition of financial relations between the commonwealth and the states.

SUMMARY and CONCLUSIONS

Does logic apply in these circumstances? If we were planning on settling a newly discovered land, having just lost access to another, would there be only one consideration? I think not! The best report to the authorities would be one that set down the present circumstances in 'our' region, and in 'our' sphere of influence, and then list all the benefits that would accrue to 'our' country, upon making the move to settle or colonise on that new land. It would be a stepping-stone, and not an end in itself.

There would be expenditures associated with the establishment, and thus a cost-benefit analysis would be set down. Even if the costs were to be diverted from another government outlet for expenditure, there would be benefits and the support for that first step would be stronger if the 'opportunity' cost in favour of the new colony was stronger and more favourable than the cost under the former expenditure.

And so it was with Cook's discovery, except the British neglected for 'cost' reasons, the most fundamental of steps–that of reconnoitring the colony before despatching the First fleet. Matra, Phillip and others had strongly suggested a 'forward party' to select the best sight, to commence preparing the sight, commence a basic building program and ensure fresh water and appropriate crops were available when the main party arrived. The authorities refused to go along with this commonsense approach and the consequences were enormous for Phillip. Cook and Banks believed, in an untested theory, that pockets of soil near the coast could support small colonies of Europeans–so long as the colonists imported their seeds, plants and livestock. Blainey concludes that Cook and Banks arrived at a good time (both month and year–1st May, 1770) for witnessing 'vast quantities of grass and vegetation'. But he suggests that they could 'not possibly assess the soil and climate during such a brief (7 day) visit. Here was a new land, lying on the opposite side of the equator and growing exotic plants; a land occupied by people whose way of life offered few clues about the land itself'.

It was on the misconception of 'rich and fertile soils' that Britain was to locate their first settlement on the new land. The choice would have been very different if the Endeavour had landed during a hot dry spell.

This analysis we mentioned being completed for the authorities listing the costs and the benefits as well As the strategic value of the land, would also have included a statement on the integral value of the land itself. However, the conclusion would and must have been that the country, by the standards of the age, was valueless.

We know now that the stony plains and hillsides conceal minerals and oils of immense value, and that pipelines and railways can move huge resources quickly and efficiently from remote and isolated areas to the nearest port. But the 17th and 18th century decision-makers did not have that knowledge. They knew the limitations of the world and sensibly ignored the new land. There seemed to be no riches near the coastline, and it did not appear to offer (as did most other colonies) energetic, docile labourers. There were no apparent new timbers, spices, vegetables or fibres. What the British desperately hoped for was access to tall pines, to flax and hemp or at least soil which could grow such crops, but it was the prospect only that caused excitement. And that excitement turned out to be badly misplaced. The new land appeared to explorers before Cook, not to even provide a port of call for refitting, restocking and refreshment.

Was this land really worth claiming, let alone settling? Blainey acknowledges in his source notes to '*A Land Half Won*' a different perspective from the one he submitted ten years earlier in *The Tyranny of Distance*. By 1980 he was able to write "my view now is that Botany Bay was settled for four distinct reasons: the search for new naval supplies, the need for a half-way house on new trade routes, the convict problem, and not least the over optimistic assumptions held about the climate and soils of Botany Bay". Blainey goes on to admit that 'further re-reading of the Cook and Banks Journals has convinced me that their mistaken deductions about the climate and soil of Botany Bay were vital prerequisites for the English settlement in Australia.

So to our conclusions about foreign policy, defence, trade and law and order considerations we should add misstatement about and misunderstanding of the new land as a significant factor in determining the final outcome.

Although the House of Commons passed the first Transportation legislation in 1717 (4 Geo I, c.11), it remained high on the agenda in Britain as both a social policy as well as an economic policy through the rest of the 18th century. It surely was a neat policy to implement and administer. Convicted felons, who had done little to deserve a 7-year transportation sentence, were handed over to contractors, who without charge to the government would ship these offenders to North America and sell them to the plantation owners in the Carolinas and Virginia. It was a winning answer for everyone involved except the prisoner, who was being sold into virtual, if not actual, slavery. The contractor made money, the government had a monetary obligation as well as a future commitment taken off its hands, and the plantation owner, for a small sum of around twenty-five pound, got a worker for life.

It was when the Americans of more independent mind saw the better opportunity came with the huge number of black slaves from Africa than the white trash and waste from England, that the Loyalists came under challenge and the War of Independence threw out the English from the colony. So Britain now needed a colony for the American Loyalists as well as the growing number of human waste being processed through the courts.

But how could the authorities locate a refuge that was under way and would offer the same benefits as the North American colony had offered. The obvious places were Canada and Africa. So the answer to the question of a transportation destination was simple. However the better answer was to locate a destination that cold assist in solving other challenges. A naval supply base, a transit base for traders, a base from which to launch interference against the Spanish, Dutch and French, who growing presence in the southern hemisphere was causing strategic concerns; these were questions awaiting an answer. When one combined with these the question of transportation destination, the answer was a new colony in the Pacific with convicts being the icing on the cake. This is when the convict system became, in essence, a form of compulsory, assisted migration. The colony's main economic activities would be suckled by the convict system.

As a revisionist theory of the colonial origins, it is not new or even original it is commonsense and logical. It made sense to the merchant pressure group in London; it made sense to the Colonial, Home and Foreign Offices within the government, and the general population who were affronted by the hulks and overcrowded prisons, the growing poverty and social disorder. The only group not enamoured with the decision were the contractors who had carted so many prisoners to the North American colonies and had no wish to travel twice the distance and through unchartered waters to an unknown destination.

Sources

Outline: From 1786 to 1850 there were many enactments by the British House of Commons, and reports from its various committees, that need assembling and commenting on. In its website 'Documenting a Democracy', the National Archives lists 15 documents that reflect early settlement in the Colony of New South Wales

Secret Instructions to Lt. James Cook 30th July 1768
Governor Phillip's Instructions on the first settlement 25th April 1787
NSW Courts Act 1787
Charter of Justice 2nd April 1787
Charter of Justice 13th October 1823
NSW Act 1823
Governor Darling's Commission 16th July 1825
Australian Courts Act 1828
Governor Bourke's Proclamation 26th August 1835
Order ending Transportation 22nd May 1840
NSW Constitution Act 1842
University of Sydney Act 1850
Crown Lands Act 1861
Seat of Government Surrender Act 1909

Additional Reading

Early Constitutional Development in Australia–A.C.V. Melbourne
Fitzpatrick, B.C. British Imperialism in Australia 1783-1833
HR NSW–Vols 1-10
Spann, R.N. Public Administration in Australia
Historical Series Library Vols 1-12
Butlin Forming a Colonial Economy
Sweet & Maxwell "A Legal bibliography of the British Commonwealth" Vol 1
Morris, Cook, Creyke, Geddes & Holloway 'Laying Down the Law' 1996
Harvard Law Reports Vol 35 pps 519-538
'Chronological Table of British Statutes 1235-1999' (HMSO)
Campbell, Poh-York & Yooher 'Legal Research–Materials & Methods'
Castles 'An Australian Legal History'
Quick & Garran 'Annotated Constitution of Australia'
Fitzpatrick 'Colonial Australia–Macquarie to Darling'
Thompson: Financial Statements from 1856-1885

Headings

The Acts of the British Parliament 1786-1850
The Reports of Standing Committees of the House of Commons
U.K. Acts of Parliament affecting the Australian Colonies
(Refer separate table of 94 Statutes)

Governors

Phillip
Hunter
King
Bligh
Macquarie

Proclamations on Currency & Finance

Currency-1814
Finance-1815
'Holey dollars'-1816
Restrictions on P.Ns-1822
Gov't accounts-1823
Adjusting tariffs (4Vict#11) 1844 (Thompson 491)
Adjusting tariffs (7Vict#24) 1846 " "
Incr'sng duties (11Vict#7) 1847 " "
Duties (14Vict#8) 1850 " "
Repealing duties (16Vict#7) 1852 " "
Duties (18Vict#24) 1854 " "
Duties (19Vict#14) 1855 " "
Package charge (20Vict# 7) 1855
Purpose of Research and Findings

It is the purpose of this essay, in making this listing of British Legislation affecting the Colonies of Australia (in particular the colony of New South Wales) to assemble a comprehensive and all inclusive listing of Statutes relevant to the Colonies, and describe each of the pieces of legislation in its context, expected outcomes and eventual effect

Background to Legislation

The United Kingdom Parliament came into being in 1801 by amalgamation of the Parliaments of Great Britain and Ireland under the Union with Ireland Act 1800 (38 & 39 Geo III c.67). The Parliament of Great Britain had come into being on 5th May 1707 as a result of the union of the kingdoms of England and Scotland, first by treaty and then by ratifying Acts. Wales had been formally incorporated into England by an Act of 1536 (27 Hen VII c.26).

Statutes of the Parliament of the United Kingdom and its predecessors are referred to as Imperial Acts. Such statutes may apply (or may once have applied) in Australia or in parts of Australia because they formed part of the law in force in England at the time the Australian colony was settled, or at such later date as was specified by Statute for the reception of English law in the colony. Imperial Acts received into Australian law this way could be repealed or amended by the local legislatures. The laws in force in Australia today, still include some of the statutes enacted by the Parliament of the United Kingdom, and before it the Parliaments of Great Britain and England.

Reporting the Statutes

"In 1800, the British Government, on the recommendation of a Select Committee of the House of Commons, appointed a Record Commission to produce an edition of all the Statutes of the English Parliament and of the Parliaments of Great Britain and the United Kingdom. Between 1811 and 1825 the Commission produced a series of nine volumes containing all the statutes enacted between 1225 and 1713. The series was entitled *Statutes of the Realm*. An alphabetical index was published in 1824, a chronological index in 1825. The whole collection was reprinted in 1963. In compiling the *Statutes of the Realm*, the Record Commissioners consulted manuscript collections and 61 printed editions of the statutes.

The *Interpretation Act 1889* made the *Statutes of the Realm* authoritative as regards Acts of Parliament passed before 1713 when cited in statutes passed after 1889. The period between 1642 and 1660, which presumed to exercise parliamentary legislative powers, are not included in the recorded statutes. This period began with the breach between Charles I and the Parliament and the ensuing civil war. After the trial and execution of the King (January 1649), a Commonwealth of England was established. In 1653 a Protectorate, under Oliver Cromwell, was established. The Interregnum came to an end with the restoration of constitutional monarchy in 1660 under Charles II "(Introduction to the Chronological Table of Statutes-HMSO)

The Colony of New South Wales

In applying British statutes to the colony, the history of the colony is laid bare. On the 22nd August 1770, Lt. James Cook, in the name of George III, took possession of the whole eastern coast of New Holland "from 30 degrees south by the name of New South Wales together with all bays, harbours, rivers and islands situate upon that eastern coast". British settlement was not to follow until 1788.

Although it is not relevant for this purpose, it is remarkable, that according to the HRNSW, neither the Cool official log nor his private log, nor any of the journals of the ship's company, mentions the name of New South Wales. It seems either to have been an after-thought, or to have originated with Hawkesworth.

Quick & Garran in 'The Annotated Constitution of Australian Commonwealth' records that "existing British laws only authorised transportation to the colonies and plantations of North America, and as the independence of the American colonies had now been recognised, further legislation was necessary". In 1784 the statute 24 Geo III c.56 was passed, intituled "An Act for the effectual transportation of felons and other offenders, and to authorise the removal of prisoners in certain cases (the Transportation Act)".

On 6th December 1786, an order in Council was made under this *Transportation Act* 1784 designating New South Wales as a place for the reception of prisoners condemned to transportation beyond the seas. The territory of New South Wales was described in the Order as extending from 10d 37m to 43d 39m south and west to 135 d east latitude. This description was repeated in the first and second commissions issued to the first Governor of the colony, Captain Arthur Phillip. Phillip and the First fleet arrived in New South Wales on 26th January, 1788 and his second commission (dated 2nd April 1787) was read publicly at Sydney Cove. The letters patent containing the commission issued Governor Brisbane extended the westward boundary to 125d east longitude. This revised area contained the later colonies of New South Wales, Queensland, Tasmania, Victoria and part of South Australia. The initial arrangements for the governance of the Colony were included in an imperial act of 1787 (27 Geo III c.2), which made provision for the erection of a Court of criminal Judicature in the colony, followed by the issuance of the First Charter of Justice. This constituted the criminal court and for the trial of civil causes. A second charter of justice was issued on 4th February 1814. Until 1823 no provision was made for a local legislature, though the governor assumed a power to legislate by instruments call Government and general Orders.

Provision was made in 4Geo IV c.96 for the establishment of Legislative Council with between 5 and 7 members. The Act also made changes to the colony's judicial system. These changes were made along with the third charter of justice on 17th May 1824. The Australian Courts Act 1828 (9Geo IV c.83) enacted 25th July 1828 increased the Council membership to 15 members. S.24 of the Act advanced the date for reception of English Law into the colony to the 25th July 1828.

In 1842, the statute 5 & 6 Vic c.76, known as the Australian Constitutions Act, further increased membership of the Council to 36 and made 24 of these members to be elected by property-owning inhabitants of the colony. Other Constitution Acts in 1850 (13 & 14 Vic c.59) and 1855 (189 & 19 Vic c.54) created a bicameral Parliament to meet on 22nd May 1856.

A resolution to various court conjecture as to what British law is 'suitable or unsuitable for the colony', was made by the Imperial Acts Application

Act of 1969, brought about by the 1967 Report of the Law Reform Commission (LRC 4 NSW) on the application of Imperial Acts. The report recommended that some acts be re-enacted in NSW, some retained in their 'ancient form' (Statute of Merton–20 Hen III c.83), and 'certain Imperial enactments to continue in force'

It was not until the 1890s that the NSW Parliament called for a chronological table of 'public acts in force'. This was first prepared by a parliamentary draftsman called J.F. Oliver and became known as 'Oliver's Statutes'. T.B. Clegg in 1898 revised the list in his 'Index to Statutes of New South Wales'.

The Clegg List is attached as Appendix B, whilst Appendix A is the author's consolidated list of all known UK statutes relating to the colony.

The 1819 Act (59 Geo. III, cap 114) establishing the first advisory (to the governor) Legislative Council commences with the preamble

"Whereas since the establishment off a Colony in New South Wales the Governor or other persons administering the Government thereof, have from time to time caused to be raised and levied certain rates and duties upon goods, wares and merchandise imported into or exported from the settlements therein: And whereas it is expedient that the said governors and all other persons who may have advised issued or executed any order with respect to the raising or levying any such rates or duties which should be protected from vexatious suits until further provisions shall be made by Parliament".

The first NSW Judicature Act was 4 Geo. IV, cap.96, gave the 1823-formed Legislative Council more influence to contest the governor's prerogatives. Clause 28 of the Act made the local revenue raising powers 'perpetual'.

As early as 1792, Phillip had sought approval for introducing indirect taxation for the colony. The British Treasury had approved the raising of charges (to be in favour of and on account of the British Treasury) but not revenue for appropriation by the governor.

The Quick & Garran Account

Quick & Garran's Recording of the 'Development of Colonial Government in Australia' offers an interesting insight into the UK statute structure relative to the colony.

This Part III section relates to the colony of New South Wales and commences with the earliest statutory authority.

"The Judicial Authority necessary for the government of the new settlement was derived partly from privilege, similarly assumed to exist. Phillip was appointed by Letters Patent. His legislative powers were assumed to be founded on and justified by the prerogatives of the Crown. Bigge in his 3rd Report to the House of Commons questioned whether the Crown had authority to delegate such a power to a governor. The court established by 27Geo IIIc.2 was similar in its constitution to a court of Admiralty in its criminal jurisdiction, and was composed of a Judge Advocate and 6 naval or military officers to be selected by the governor. There was ample statutory authority for the administration of criminal law in a penal settlement but not for a free colony. There was no statutory authority to create civil courts, and so by Letters Patent the Crown created a civil court having jurisdiction to deal with 'personal actions, probate and administrations according to the law of England' (Letters Patent).

The governor was endowed with almost absolute power. His rule was despotic and was only liable to be called to account by the Parliament of the United Kingdom for maladministration. His oath required him to observe the law relating to plantations and trade (the original laws relating to American colonies. Two other acts of George (59 Geo III c.114 and 2 George IV c.8) gave the governor limited powers to impose local taxation by way of customs duties on spirits, tobacco, and other imports.

Basic self-government was enacted through 4 Geo IV c. 96 in 1823, and Governor Brisbane implemented this legislation intituled 'an act for the better administration of justice and for more effectual government'. The old military courts were abolished, and a Court of Appeal and a Supreme Court were authorised. The 5 to 7 Legislative Councillors served at the pleasure of the Crown and could advise but not overrule the governor. In 1824 a (First)

Charter of Justice appointed Francis Forbes as Chief Justice. The Act also separated VDL from NSW and set a charter of government for VDL.

The second charter of government came in 9Geo IV c.83 and advised Governor Darling to amend civil and criminal jurisdictions of the court and create trial by jury, in all criminal cases. It also allowed the governor to not give sanction to acts of the Legislative Council that he did not consider were sound policy.

The official staff of the governor included the Chief Justice, the Colonial-Secretary, Attorney-General, Collector of Customs, Auditor General, Chief Surgeon and Surveyor General, and effectively constituted an executive council. The governor under 9 Geo IV c.83 was authorised to "make laws and ordinances for the peace, welfare and good government of the colony". This act did not grant Responsible Government but was a sound first step for the self-government, which was to come in 1855. The governor remained prime minister and his departmental heads, acted as his council or cabinet, and they all relied not on the pleasure of the Legislative Council, but of the Crown. Sir George Gipps opened the new council in 1843 and its elected members include W.C. Wentworth, William Bland, John Dunmore Lang Richard Windeyer and George Robert Nichols.

The 1850s brought demands for responsible government and despatched an address to the Secretary of State for the Colonies in London. A committee was authorised by London to draft a constitution and Wentworth chaired that body. The Crown rejected the first draft but amendments and the finished product were incorporated in the Constitutional Bill of 1850. Because the bill exceeded the authority and power of the authorising legislation, it was rejected. A final bill was passed in Westminster and received royal assent on 16th July 1855 (18 & 19 Victoria c.54).

Governor William Denison opened the first Parliament of NSW on 22nd May1856 under the new constitution. Stuart Donaldson was Secretary and Premier, Thomas Holt was Treasurer."

-Quick & Garran–*Annotated Constitution*

GENERAL BIBLIOGRAPHY

1 Abbott & Nairn (Eds) 'Economic growth in Australia 1788-1821'
2 Abbott, G.J. 'The Pastoral Industry, in,
3 Alexander, Michael. "Mrs Fraser on the Fatal Shore:
4 Almanacs: NSW 1813-1852
5 ANU: 'Working Papers in Economic History' #s 55,57
6 Appendix to the Bigge Report 'Returns from the Periods (AJCP)
7 Appleyard, R.T. "Australian Financiers-Biographical Essays"
8 Atkinson, M (Ed) Australia: Economic & Political Studies
9 Austin, A.G. (ed.) "Australian Educations 1788-1900"
10 Australians-A Historical Library-in eleven volumes.
11 Barcan, Alan. "A History of Australian Education"
12 Barnard Eldershaw, M. "A House is Built"
13 Barnard Eldershaw, M. "Phillip of Australia"
14 Barnard, M 'Macquarie's World'
15 Barnard, M. 'Visions & Profits: studies of Thomas Mort'
16 Barnard, M.F. 'Australian Outline'
17 Barnard, Marjorie. "A History of Australia"
18 Barnard, Marjorie. "Sydney, The Story of a City"
19 Barton, G. B. 'The Life & Times of W. C. Wentworth'
20 Bate, Frank, R.M. "Samuel Bate-Singular Character"
21 Beaglehole, J.C. 'The life of Captain James Cook' (+ 4 vols of Journals)
22 Bessant (ed.) "Australian History-The Occupation of a Continent"
23 Bigge, J.T. 'Report on the Judicial Establishments of NSW'

24 Bigge, J.T. 'Report of the Commissioner of Inquiry in State of Colony of NSW'
25 Blaikie, George. "Remember Smith's Weekly?"
26 Blainey, Geoffrey 'The National Australia Bank: A History'
27 Blainey, Geoffrey. "A Land Half Won"
28 Blainey, Geoffrey. "All for Australia"
29 Blainey, Geoffrey. "Triumph of the Nomads"
30 Blainey, Geoffrey. "The Tyranny of Distance"
31 Bolton. G (Ed) 'Creating Australia-Changing Australian History'
32 Brett, Bernard. "Captain Cook"
33 Bridges, Peter. "Foundations of Identity-Building Early Sydney 1788-1822"
34 Broadbent, James. "Francis Greenway Architect"
35 Brodsky, Isadore. "Sydney Takes the Stage"
36 Brodsky, Isadore. "Sydney's Little World of Woolloomooloo"
37 Broeze, Frank. "Mr Brooks and the Australian Trade"
38 Buckland, Jill. "Mort's Cottage" (1838-1988)
39 Burgmann, Vickie 'Constructing a Culture-The People's History of Australia since 1788'
40 Butlin, N.G. "Forming a Colonial Economy-Australia 1810-1850"
41 Butlin, N.G. 'Investment in Australian Economic Development 1861-1900'
42 Butlin, N.G.; Ginswick & Stratham 'The Economy before 1850', in Australians Historical Series
43 Butlin, S. J 'Australia & New Zealand Bank: A History'
44 Butlin, S.J. "Foundations of the Australian Monetary System 1788-1851"
45 Cannon, M 'The Land Boomers'
46 Cannon, Michael "Australia-Spirit of a Nation-A Bicentenary Album."
47 Cannon, Michael. "Life in the Country-Australia in the Victorian Age Vol 2"
48 Carter, H.B. "His Majesty's Spanish Flock 1788"
49 Chambers, John H. "Australia-A Traveller's History"
50 Clark, C.M.H. "A History of Australia"-V1-6
51 Clark, C.M.H. "A Short History of Australia" 1963
52 Clark, C.M.H. "Occasional Writings & Speeches"
53 Clark, C.M.H. "Select Documents in Australian History 1788-1850

54 Clark, C.M.H. "Select Documents in Australian History 1851-1900.
55 Clark, C.M.H. "Sources of Australian History"
56 Cleverley, John F. "The First Generation-School & Society in Early Australia"
57 Cobley, J 'The crimes of the first Fleeters'
58 Cobley, John. "Sydney Cove 1788"
59 Cobley, John. "Sydney Cove 1789-1790"
60 Cobley, John. "Sydney Cove 1791-1792"
61 Cobley, John. "Sydney Cove 1793-1795"
62 Cobley, John. "The Crimes of the First Fleet Convicts"
63 Coghlan, T.A. "Labour and Industry in Australia"(4 volumes)
64 Coghlan, T.A. 'A Statistical Account of the Seven Colonies of Australasia 1890-1904 (11 vols)
65 Coghlan, T.A. 'The Wealth & Progress of NSW 1886-1900' (13 vols)
66 Collins C.R. "Sage of Settlement"
67 Collins, David. "An Account of the English Colony in N.S.W." (Vols 1 & 2)
68 Colonies: Australia #3 (Irish University Press Series)
69 Coltheart, Lenore. "Significant Sites-History and public works in New South Wales"
70 Copland, D.B. "The Australian Tariff" 1929.
71 Copland 'Australian Trade Policy: A Book of Documents 1932-1937
72 Copland, D.B. 'Cross-currants of Australian Finance: A Book of Documents'
73 Crawford, R. M. 'Australia'
74 Crime & Punishment: Transportation # 1 (Irish University Press)
75 Crisp, L.F. "The Parliamentary Government of the Commonwealth of Australia"
76 Crowley, Frank "Colonial Australia 1841-1874"
77 Crowley, Frank (ed.) "A New History of Australia"
78 Crowley, Frank. "Australia's Western Third-A History of W.A."
79 Crowley, Frank. "Colonial Australia 1788-1840"
80 Crowley, Frank. "Colonial Australia 1875-1900"
81 Davidson, Rodney. "Australian National Trusts-Historic Houses"
82 Davison, Graeme. "The Use and Abuse of Australian History"
83 de Vries-Evans, Susanna. "Historic Sydney as Seen by its Early Artists"

84 Deakin, Alfred. "And be One People"

85 Deane, Phyllis "The First Industrial Revolution"

86 Declared Accounts in Colony of NSW (AJCP)

87 Declared Accounts in the Commissariat (AJCP)

88 Dickey, Brian. "No Charity There"

89 Dickey, Brian. "Politics in New South Wales 1856-1900"

90 Dunn, Michael. "Australia and the Empire-from 1788 to the present"

91 Dyster, Barrie (ed.) "Beyond Convict Workers"

92 Eggleston, F.W. (ed.) "The Peopling of Australia"

93 Ellis, M. H. "Francis Greenway"

94 Ellis, M. H. "John Macarthur"

95 Ellis, M. H. "Lachlan Macquarie"

96 Emanuel, Cedric. "Historic Buildings of Sydney Sketchbook"

97 Emanuel, Cedric. "Historic Sydney Sketchbook"

98 Emanuel, Cedric. "The Rocks-Sydney's Most Historic Area"

99 Emanuel, Cedric. "Sydney Harbour Sketchbook"

100 Evatt, H.V. "Rum Rebellion"

101 Farrer, T. H. "Free Trade vs. Fair Trade"

102 Fitzpatrick & Munday 'Colonial Australia' Vols 1-8

103 Fitzpatrick, B.C. The Australian Commonwealth

104 Fitzpatrick, B.C. 'The Australian People 1788-1945'

105 Fitzpatrick, B.C. 'The British Empire in Australia: An Economic History'

106 Fitzpatrick, Brian C. 'British Imperialism and Australia 1783-1833'

107 Fitzpatrick, Brian. "The Australian People 1788-1945"

108 Fitzpatrick, Brian. "The British Empire in Australia-An Economic History 1834-1939.

109 Flannery, Tim. "The Birth of Sydney"

110 Flannery, Tim. "Watkin Tench 1788"

111 Fletcher, B.H. 'Colonial Australia before 1850'

112 Fletcher, Brian H. "Ralph Darling-A Governor Maligned"

113 Flower, Cedric "Treasures of Australia"

114 Fogarty, Br. Ronald. "Catholic Education in Australia 1806-1950"

115 Fowles, Joseph. "Sydney in 1848"

116 Frost, Alan 'Botany Bay Mirages'

117 Gamble, Allan. "Botany Bay Sketchbook"

118 Gamble, Allan. "Setting for a Campus"

119 Gamble, Allan. "St Mary's Basilica-Sydney"
120 Gamble, Allan. "University of Sydney Sketchbook"
121 Garran, Andrew (ed.) "Australia-The First Hundred Years"
122 Gayer, A.D., Rostow & Schwartz: 'The Growth and Fluctuation of the British Economy 1790-1850'
123 Ginswick, J. 'A select bibliography of pamphlets on Australian Economic & Social History, 1830-1895'
124 Gould, Nat. "Town and Bush"
125 Grattan, C. Hartley (Ed) 'Australia' (1947)
126 Grattan, C. Hartley. "Introducing Australia"
127 Grattan, C.H. 'Introducing Australia'
128 Greenwood, G. 'Australia: A social & Political History'
129 Greenwood, Gordon. "Australia-A Social and Political History"
130 Hainsworth, D.R. 'The Sydney Traders: Simeon Lord & His Contemporaries 1788-1821'
131 Hall, A. R. 'The London Capital Market & Australia 1870-1914'
132 Harris, Alexander 'Settlers & Convicts'
133 Harris, Max. "The Land that Waited"
134 Haskell, Arnold, L. "The Australians-The Strategic Position"
135 Herman, Morton. "Historic Building of Parramatta"
136 Herman, Morton. "The Blackets-An Era of Australian Architecture"
137 Historical Records of N.S.W. 1762-1811 (9 vols.)
138 Historical Records of Victoria-Vol 7.
139 Holder, R.F. 'History of the Bank of NSW (2 vols)'
140 Holder, R.F. 'Bank of NSW: A History' 2 Vols
141 Horne, Donald. "Billy Hughes
142 Howe, Robert. "The Sydney Gazette 1803-1842"
143 Hughes, Robert. "The Fatal Shore"
144 Illustrated History of Australia
145 Ingleton, G.C. (Ed) 'True Patriots All'
146 Inglis, K. S. "The Australian Colonists"
147 Ingpen, Robert. "Pioneer Settlement in Australia"
148 Jackson, R.V. 'Australian Economic development in the 19th century'
149 Jose, Arthur W. "History of Australasia"
150 Joy, William "The Exiles"
151 Karskens, Grace. "The Rocks-Life in Early Sydney"
152 Keesing, Nancy. "John Lang and the Forger's Wife"

153 Kiddle, Margaret. "Caroline Chisholm"
154 King, Jonathan. "The First Fleet"
155 Kingsmill, A.G. "Witness to History"
156 Kingston, Beverley. "The Oxford History of Australia-Glad, Confident Morning 1860-1900"
157 Klugman, K. "The Australian Presence in the Pacific"
158 Kociumbas, Jan. "The Oxford History of Australia-Possessions 1770-1860"
159 Lacour-Gayet, Robert. "A Concise History of Australia"
160 Laidlaw, Ronald. "Mastering Australian History"
161 Lane, P.H. "An Introduction to the Australian Constitution"
162 Lang, J.D. 'Historical & Statistical Account of NSW'
163 Langley, Michael. "Sturt of the Murray"
164 Lawson, Will. "When Cobb & Co was King"
165 Library of Australian History, Sydney 1980
166 Lourandos, Harry. "A Continent of Hunter Gatherers"
167 Loveday & Martin "Parliament Factions and Parties"-1856-1889
168 Lyne, Charles. "The Industries of New South Wales"
169 Macarthur Onslow, S (Ed) 'Early Records of the Macarthurs of Camden'
170 Macintosh, Neil K. "Richard Johnson-Chaplain to the Colony"
171 Macmillan, David S. "The Debtor's War"
172 Madgwick, R.B. 'Immigration into Eastern Australia 1788-1851'
173 McIntyre, W. David. "Colonies into Commonwealth"
174 Melbourne, A.C.V. "Early Constitutional Development in Australia"
175 Melbourne, A.C.V. "William Charles Wentworth"
176 Menzies, R.G. "Post War Reconstruction in Australia"
177 Moorhouse, Geoffrey. "Sydney"
178 Mudie, James 'The Felonry of NSW' (1837)
179 Mulvaney, J. "A Good Foundation-Reflections on the Heritage of the First Government House, Sydney"
180 Murdoch, Walter. "Alfred Deakin"
181 Nichols, S. (Ed) 'Convict Workers: Reinterpreting Australia's Past'
182 Oats, W. N. "Backhouse & Walker-A Quaker View of the Australian Colonies 1832-1838"
183 O'Brien, E.M. 'The Foundations of Australia 1786-1800'
184 O'Donnell, Dan. "James Hannell 1813-1876 Currency Lad"
185 O'Hara, J: 'The History of NSW (1818)

186 Palmer, Vance. "National Portraits"
187 Park, Ruth. "The Companion Guide to Sydney"
188 Park, Ruth. "The Companion Guide to Sydney"
189 Philips, David (Ed.) "A Nation of Rogues?"
190 Portus, G.V. 'Australia: An economic interpretation'
191 Price & Hammond 'Elder, Smith & Co-the first 100 years'
192 Quick & Garran, "The Annotated Constitution of the Australian Commonwealth"
193 Reynolds, Henry. "The Law of the Land"
194 Reynolds, John. "Edmund Barton"
195 Richards, Thomas. "An Epitome of the Official History of New South Wales 1788-1883"
196 Roberts, S.H. 'History of Australian Land Settlement 1788-1821'
197 Roberts, S.H. 'The Squatting Age in Australia 1835-1847'
198 Robson, L.L. "The Convict Settlers of Australia.
199 Royal Colonial Institute (now Royal Commonwealth Society) 'Subject Catalogue' (4 Vols)
200 Russell, Eric. "Thomas Moore & The King's Dock Yard 1796-1816"
201 Rutter, O. 'The First Fleet: The Record of the Foundation of Australia from its conception to the Settlement at Sydney Cove'
202 Scott, Geoffrey. "Sydney's Highways of History"
203 Shann, Edward. "An Economic History of Australia"
204 Shaw, A.G.L. The Story of Australia
205 Shaw, A.G.L. "Great Britain and the Colonies 1815-1865"
206 Shaw, A.G.L. "The Economic Development of Australia"
207 Sherer, John. "The Gold-Finder of Australia"
208 Sinclair: 'The Process of Economic Development of Australia'
209 Smith, Robin (ed.) "Australia's Historic Heritage-The birth of a nation"
210 Souter, Gavin. "Lion and Kangaroo-Australia: 1901-1919"
211 Souter, Ngaire. "Around the Quay"
212 Steven, Margaret. "First Impressions-the British Discovery of Australia"
213 Steven, Margaret. "Merchant Campbell 1769-1846"
214 Stone, R.D.J. "Makers of Fortune"
215 Sullivan, Martin. "Men & Women of Port Phillip"
216 Summers Anne "Damned Whores and God's Police"
217 Tennant, Kylie. "Australia: Her Story"

[218] Terry, F.C. "New South Wales Illustrated"
[219] The Australian Encyclopaedia-in six volumes.
[220] The Macquarie Book of Events
[221] The Sydney Gazette (facsimile copied in 5 vols)
[222] Thomson, James. "The Financial Statements of N.S.W. 1855-1881"
[223] Toohey, John. "Captain Bligh's Portable Nightmare"
[224] Turnbull, L. H. "Sydney-Biography of a City"
[225] Twopenny, Richard. "Town Life in Australia"
[226] Vample (Ed) 'Australians: Historical Studies'-series
[227] Van Sommers, Tess. "Sydney Sketchbook"
[228] Wadham, Samuel. "Land Utilization in Australia"
[229] Walker, Mike. "Australia-A History"
[230] Wannan, Bill. "Very Strange Tales-The Turbulent Times of Samuel Marsden"
[231] Ward &Robertson: 'Select Documents in Austn Social History 1788-1850 (Vols1,2)
[232] Ward, John M. 'The Triumph of the Pastoral Economy 1821-1851', found in
[233] Ward, R. 'The Australian Legend'
[234] Ward, Russel (ed.) "The New Australia-Edmond Marin La Meslee" (1883)
[235] Ward, Russel. "Australia"
[236] Wentworth, W.C. 'A Statistical Account of the Colony of NSW Vols 1-2'
[238] White, Unk. "The Rocks Sydney"
[239] Williams E. N. (ed.) "The Eighteenth Century Constitution"
[240] Wood, G. Arnold. "The Discovery of Australia"
[241] Wood, G.L: 'Borrowing & Business in Australia'
[242] Wood, F.L.W. "A Concise History of Australia"
[243] Yarwood, A.T. "Samuel Marsden-The Great Survivor"